DǍ

KWǍNDUR

GHÀY

GHÀKWADÎNDUR

KWANLIN DÜN

KWANLIN DÜN

DĂ KWĂNDUR
GHÀY GHÀKWADÎNDUR

Our Story in Our Words

Figure.1
Vancouver / Berkeley

XXXXXXXX XXXXXXXX

On the endpapers of this book, and at various places within, you'll see decorative designs and patterns drawn by Dr. Ukjese van Kampen. These come from the Geometric period of Yukon First Nations' art history, prior to the 1897 Klondike gold rush. Geometric motifs and symbols representing celestial bodies, world and spiritual patterns were applied to clothing, drums and tools, in patterns that seem to have been unique to individual artists. The "X" motif was common, with the earliest known example, from the Upward Sun River archaeological site in Alaska, dating to 11,500 years ago. This early Yukon First Nations art fell out of use with the advent of beaded floral designs in the late nineteenth century, but has recently been revived by various First Nations.

Cataloguing data is available from Library and Archives Canada

ISBN 978-1-77327-078-4 (hbk.)
ISBN 978-1-77327-079-1 (pdf)

Design by Jessica Sullivan
Editing by Michael Leyne
Copy editing by Audrey McClellan
Proofreading by Lucy Kenward
Indexing by Stephen Ullstrom

Front cover photo: Joshua Stendahl / Alamy Stock Photo
Back cover photo: Fritz Mueller, Kwanlin Dün Cultural Centre

Page 8: Aerial view of Monkey Point on the west side of Tàk-wädàdhà (Marsh Lake), opposite Kuk'aheeni Tlein (Judas Creek), July 2016. Kuk'aheeni Tlein means "big fishtail creek" in Tagish.

Printed and bound in Canada by Friesens
Distributed internationally by Publishers Group West

Figure 1 Publishing Inc.
Vancouver BC Canada
www.figure1publishing.com

As Kwanlin Dün we dedicate this book
to our ancestors—the ones who have
gone before us—in recognition of their
love and their vision for a better future
for all our children. They broke the trails,
crossed the windfalls and built the
bridges that led us back to our rights as
self-governing people. What we know
today came from what they preserved
and passed down to us. What we know
about ourselves came from them. The
more we examine our heritage, the more
we understand the depth of their gifts
to us. We also dedicate this book to our
youth, who will keep their vision going.

KAJÈT (RAVEN OR CROW)

According to our traditions, Kwanlin Dün have lived as a matrilineal society for countless generations, with daughters and sons following their mother's clan lineage. Our clans—Kajèt (Raven or Crow) and Aguna (Wolf)—form the two sides of our moiety system (from the French word *moitié*, meaning "half"), defining important reciprocal relationships among our people.

AGUNA (WOLF)

Our songs, stories, artwork, regalia, personal names, ceremonial protocols and obligations to one another are defined by our clan heritage. According to our traditions, a Kajèt person must marry an Aguna person to keep the proper balance in our community. Our Kwanlin Dün First Nation logo carries forward that tradition, representing Kajèt (Raven or Crow) and Aguna (Wolf) as the two sides of our Nation joined together in a continuous circle of life.

Contents

4 141 Yúk'e Kwàch'e (It is winter time): 1940–1973

5

Dahts'ì' dahkwundêts kwudīdêts
Da Na Kundur Nàniithan
Dá naw huney Nániithan
Yì.în shakhwkhwałtułnîk

WE WILL TELL ALL OF YOU OUR STORIES

COUNCIL

Kwanlin Dün First Nation Council is pleased to welcome this wonderful book after many years of work by our Elders, youth, citizens and staff members. It is a key component of our Final and Self-Government Agreements—part of our Nation's "Return to the River" to reclaim our heritage and to secure our rightful place in the presentation of history about our homeland.

This book documents the knowledge, wisdom, courage, strength and resiliency of our ancestors. They ensured that our languages and culture would survive to provide guidance for us and for all future generations. We owe so much to them for persevering through difficult times to look after us. They protected our lands and waters too, giving us the opportunities we have today to make a good life for our families. They created a foundation for us to reclaim our identity and to bring forth our heritage to celebrate—and to share—with our neighbours and visitors so they will better understand our history and our culture.

This book is especially important as a record of our stories and experiences along the Whitehorse waterfront and surrounding areas. Images and narratives found within these pages are the contributions of our grandmothers and grandfathers from past to present. Many of our people today never had the opportunity to hear our history firsthand from Elders. Our children and grandchildren, and the many generations coming after us, will be able to learn from this record of our stories.

As Council, it is clear that one of our most important responsibilities is to preserve connections with our culture. Moving from our former

Indian Act Band status to a self-governing First Nation with a modern treaty presents many challenges. We still have a lot of work to do to implement our agreements and fulfill the needs of our people. Our goal is to see all our people enjoying healthy, happy, peaceful and productive lives. Our history is an essential tool for building up all our new institutions for education, health, economic development, governance, recreation, housing and much more. Our grandparents' work is our motivation for continuing to implement our treaty in a good way for all our people.

Kwanlin Dün First Nation is like a beautiful bowl of mixed berries— our citizens have come from many communities to join the original Tagish Kwan to create the vibrant Nation we are today. We appreciate every one of our members and the unique knowledge they bring. We have faced prejudice, discriminatory policies, restrictions and losses through the years. We still experience many challenges with harmful influences in today's global environment. We will go forward secure in the knowledge that we come from strong, good and resourceful people. That is our legacy from our ancestors and the gift we send onward to our children and grandchildren, and all those yet to be born.

ELDERS COUNCIL

Our Kwanlin Dün Elders Council congratulates everyone involved in producing this book about and for our Nation. It documents our journeys together with many beautiful stories and images. We can all be very proud of our achievements as a people. We must continue to work together to preserve our culture, our languages, our strength and our unique knowledge to pass on to our descendants.

As Elders, we remember the times when many of our people lived along the waterfront in Whitehorse with few services and often in tough circumstances. We were moved from our homes numerous times, with little notice and with no place to go. We also cherish memories of good times there, sharing songs, drumming, food, laughter and the love of family and friends. Today we have reclaimed a new place and a new purpose on the waterfront with our Kwanlin Dün Cultural Centre, where we welcome our neighbours and people from around the world to experience our heritage.

Through the years we have found many new ways to survive and thrive while still practising our traditions. Today we are rebuilding our Nation with a new vision that combines past strengths and new opportunities. This book will help us to be mindful of who we are and where we come from. It tells about our traditional ways of living, with our profound respect for our matrilineal Wolf and Crow Clans. In the fast-paced and ever-changing environment that is our current reality, our grandchildren need to understand who they are so they don't lose their identity and their way in the world.

This book presents our hopes for the future. We want to see our people prosper in all their endeavours—to be happy, healthy, well-educated and peaceful. The work that we have done together to negotiate our land claims, establish our self-governing First Nation, build homes and initiate programs for our people—bound together with our ancestors' wisdom—is a firm foundation for building a bright future for all our people.

YOUTH COUNCIL

As Kwanlin Dün youth, we welcome this book. It will be so important in helping younger generations now and in future years to learn about our unique history. We are pleased to see so many wonderful images and stories shared by our people. The book gives us the chance to understand the ways that our Elders lived in past years and how hard they worked to make the good life we live today.

Often people from outside our community only hear stories about the gold rush. We want them to know that First Nations people lived here long before those events, and we have accomplished so much since then. We had and still have our own languages, traditions, beliefs and knowledge that guide us to live respectfully in this beautiful land. Sharing our Elders' knowledge is important in planning a good future for all the people who live here.

Sometimes we don't realize how privileged we are today. Life is so easy compared to the hard times our Elders experienced just a few years ago. They had to withstand prejudice, injustice and many losses as rapid change overtook our lands and our culture. They remained strong and resilient in those times—always searching for ways to overcome the many challenges confronting our people.

Through our Final and Self-Government Agreements we now have opportunities to right past wrongs and to build upon our strengths as citizens of Kwanlin Dün First Nation. There are so many great things happening today! As youth, we can speak with our own voices to our leaders—and our ideas are welcomed. We travel on our rivers and across our lands, learning our languages, history and culture, experiencing the beautiful environment that is also part of our heritage to enjoy and to protect. We are working hard to erase negative stereotypes about Kwanlin Dün held by some people outside our community. Our dream is to be fully accepted as equal and valued citizens in our city, in the Yukon and everywhere in our country.

This book is a celebration of our people—we've come so far and we have so much more to do. Our Cultural Centre marks the beginning of our return to the river. If we could still live there, we would because the river is so crucial to us. Thank you to all our Elders and people who brought forth this book. Listening to the old stories helps us fight for what is important for our future.

TECHNICAL REVIEW TEAM

This beautiful book is a gift to our people today and for all future generations. It has been a long time in the making and many people have contributed to its completion. Our Elders of long ago told stories about our land and the right ways to live here. Families gave their photos and histories, adding their experiences to this record. Our youth brought fresh ideas about our world today and their dreams for tomorrow. Together we have created a distinctive history of Kwanlin Dün—told in our own words.

As members of the Technical Review Team, we have a number of intentions for this book. We want readers to understand our identity as a self-governing First Nation with roots throughout the southern Yukon. Our original families were the Tagish Kwan people, who lived and travelled extensively from Tagish Lake through to the Big Salmon River and in the surrounding areas to the east and west. As Whitehorse grew from a small settlement to the capital city of today, many families moved to this community from other areas. We welcome them all as part of our diverse and vibrant First Nation.

The rich beauty of this land and our close relationship with the environment is vital to our people. Changes are happening all across our Traditional Territory at an increasing rate. It is critical that we recognize the places where our ancestors made their living and understand how hard they worked. Many of the places they knew have disappeared with the fast-paced developments of the past century.

In our lifetime we saw the blueberry patches around Whitehorse Rapids swept away forever, along with our rich salmon fishery at Marsh Lake after the building of the power dam. Hunting and trapping areas also disappeared as the rapidly growing city of Whitehorse took shape in our midst. Newcomers arrived in greater numbers with each passing year, bringing new ideas, laws and influences that challenged our rights and freedoms. We want people to understand the impacts these events had on us.

Our people have faced dramatic change over a few short generations. With the steadfast faith of our Elders and the ongoing ingenuity of our people, we have adopted some new ways and adapted others to suit our needs. We have pursued opportunities for wage employment, starting with the early explorers, prospectors, steamboats and wood camps, and continuing to this day with high-tech innovations in our community.

Throughout our history we have relied on our belief in family and clan connections, our love for our land and our respect for all living things to ensure we would always have a good place to call home. Our traditional values remain a key source of strength and pride. Our modern self-government is founded on those values.

Tagish and Southern Tutchone are the languages acknowledged in the Kwanlin Dün First Nation Final Agreement. Some of our people speak Northern Tutchone and Tlingit. These four Yukon First Nation languages express our knowledge, history and beliefs in ways that are unique to us. We developed the first chapter of this book to give future generations a ready source for traditional stories in each of these languages. For all time, people will see and hear the ways in which our Elders understand the world. Other chapters are built on the true words and narratives of our people of all ages.

We give thanks to everyone who made this book a reality—our Elders, leaders, citizens, youth, workers, friends and neighbours of all backgrounds. We believe it will set a new course for teaching and understanding our history, as well as our place in this community. We are proud of our heritage and happy to share our stories with the world.

GÙNÈŁCHĪSH
SHÄ̀W NÍTHÄN
MÁSỊ CHO
GUNEŁCHÎSH

A Note on Languages

facing This map shows the approximate distribution of the eight First Nation languages spoken in the Yukon, several of which extend beyond the contemporary political boundaries of the territory. Inuvialuktun is spoken on the north coast by Inuvialuit who travel there but reside in the Northwest Territories.

Elders, language holders and specialists provided assistance with identification and spelling for place names, personal names and phrases in the four languages recognized by the citizens and beneficiaries of KDFN (Tagish, Tlingit, Southern Tutchone and Northern Tutchone). In some cases the name provided in one of the four languages has the same meaning in English, and that has been noted. In other cases the English name is unrelated to the name in the First Nation language, so both the First Nation name and the English translation of it are noted, along with the English name.

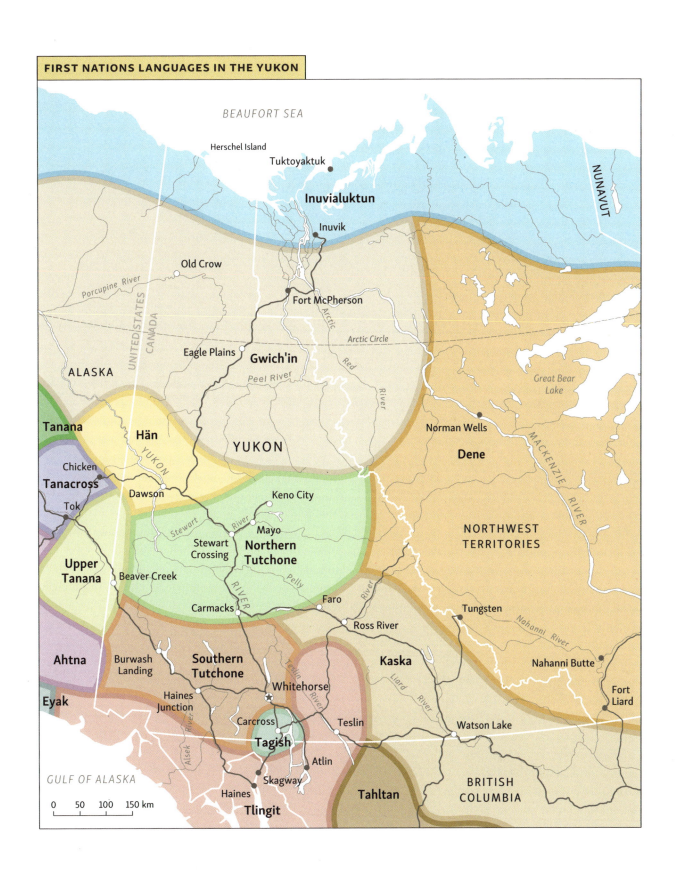

FIRST NATIONS LANGUAGES IN THE YUKON

BEAUFORT SEA

Herschel Island

Tuktoyaktuk

Inuvialuktun

NUNAVUT

Inuvik

Old Crow

Porcupine River

UNITED STATES / CANADA

Fort McPherson

ALASKA

Eagle Plains

Gwich'in

Arctic Circle

Peel River

Red

River

Great Bear Lake

YUKON

Norman Wells

Tanana

Hän

Dene

YUKON

Chicken

Tanacross

Dawson

Keno City

MACKENZIE RIVER

Tok

Stewart

River

Mayo

Stewart Crossing

Northern Tutchone

NORTHWEST TERRITORIES

Upper Tanana

Beaver Creek

Pelly

RIVER

Carmacks

Faro

River

Tungsten

Nahanni River

Ross River

Ahtna

Burwash Landing

Southern Tutchone

Kaska

Nahanni Butte

Whitehorse

Teslin River

Liard River

Fort Liard

Eyak

Haines Junction

Carcross

Teslin

Watson Lake

Alsek River

Tagish

Atlin

GULF OF ALASKA

Skagway

Tahltan

BRITISH COLUMBIA

0 50 100 150 km

Haines

Tlingit

Adaalàl Kwàch'e Kwadą̂y

It is spring time long ago

Our Elders tell of how
the world began long ago …

overleaf A misty morning at Atlin Lake.

facing Looking west towards Ibex Mountain, this area near Fish Lake has deep cultural significance as a travel route for thousands of years and as important habitat for moose, woodland caribou and Dall sheep. Elder Rose Charlie tells of how this landscape was formed by two giant bull moose fighting long ago.

SPRING IS THE TIME of birth and new beginnings. Our Elders tell of how the world began long ago when the land, waters, peoples and other living beings came to be. Their stories teach about our matrilineal moieties—Kajèt (Raven or Crow) and Aguna (Wolf)—and how we should hold up our people through respect, harmony and proper behaviour. Our worldview today is based on these ancestral beliefs passed down through countless generations. The stories told in our Tagish, Southern Tutchone, Northern Tutchone and Tlingit languages are an integral part of our identity. They guide our actions toward animals, the land and other people. This is how we understand our world.

This chapter presents stories in each of our languages, told in the traditional way first. English translations provided underneath each word or phrase illustrate the way our languages express meaning, which is followed by an English interpretation of the story.

Ch'óonehte' Má—Stóow—Angela Sidney

Angela Sidney, known as Ch'óonehte' Má in Tagish and Stóow in Tlingit, was born near Tagish in 1902. Her mother, Ła.oos Tláa (Tagish)—Kaax'anshée (Tlingit)—Maria Johns, was of the Deisheetaan Clan of Inland Tlingit people, descended from Coastal Tlingit at Angoon, Alaska. Her father was Haandeyéil (Tagish)—Ḵ'aajinéek' (Tlingit)—Tagish John of the Dak'laweidí. Angela spoke Tagish and Tlingit fluently and knew the Southern Tutchone and English languages as well. She lived at Carcross and Tagish as a child, travelling extensively with her family, hunting, trapping and fishing around the big lakes in the southern Yukon. She was a renowned storyteller who travelled to southern Canada to share her stories and knowledge and was one of the founders of the Yukon International Storytelling Festival in Whitehorse. She passed away in 1991.[2]

XĪ`H MĀ (GAME MOTHER)

Told by **Ch'óonehte' Má—Stóow—Angela Sidney**[*]

Kwoda'ę̀ · 'ak'ānāzhe lèh · ihghānākādēdl · dechìdle · yèh
Long ago · they just grew up · they stayed together · his younger brother · with

łigidè · ghadenè · kàske.
one · woman · they stayed with her.

Kūyeh · nàdedèhxai · kàk'e · nakindēd
At that time · it was getting to be fall · at that time · they stayed there

kidādêł.
they were preparing to go.

'Āh · kīdogho · yéhchį̄.
Snowshoes · for them · he made it.

Sòsan · echį̄ · dits'àn' · ghènilā · kàk'e · daxēdlī.
Well · he made · to her · he gave her · that · evening.

Ezìs · dik'āle · kè̀schùs, · wadzīhzìs · dik'āle.
Hide · white · she brought out, · caribou hide · white.

Yik'ēdàsdèts · kàk'e · nīnìlā · detsìlādl.
She wrapped it · that time · she put it · [above] her pillow.

"Nādinūt'at · dè," · yèhndī.
"Undo yourself · then," · she said to it.

K'amā · nitsitkidizhā · nādenest'at.
In the morning · when they woke up · it was undone.

K'à̀'āt'į̄ł.
It will happen like that all the time.

Wachidle, · "Ninī · nihchįh · dò̀t'esìā?"
His younger brother, · "You · you make it repeatedly · how is it going to be?"

Łǭ · wachidle · 'āh · kadèzhà̀.
Even so · his younger brother · snowshoes · he went to get.

Łāyālēł.
He brought them.

*Told in the Tagish language by Ch'óonehte' Má—Stóow—Angela Sidney, who told the "Game Mother" story on many occasions throughout her long life. She said that she first heard the story in 1912. This version was transcribed phonetically by Victor Golla. Patrick Moore wrote and edited the text in Tagish. He reviewed the text with Angela Sidney's daughter Ida Calmegane, who provided assistance with Tlingit words and English translation. James Crippen provided interpretation for Tlingit words. Tlingit and English words in the text are written in italics.[3]

'Ī · yèhchį̄ · *k'adéin* · yèhchį̄.
That · he made it · well · he made it.

Yighenìlà · t'è' · dats'ān' · yighenìlà.
He gave them to her · then · his wife · he gave them to her.

Dichū · dè · azìs · dik'ale · detsìlā · ninìlà.
Again · then · hide · white · his pillow · she placed [on].

"Nādinūt'at · dè!" · yèhndī.
"Undo yourself · then!" · she said to it.

K'amā · nitsidkidīzhāgè · nầdìnest'àt.
In the morning · when they woke up · they had undone themselves.

Kầkat'į̄.
It's like that all the time.

Yásk'è · *tsu* · kondiye · *don't know* · 'āh · kīghayèhchį̄.
In the winter · again · older brother · doesn't know · snowshoes · they made for her.

Łigide · nakandē · *chá* · *yaa* · *dachóon* · nầzheł, · nầzhel
One place · they stayed · just · along · forward · she was growing, · growing

wáa sá · dene · dunin · yèh · et'ē.
somehow · person · child · with · she was.

At'ānezhā · "'Āh'às · tl'akų̀!
Leaf Moon (May) · "You two go away · now!

'Esghāh · tìkầsầhdēdl.
For me · you are making it hard.

'Edū · dene · là'ầst'e," · yèhndi.
Not · person · I am," · she said.

"'Adū · dene · là'ầst'ē.
"Not · human · I am.

'Āh'às!
Go away!

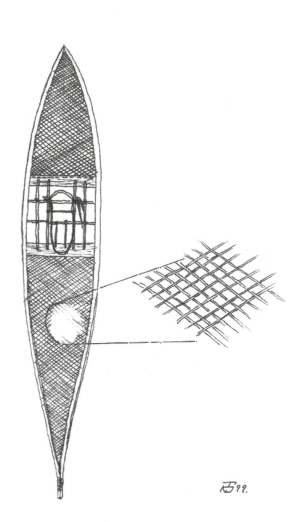

above An ah' (traditional snowshoe) still in use today, with detail of webbing.

'Adū · nisàd · eshk'ánahta · nàhsin · dege."
Not · far · you [plural] watch me · you think · for."

Kà'āk'e · dū · nisàd · koch'įh · kik'ànehtā
And then · not · far · from · they watched her.

Kà'āk'e · Xandē · kaēzhā.
And then · Moose · he came out.

Wadè'... · yèkàkūndèdl · Dendìgì · kè̀ · wadè' · yich'įh
His horns . . . · she told him to come back · Bull Moose · also · his horns · from him

yeslā · maghù̀ ' · chū.
she took · his teeth · also.

Shash · ghù̀ ' · là · dik'àt'ēn, · shash · ghù̀ ' · yich'įh · idēslā.
Bear's · teeth · assert · looks like, · bear's · teeth · from him · she took.

Yī · tlà̧geh · áwé · Shichdzísk'w · chū · yī · tlà̧ge' · Wajīh · tsu
That · after so · then · Cow Moose · also · that · then · Caribou · also

just the same way · kà'ayilā · wadè'.
just the same way · she did like · his horns.

"Nānù̀ leh · t'è̀ · nidè̀ · 'adū · ch'u · tlákw · 'ūsìndōde!"
"Put them away · then · your horns · not · just · always · you wear it!"

yèhndì̀ · du · yatx'i
she told him · her · children:

Xandē · tsu · Caribou · tsu, · yī · tlà̧ geh, · Mbegè · tsu,
Moose · also · Caribou · also, · that · after, · Mountain Sheep · also,

'īyit · tsu · meghù̀' · yà̧kù̀lį̄.
that one · also · his teeth · exist.

Wayè̀ t'ānè' · ghighanìlā.
His leaves · she gave him.

Xandē · at'āne · dambèdè' · dogha · t'ē' · at'āne.
Moose · leaves · its food · for · it is · leaves.

Wajīh · tsu · majīhdè' · ūzhē · yíghenìlà̧.
Caribou · also · caribou lichen · it is called · she gave it to him.

"Nindiye · dogha · t'ē," · nī.
"Your food · for · it is," · she said.

Kù̀hyeh · Mbegè · tsu · ts'įh · áyá · chanatīn · kots'įn · de,
And then · Mountain Sheep · also · from · focus · she was sleeping · from · then,

dè̀ghāghà · kots'į̄ · lā · tl'ò̀ we · ghighenìlā · tè̀.
beside it · from area · assert · grass · she gave him · then.

"Dejā · jù ' · nindīyè' · dogha · et'ē · nin," · yèhndìh.
"This · also · your food · for · it is · you," · she told him.

'Ī · tl'ōw · ghighenīlā · yī · tlą · shīndigì · kwots'į̄h · łech · yèht'ût.
That · grass · she gave to him · that · after · fireplace · from · ashes · he licked.

Aadáx · áwé · Jenò · 'ayū · xìh · 'ūzhē · yìdìtsų
And · then · Mountain Goat · different · animal · they call it · that one too

wandīyè' · sákw · nìlā.
his food · for · she gave him.

Wetl'ą̀ge · tle · hóoch'i · aa · át · áwé · Shash · kēzhà̀ · 'ī · chū.
After that · then · last · one · thing · focus · Bear · came out · that one · too.

Jìje · yeghìlà · yeghìlà, · jìje, · jìjest'ēza.
Berries · she gave him · berries, · blackberries, · moss berries.

Deghù̀ ' · yich'ánèsyù̀ t.
His teeth · he held on to them.

"Łō! · 'Amā, · łō! · Yē · yèh · ūst'į̄ · dōnih'į̄?" · yèhndī.
"Don't! · Mother, · don't! · What · with · I will be · to have?" · he said to her.

"Dū · den · dogha · nighù̀ ' · nighāneslā," · yèhndī.
"Not · people · for · your teeth · I gave you," · she said to him.

"Dene · kijūdliht'è'.
"People · you must love them.

Łō · dūshà̀'nèsen, · 'ī · dene," · yèhndì.
Don't · be mean, · those · people," · she said to him.

Yī · tlą̀ k'e · Agayh · yeisú.
That · after · Wolf · still.

Agayh, · Agayh · kàèzhà̀.
Wolf, · Wolf · came out.

Aadáx · áwé · wakàge · nàkots'ìt.
After that · focus · on it · a year passed.

'Akēyi · yidogha · kī · dase'à̀.
Swing · for them · also · she put up.

'Akēyì · xandē · dendigīzìs, · xandē · 'ūghìdō · di · 'akēyì · yi'āy'à̀.
Swing · moose · bull moose hide, · moose · for them · this · swing · she put up.

Watl'ūlè' · Tàghàhi · kots'ìn · nit'į̄ · tléix' · aa.
Its rope · Facing the Water (Grey Ridge) · to · it was tied · first · one.

Tātl'à̀ · Sàts'ī'.
Forehead · Blowing (Caribou Mountain).

facing top A wajīh (caribou) at Tagish.

facing centre A young mbegè (mountain sheep), also known as Dall sheep, in Kluane Range.

facing bottom Two wajīh (caribou) on a ridge near Primrose Lake.

top Majīhdè', or caribou lichen, also known as caribou moss. Majīhdè' translates literally to "caribou horn."

above Moss berry, crow berry, or, sometimes, black berry.

Aadáx · *áwé* · tōdē · Wajīh · Dzełè'.

After that · focus · the third · Caribou · Mountain (Nares Mountain).

Yī · tlą̀k'e · *Aadakoon.áa(gen)* · Chilì · Dzełè' · ts'àn

That · after · [Tlingit word for Montana Mountain[4]] · Gopher · Mountain [Montana Mountain] · to

dakīnētl'ų̀.

it is tied to.

K`ầk'ehūt · Xandè̀ · "'Ī · ts'àn · āshầl."

And then · Moose · "That · toward · I walk."

'Ī · xin · yèh · 'ejin.

That · song · with · he sings.

BULL MOOSE SONG:[5]

Yē-ē-ē · chū-ū-ū · dene · shechὺzhā-ū-ū

What · small · people · put up [the swing]

Yē-ē-ē · chū-ū-ū · dene · shechὺzhā-ū-ū

What · small · people · put up [the swing]

Mets'èn · eshshāle · na'inà'ą.

To it · I'm going · somebody sees me.

Īyē'ēīyē'ēīyē'ēīyē'ē
Ā'ō'īīē īyē'ī
Ā ā ā ēāī ye āī ya!
(Song repeats)

Xandēmā · *tsu* · dachīga · ket'į̄ · kầ'àk'i.

Cow Moose · also · her calf · she has · already.

'Ì yet · kầ'àk'i · *áwé* · 'ī · doghe · ejin · dichīgi · dō.

That one · at that time · so · that · for · she sang · her calf · for.

All · *tléix'* · *gaa* · *a* · *kaadé* · nā'àt · ghīghènàkwazhā

All · one · each · it · toward · they got · she played with them

denunin'è · keh.

her children · all.

Tlą̀ hū · yighà · dèszhā · dohon · gāł k'ets'ìd.

After · from them · she left · finally · she was tired out.

Kā · *áwé* · 'ī · Chilì · Dzełè' · kotānde · Chilì · Dzełè'.

That's · so · that · Gopher · Mountain · above · Gopher · Mountain.

'Ī · yidi · t'e · nestī̦.
That · there · then · she camped.

Yī · tlà̦ · nitsidītą̦ · geh · *next day* · Wajīh · Gū'e'.
That · after · she woke up · then · next day · Caribou · Worms (cirque).

Ů̦ zhē · 'Ī · zhū'ů̦ ghē · nèstī̦ · so · wakandigì · kolī̦.
It is called · that · that's where · she camped · must be · her place · exists.

'Adū · sò̦ sin · chanestī̦ · *shóox'* · aa · *káa* · *áwé* · yīyek'ą̦ngēt'e.
Not · well · she slept · first · one · on · it is · close by.

Dixonh · nachanestî̦.
Again · she lay down again.

Kookáa · *áwé* · chandāł · yìke · wak'andīgì · kù̦lī̦ · Wajīh · Gū'è'
For · it is · in two · places · her place · exists · Caribou · Worms

Dzełè' · kāge.
Mountain · on.

'Ī · kots'ī̦h · dèhzhā · k'eh · *áwe* · Teslin.
That · from · she took off · following · it is · Teslin.

Tléinaáx · *Tawei* · Łìgìde · Mbegè · 'uzhē,
Lone · Sheep (Three Aces Mountain near Teslin) · One · Sheep · it's called,

Dzeł · 'Ī · *hóoch'í* · aa.
Mountain · that place · last · one.

Áadáx · dèhzhā · nèzhū · *tle* · *hóoch'* · *tléil* · *xwasakú*.
From there · she went · where to · then · last · not · I know.

Jà̦ · kots'ī̦h · 'adū · kēsìn.
Here · from · not · I know.

Jè' · alī̦ · yūdin.
That's · all · I know of it.

ENGLISH INTERPRETATION

Long ago two brothers lived with a woman.
It was getting to be fall time and they were preparing to go.
The younger brother made snowshoes for them.
He made them well and, in the evening, he gave them to his wife.
She brought out a white hide, a white caribou hide.
She wrapped the snowshoes in the hide and put it on her pillow.

"Undo yourselves!" she told them [the snowshoes].

In the morning when they woke up, the snowshoes were undone.
This happened repeatedly.

The older brother said to his younger brother, "What's the use of making them?"

Even so, his younger brother went to get snowshoes.
He brought them back.
He made them; he made them well.
He gave them to her then; he gave them to his wife.
Again, she put them in the white hide and placed them on her pillow.

"Undo yourselves!" she told them.

In the morning when they woke up, they had undone themselves.
It was like that all the time.
In the winter time they made snowshoes for her.
They were staying at one place and she was growing bigger and bigger;
    she was pregnant.

In May she told her husbands, "Go away now!
You are making it hard for me.
I am not like other people," she told them.
"I am not like other people.
Go away!
If you want, you can watch me from nearby."

They watched her from nearby.
Then Moose came out [was born].
She told him to come back and she took his horns and his teeth.
His teeth were like a bear's and she took those from him.

She did the same thing to the horns of Cow Moose and then Caribou.

facing top Dendìgì (bull moose).

facing bottom Dendìgì (bull moose).

above Two male mbegè (mountain sheep), also known as Dall sheep.

"Put your horns away and don't wear them all the time!" she told her children:
Moose and Caribou, and after that Mountain Sheep,
that one [Mountain Sheep] also had teeth.

She gave him leaves [to eat].
Leaves, leaves were the food for Moose.
Caribou too, she gave him caribou lichen.

"That's your food," she told him.

And then from right beside where she was sleeping,
she gave Mountain Sheep the grass that was growing there.

"This is your food," she told him.

She gave him grass and after that he licked ashes from the fireplace.
And then Mountain Goat, a different animal, that one too, she gave him his food.
After that, at the end, that one last thing, Bear, came out.
She gave him berries, moss berries.
He wouldn't give up his teeth though.

"Don't! Mother, don't! What will I have left?" he said to her.

"I didn't give you your teeth to use on people," she told him.
"You have to love people."

"Don't be mean to those people," she told him.

After that, Wolf was still to be born;
then Wolf came out.
After that a year passed.

She put up a swing for them then.

She put up a big trampoline for them made of moosehide, bull moose hide.

The first rope was tied to Tằ ghàhi (Grey Ridge).

The next was to Tatl'ằ Sach'ī (Caribou Mountain).

After that the third was to Wajīh Dzełè' (Nares Mountain).

After that a rope was tied to Ādakōn'ā, Chilì Dzełè' (Montana Mountain).

Then Moose said, "I'll walk toward it [trampoline]."

[sings Bull Moose song]

Cow Moose already had a calf.

At that time, she sang for her calf.

Game Mother played with each of her children.

Then finally she was tired out.

She camped above Chilī Dzełè' (Montana Mountain).

After she woke, the next day she camped at Wajīh Gū'è' (cirque on Mount
    Lanning), and her impression must still be there.

She didn't sleep well at first so she lay down again close by.

That's why there are two places where her impression was made on Wajīh Gū'è'.

From there she took off toward Teslin.

Tléinaáx Tawei [Tlingit] Łìgìde Mbegè [Tagish] (Three Aces) it's called;
    that was the last place [she rested].

Where she went from there I don't know.

I don't know what happened from there.

That's all I know of it.

Áyenjiátà—Louie Smith

Áyenjiátà—Louie Smith of the Crow Clan was born in 1932 on the Teslin River at Tatl'ane (Dog Salmon Slough). His mother, Tàshura—Mary Smith, was from the Little Salmon area and was the daughter of Big Salmon Charlie. His father, Tl'ukshan—Charlie Smith, was from the Lake Laberge area. The family set fishnets at Dog Salmon Slough in summer. They also had a cabin at T'äw Tà'är (Winter Crossing) and a home in Whitehorse. Áyenjiátà means "Experienced Daddy" in Southern Tutchone. Louie has learned many different skills throughout his long life—trapping, hunting and fishing with his parents, later working as a labourer on the Whitehorse waterfront and in highway construction. He and his brothers all played fiddle and guitar, holding dances at his father's home in Whitehorse. From his earliest years, Louie listened to his father and other Elders telling their traditional stories in their languages, along with the history of the region and their travels. Today Louie continues to delight people with his fiddle and his stories—generously sharing his knowledge with anyone who wants to learn.[6]

Nindal Kwädīndür
(I'm going to tell you a story)

TS'URK'I YÈ MURK'ÀY (CROW AND GULL)

Told by Áyenjiátà—Louie Smith*

Ni na · kŭndûr · nĭthan.
Your presence · I'll tell story · I think/wish.

Maggie Broeren · ghana · kwandûr, · dunèna · 'ĭlhî · k'e'.
Maggie Broeren · it about · she told, · child · I was · when.

Maggie Broeren · Jim Boss · u maat · 'ach'e' nà.
Maggie Broeren · Jim Boss · his older sister · is was.

Ayet · Ts'urk'i · ghana, · ayet · Ts'ark'i · jenàch'ur, · ayet · k'ànat'äy.
That · Raven · about it, · that · Raven · it was black, · that · was flying around.

Kààthe · tààkejêl · k'e · chu · zhą · kwàlį.
At first · they came up · when · water · only · there was.

Chu · kààshe · ch'âw · dadįtàr · nà · Nan käy, · 'ani.
Water · everywhere · it was · flood · was · Earth on · she said.

El · dadįtàr · kwàch'e · nà.
Ocean · flooded · it was · done.

Ayet · Ts'urk'i, · u ghana · kwĭndur, · aju · chu · däw · 'ăsį · ch'e'.
That · Raven, · about · I'm talking, · not · water · for · made · it was.

Ayet · Ts'urk'i · aju · chu · däw · 'ăsį.
That · Raven · not · water · for · made.

K'ànat'â · däw · 'ăsį · ch'e'.
Flying about · for · it made it · it was.

Kànat'â · k'e · aju · nan nànut'aâl · kwàlį, · chu · zhą · ch'e' kwàlį.
Flying around · when · no · to land on · existed, · water · only · there was.

Thaanshäw · k'ànat'â · k'e · u t'à · nàndhat.
Alone · flying around · when · his wing · it became sore.

Chu · yì · tanìĭtth'ât ch'è', · 'adĭchàl · nįdhan.
Water · in · I will, · I might die/drown · it thought.

K'atthù · k'ànààt'a, · nan · ka · nànătâ · k'e'
In vain · it flew around, · land · for · it looked around · when

*Áyenjiátà—Louie Smith told this story in English at the Kwanlin Dün First Nation Waterfront Heritage Project Story-Weaving Workshop on March 17, 2017. Daniel Tlen translated the transcript into Dän K'é (Southern Tutchone), with word-for-word English translations, by Nakhela—Hazel Bunbury in collaboration with Louie Smith in November 2019. The English interpretation is an abridged version of the 2017 Story-Weaving Workshop transcript.

jûch'â · dak'ala · ǎ'ą · nǎ'į · chu · käy.
suddenly · white small · object · he saw it · water · on.

Ye · ch'i · k'ànaatth'uh · ayet? · Nǔ'į · ni, · nįdhį.
What · is it · moving about · that? · Let me see it · let, · it thought.

Ätl'a · Murk'ày · 'ach'e · ną.
It was · Gull · it was · was.

'Iyèńjì · Murk'ày · ǎch'e · yiw · k'ànaame.
It knew · Gull · it was · there · swimming about.

'Iyèńjì · Murk'ày · chenaada · yiw.
It knew · Gull · could diving · there.

Murk'ày · chu · t'äy · dezhì · ch'e'.
Gull · water · under · breathe · it could.

Àk'e · Murk'ày · tl'awa · yè · lhùr-tth'àl
Then · Gull · grass · and · mud

above Murk'ày (seagull) sitting on the nest she made for herself.

dë dhê · yè · taàla · taatl'äy · kwa-ts'an. · Njuha · 'idäw · ǎsį.
its mouth · with · brought up · bottom · area from. · Island tiny · it for · it made it.

'Ùtlǎy · tl'aw · shų · yè, · kwa-ghą · daalal. · Àk'e · njuha · dàlal.
Lots · water weeds · also · with, · it for · it floated. · Then · island little · it floated.

Murk'ày · ghar · dààch'ėl · kwadìkhaan.
Gull · babies · it was going to have · pretty soon.

Aju · 'iyeǹli · chu · käy · kwàdlè · yiw.
Not · it wants · water · on · they born · there.

Nan · käy, · njuha · käy · ghàkwìndlį.
Land · on, · island tiny · on · they were born.

Murk'ày · ghara · ghànìkhe, · murk'ày · ghara.
Gulls · little · she was raising them, · gulls · little

Ts'ark'i · kwaǹkhaan · kànaat'ây · k'e, · yèni, · "Ye · ń'į · ayet?
Raven · close by · it flew by · when, · it said to it, · "What · you got · that there?

Ye · ń'į 'u käy · ńda, · ayet 'yiw?"
What · on top · you are sitting, · there?"

"Shän, · ʼïsị ch'e · taatl'äy · kwa-ts'an, · lhùr-tth'àl ts'an."
"I made it, · is me · bottom · area from, · mud from."

Ts'urk'i · nịdhan, · Dukât · shị̀.
Raven · thought, · I'll ask it · I will.

Ts'urk'i · yedăkat, · "Njuha · k'à · ʼă-ghạ · ʼụsi · shị̀?
Raven · asked her, · "Island small · can you · me for · you make · will?

ʼĂ näw kwàzhà," · ʼăni, · "ʼă t'à · àndhat."
I am tired," · he said, · "my wings · played out."

Murk'ày · ʼăni, · "ʼAjù'! · ʼAju · ʼakàdǐch'ạ̀l'."
Gull · said, · "No · not · I'm going to do that."

ʼÀk'e · nị̀dhị̀ · Ts'urk'i, · dùŭlhê · shị̀ · ayet · Murk'ày?
Then · it thought · Raven, · what should I do · I will · with that · Gull?

Oh! · ʼUyìńjì · dadǐlhèl · yiw. · ʼU ghara · àtlạ · kwàlị.
Oh! · I know · what I'm going to do · there. · Its young · many · there are.

Ts'urk'i · nă̆ị̂ · murk'ày · ghara · ch'û, · murk'ày · ghara · nedǹchị̂.
Raven · saw it · gulls · small · soon as, · gull · small · he grabbed one.

Ts'urk'i · säl · yè · gă · nadèlè · k'è, · murk'ày · ghara · nedǹchị̂.
Raven · gopher · and · rabbits · picked up · like, · gull · young · it picked it up.

Murk'ày · ghara · nadìchi.
Gull · little · it picked it up.

"Ni ghara · nedìchi, · aju · ni · ghààdǐchal'.
"Your little one · I'm taking it, · not · you to · I'm giving it back.

Nan · 'ă · ghàń'ą k'e, · ni · ghànuchâl · shì."
Land · me to · you give, · me then · you to I'll give it back · will."

Murk'ày · k'ààyenăt'a, · k'athù · yedăkat.
Gull · flew after it, · in vain she tried · to ask it.

Kwadàdhat · k'ààk'et'â · ch'û.
After a long time · they flew about · as.

Dàkhwàn · 'ăni · Murk'ày, · "'Ă ghara · cheduchèl'."
Finally · said · Gull, · "My little one · you might lose it."

'Àk'e · dàkhwàn · 'ăni · Murk'ày, · "Àghây',
Then · finally · it said · Gull, · "Yes,

Nań · nu'aal, · 'ă ghàńchè'.
land · I will give you it, · me to give it back.

Taatl'äy · ts'an · ni ghą · 'ù kushà · shì."
Water bottom · to you · for it · I'll get it · will."

Kwadàdhat · Ts'urk'i · 'i däw · 'adâ · ch'û · ayet · 'yiw.
After a long time · Raven · it for · it waited · a while · that · there.

'Àk'e · Murk'ày · dàkhwàn · dây · kànààzha
Then · Gull · finally · up · came back

dë dà · yè · sana · daa'aal, · tl'äw · shu.
its beak · with · soil · it carried it, · water weeds · too.

Chu · käy · 'i yedńjì'. · 'Àk'e · Murk'ày · 'ăni, · "Nà'! · ń'ay · ach'e.
Water · on · it let them go. · Then · Gull · she said, · "Here! · your object · it is.

'A-dan · yiw · kwìsi, · äju · kwinkhan."
Different · place · you make it, · not · close by."

Ts'urk'i · 'ăni, · "'Àghây'! · Shàw · nǐthan, · atl'a · 'u yenìlhi · ch'e'."
Raven · it said it, · "Yes! · Good · I think it is, · that is it · I wanted it · it is."

'Ăhù · dë nân · käy, · njuha · ńlį, · käy · daada · Ts'ark'i.
Now · own land · on, · island little · it became, · on · it sat · Raven.

'Àk'e · shàw · nèkwìn'ą. · Tl'ă hù · kwàch'e'.
Then · he fix · things up. · End now · it is.

ENGLISH INTERPRETATION

What I want to tell that story about, Lake Laberge and Maggie Broeren, it's Jim Boss' sister. When I was a kid, and I hear that story, she tell us about it. 'Bout Crow, you know those crow, that black one that, flyin' around? And the Seagull too. When they first come through this part of the area. There was this part of the area alright, but just nothing but water, that's what she say. It's the ocean. Lots of water everywhere.

So, well, that Crow, that Raven, that's what I'm talking about. He don't made for water, that Raven. Well, they made it just flying around. And so, they sit on top of the tree on top of hill like that, over there, on the side of the cliff. Sit down on top of that, in the tree. Then he making that noise like "Gaw, gaw, gaw, gaw," he says.

Then, he want to fly around. Then, where he got to the place is, nothing but water, he got no place to land. Next thing, he flyin' around. Just by himself. But, you see the arm get played out. Not the arm, a wings. All old, played out, here. Pretty soon he gonna go down to that water down there. He don't wanna fall in that water there. He gonna drown there. So he flyin' around everywhere. Pretty soon they see some kind of white little mark in the, in the water. So he wanna see what's that. That was moving around there, moving his head around. There was a seagull.

Yeah, he know, he know a seagull could swim around in the water and he dive, too. Seagull could stay long time underwater. And he dive in. What he did, he get little piece of grass or ground, he pick it up from down the bottom of the water. Got him in his mouth, and to bring it up over there. And he fix a little, he put it together, pretty soon a round little, round little thing like that. He make a ground there. Here, he start free floating, that thing. Lots of grass in that little bit, and he float. So, because he gonna have a baby pretty soon. Well, he can't have it in the water. So he have it in, in that little ground, something like a little island. And he was growing up little ones, small little one. Little, little seagull.

Then he [Crow] fly right close to this, that Seagull. Then he tell him, "Hey, hey, Seagull, what do you got there, what do you sit on top there?" he said.

"Oh," he said, "I make it," he says, "I made it myself. I got it from the bottom of ocean."

Then he fly around there. What shall I do with, with that, Seagull, do you figure? Mmm, well, I'm gonna ask him "Hey, Seagull," he said. "Would you build me one of that little island you got there? I'm played out now," he say. "My wings are just all played out. I don't wanna hit that water. I don't know how to swim either."

So Seagull says, "No! I'm not going to do it," he say.

Well, he think, you're not gonna do it? Then he think about, what shall I do with that Seagull anyway? I wanna, oh, I know what to do. He got a little baby there, small little one, see it little one, walking around everywhere. So far, where he could get a chance, that little one over there, that little seagull, looking after little ones there. One of them seagull walking around over there, small little one. The Crow got his chance, then. So he just, he dived just like a eagle when he wanna catch rabbits or gopher. Just—*woof*—just like that. That's what he did. He pick it up. He pick up little seagull.

"What you gonna do with it?" Seagull said.

"Well," he say, "I'm gonna take this little one," he say. "I'm not going to give you back," he said. "You gotta give me that ground," he tell him, "then I give it back to you."

The Crow and the Seagull follow him all over the places. Then they fly around lot of places. And he keep on beg him, flyin', flyin'. Finally, he said, "Okay," he say. Pretty soon they gonna lose that little one. And the Seagull says, "Okay, I get you same kind what I got there. I gotta go down in the ocean. On the bottom. Gimme back. Okay, put him back on that little island, then." So he put him back on the little island. Then he watch it, I think, the little seagull, they stay right on that little island, a little world.

Then, pretty soon, the Seagull gone long time, him, he just wait there. He give him that little seagull back already. So he waited there. Looking for Seagull, finally he come out. "I got this," he say. "Okay, here." He took it out of his mouth, chunk of dirt little bit and, ah, grass, on the bottom, he put him on top that little island.

"Okay, this is yours now," he said. "Okay, go fix it someplace else, not too close," he says, "go a long ways."

"Yeah. Okay," he says. "Thank you," he says. "That's all I wanted."

Now, while he was on top of that world, that little island, when he fix it there, he put a lot of little creek, like a little river, and a small little creek. Then he fix it, he put a lake on top there too, like, water. He's got a miracle, too, that Crow, you know, just like God. When God says you want something, that's done. And "You come into be a lake," he said. Then, when that thing it started grow, little lake, how shall I put a fish in there? Then they try to look around for a fish, next, then they got a fish, and the scale, the fish scale, got him in his mouth. So, then, he find that little fish, and he took the little scale out. "Okay, I want this here to be a salmon," and he name all those little fish, like graylings, whitefish, pike, all these things like that, then he put him in that little lake. "Grow," he says. And he started growing, and that's how come a little fish is like in Teslin, they got a lot of fish in there. So does Big Atlin, too. And even Marsh Lake, you see, Lake Laberge and Kluane Lake, they all got fish. Well, that's, that's how.

He say, "I want this here, this little island to grow," he say. And that island start grow, bigger and bigger and bigger. Pretty soon, he had one mile that way, another mile this, across. Pretty soon, little bigger and bigger. Look how big a world is it now. That's the way that the story said it goes, anyway.

facing top T'awa (grayling).

facing bottom "Jua nighè" ani. Aju kwädàdhat ch'u ju shäw. ("I want this here, this little island to grow," he say. And that island start grow, bigger and bigger and bigger.)

Nakhela—Hazel Bunbury

Nakhela—Hazel Bunbury of the Aguna (Wolf) Clan was born at Tàa'än Män (Lake Laberge) in the 1940s. The name Nakhela means "crocus" and was given to her because she was born in the spring. Her mother was Ukàts'enatäy—Irene Adamson, which means "looking for it" in her Southern Tutchone language, and she was raised at Lake Laberge. Nakhela's father was John Adamson, whose mother came from Shäwshe (Dalton Post) and had connections to Coastal Tlingit people. Nakhela went to the Whitehorse Indian Baptist Mission School as a young child in the 1940s and '50s, but she never forgot her language and the stories of her ancestors. She worked for many years as a Native Language Instructor in Whitehorse schools and continues to share her culture, language and knowledge with all who want to learn.[7]

Nindal Kwädīndür
(I'm going to tell you a story)

CHÙNÄY YÈ TS'URK'I KWÄNDUR (EAGLE AND CROW STORY)

Told by **Nakhela—Hazel Bunbury**[*]

Kwadą̂y · kwàzhà · 'äni, · 'ä mà̧, · chu · dadı̧tàr kanùr · nan · käy.
Long ago · it was · she said, · my mom, · water · flooded · earth · on.

Aju · nan · kwadä́ı̧.
No · land · area seen.

Chùnäy · yè · Ts'urk'i · tàduh · käy · dakeke.
Bald Eagle · and · Raven · driftwood · on · they sat.

Lhŭa · yè · taatlèt · yekĕna, · ayet · t'ù̧ · kekenjì'.
Fish little · and · seaweed · they eat, · that · by · they lived.

"Shań · 'A Shäw · ĭch'e," · 'alhèkeni.
"I/Me · Elder · I am," · they said to each other.

Ts'urk'i · 'äni, · "Ä lä! · Shän · 'A Shäw · ĭch'e."
Raven · said, · "Brother-in-law! · I/me · the Elder · I am."

'Àk'e · 'äni · Chùnäy, · "Ajù'! · Ajù'! · Shän · 'A Shäw · ĭch'e."
Then · said · Eagle, · "No! · No! · I/me · the Elder · I am."

Chùnäy · 'äni, · "Shän · 'A Shäw · ĭch'i.
Eagle · said, · "Me/I · the Elder · I am.

Ye kû̧ · 'ä thì · dak'al · nį̧'ı̧a?"
My · head · white · you see?"

'Àk'e · 'alhèkeni, · "Ts'aăt · thadŭt'aâl · ni.
Then · they said to one another, · "Hat · let's put it on · let's.

Ma · u yè · kwajentl'ùr · 'A Shäw · ŭch'è · shı̧'."
Who · it with · make it get dark · the Elder · to be · will."

'Àk'e · Ts'urk'i · ts'aăt · tthàdàt'ä̧ · k'e, · aju · 'àkwàzhà'.
Then · Raven · hat · put it on · when, · nothing · happened.

Shak'â · kèkwadàch'į.
Still was · light out.

K'athù̧ · ts'aăt · yî · yèch'ì.
Tried · hat · down · it he pulled.

*Told in the Southern Tutchone language by Nakhela—Hazel Bunbury. Hazel often tells this humorous story to schoolchildren and other audiences, and published an English version of the story in her book *Dashäw Ts'an Kwändür Stories From Our Elders* (Whitehorse: Ta'an Kwach'än Council, 2012). Daniel Tlen wrote the version below, in collaboration with Hazel, for this publication in 2019. The English interpretation is from her book.

Shàk'a · kèkwadach'į, · aju · 'àkwàzhà.
Still · light out, · nothing · happened.

'Àk'e · Chùnäy · dë thì · käy · ts'aăt · thadà'ą.
Then · Eagle · his head · on · hat · put.

Dë thì · käy · dàye'ą̆ · ch'û, · kwäjentl'ùr.
His head · on · put on · soon as, · it began to get dark.

Yî · yèch'ì · k'e, · kwajenàtl'ùr', · kwajenàtl'ùr'.
Down · he pull · then, · it got darker, · it got darker.

Ts'urk'i · 'ăni, · "'Ă lă? · Ă lă?"
Crow · said, · "Brother-in-law? · Brother-in-law?"

Chùnäy · aju · 'i ts'àn · kàkwįna.
Eagle · not · him to · he spoke back to it.

Kwatl'ą̆y · Ts'urk'i · neêzhat, · 'ààk'e 'ashâw · kįzhal,
After a while · Crow · got scared, · real loud · he yell,

"'Ă lă! · Ă lă! · Tlą dįni nâ, · nań · 'A Shäw · niche na."
"Brother-in-law! · Brother-in-law! · True, · you say · Elder · you are."

'Àk'e · Chùnäy · ts'aăt · thàjedàt'ą,
Then · Eagle · hat · he began to take it off,

thaayedaat'aâl · ch'û · kèkwadàch'į.
taking it off · as it was · it became light out.

Shàwuthân · tthayedata' · k'e · dzĕnù · lakwàzhà.
Good · took it off · then · day · it became.

Kwàka · ch'e' u yè kwanjì · kàanùr · nan käy
That's why · it is known · all over · earth

Chùnäy · 'A Shäw · 'ach'e · yiw.
Eagle · the Elder · it is · that.

Adaalàl Kwàch'e Kwadą̂y (It is spring time long ago)

ENGLISH INTERPRETATION

This was one of my favourite bedtime stories as a child, told to me by my grandma Tuchàtk'e and my mom, Ukàts'enatäy. This story happened long, long ago when the world was young, still covered with water, and the land was still being formed. Ts'urk'i (Raven) and Chùnäy (Bald Eagle) were the only creatures on earth.

Ts'urk'i and Chùnäy were sitting on a piece of driftwood, arguing about who was the older of them. Ts'urk'i said, "I am the older one, Brother-in-law. I am older than you." The Chùnäy said, "No, I am the older one. Can't you see my white head? I am the oldest creature on earth." They argued back and forth like this for a while as they sat on the floating wood. Finally, they decided to have a contest to see who was the oldest. The Chùnäy said, "We will put on a hat. If it gets dark when we put on the hat, it will prove who is the oldest!" So the Ts'urk'i put on the hat first, and nothing happened. He pulled the hat further down on his head, and nothing happened. Finally, he crammed it all the way down over his head, and still nothing happened. Then the Chùnäy put on the hat. As soon as he put it on, it became overcast. As he pulled it down further on his head, it became darker and darker. When he pulled it all the way down, it became black as night and there was total silence. They sat there for a while in darkness and silence, except for the water lapping on the log.

Finally, the Ts'urk'i called out into the darkness, "Ála! Ála! Brother-in-law." The eagle did not answer him. The raven called out again, "Ála! Ála!" Still, the Chùnäy did not answer. Finally, the Ts'urk'i began to panic. He yelled out loudly into the darkness, "ÁLA! ÁLA! You were right, Brother-in-law! You are older! You are the oldest!" The Chùnäy began to remove his hat. As he slowly took it off, it began to get light out until it was completely daylight! That's how they knew that the Chùnäy was the oldest.

The oldest creature on Earth.

Tl'ahụ

facing top Chùnäy (bald eagle).
facing bottom Ts'urk'i (raven).

Ka'ewa—Emma Ina Shorty

Ka'ewa—Emma Ina Shorty
of the Crow Clan was born in
Carmacks to Violet and Old
McGundy in 1926. Her father
died before she was born,
so her elder brother, Taylor
McGundy, had a big influence
on her childhood, along with
her mother. They taught her
stories and traditional lifeways on the land. She married
George Shorty and they had ten
children, travelling on their seasonal rounds with their large
family and looking after many
more children who needed help.
They hunted, fished, trapped
and gathered foods year-round,
living in many different places
from Carmacks to White-
horse. Northern Tutchone was
Emma's first language and she
maintained lifelong fluency,
contributing to programs at the
Yukon Native Language Centre. She passed away in 2016,
leaving a legacy of storytelling,
kindness and generosity.[8]

TS'AW CHO AN (BIG FROG DEN)

Told by Ka'ewa—Emma Ina Shorty*

Eyet · Ts'aw Cho · nánji · hūch'i, · hunįn, · ă-dáát
Those · Frogs Big · lived · it was, · they say, · place downstream

eyet · Ts'aw · Cho · An · úyi · henįn · Eagle Rock · heyénįn.
that · Frog · Big · Den · its name · they said · Eagle Rock · they call it.

Enę · enāw · Hunäy · k'e · Ts'aw · Cho · u t'át · nánji · ch'i · ni.
They said · tell me · Story · when · Frog · Big · inside · lived · was · said.

Eyet · hech'i · eju · Dän · yéch'a · néjí · heyénįn · nę.
That · was · not · People · affair · they lived there · they said · did.

Dän · a-nú · a'áw, · tth'äy · eyet · Khwän · yí · Khwän.
People · toward us · floated, · heard · that · Raft · with · Raft.

Há k'e · nįn, · "Ts'oyę nę́!" · hénįn, · tth'ą̈ y.--
After that · they said, · "Let's kill them all!" · they said, · was heard.

"Ts'oyę nę́! · Ts'oyę nę́! · Eyet · Ts'aw."
"Let's kill them! · Let's kill them! · Those · Frogs."

Dän, · Khwän · yí · téhe'äw, · Dän · tl'akú, · Dän,
Person, · Raft · with · come to shore, · People · all, · People,

Dän · u ts'ín · tééjaw. · Tth'äy, · a-däy. · Eyet · Dän
People · it to · came to shore. · Heard, · up above. · Those · People

k'e, · sék'ē · Khwän · ka · détth'i · do · įnch'í · heejäw,
then, · still · Raft · on · they sat · for · they went · without them,

įnch'e · héejaw · a-däy · Ts'aw · Cho · An · ts'ín · tééjaw.
they went · without them · above · Frog · Big · Den · to · they went up.

Eyet · akú · Tso · yáálāw · k'e, · húyū · ts'ín · adäw
That · now · Wood · they carried · there, · area to there · to · they went

tth'ä̈y, · Dän. · Akú · u Aan · u ts'ín · nânjäw · k'e, · ja!
they say, · Person. · Now · its Den · it to · they came there · when, · where!

*Ka'ewa—Emma Ina Shorty recorded this story in Northern Tutchone with her daughter Enkhume—Anne Ranigler at the Yukon Native Language Centre on Wednesday, January 31, 2007. Anne transcribed the Northern Tutchone version and translated it into English on February 1, 2007, and revised it in March 2020 for this publication with assistance from Daniel Tlen.

Dän · yi · hīī'yááw, · tth'äy, · "Khuu!"
People · with · it breathed out toward them, · they say, · "Khuu!"

Nịn · łôa · eyet · Dän · a-tthi · tänitl'et, · tth'äy.
It said · truly · those · People · downhill · they fell into water, · they say.

Hatl'a choa · eyet · Khwân · ka · détth'i · hatl'a choa · adeêgę.
All of them · that · Raft · on · they sat · all of them · were killed.

Hu yu · ts'in · hêeje · eyet · Ts'aw · Cho · Tagé · gé · han'rą · k'e,
Area · from · did · that · Frog · Big · River · along · went · then,

dé'rą, · tth'äy. · Dän · łänthät, · Dän · hudégę, · huts'ụa
they left, · they said. · People · got hurt, · People · killed, · that is why

de'ra ts'ọa · ch'i · né. · U tl'áán · haju · húyū, · haju nánji.
they went away · was · did. · After that · nothing · there, · nothing live there.

Etsía · ịntǎ · huyinye, · tth'äy, · hutl'áán · eyet · Ts'aw
My grandpa · inside · he saw, · they said, · it after · that · Frog

de'ra · tl'aan. · Dech'äw · huyinyę · lik'e · je · ukek
they went away · after that. · Porcupine · went in · because · in · tracks

ukek · huyinye, · tth'a'ÿ. · Ts'éna · hetę lọ · eyet · dịnk'ę
tracks · went in, · they say. · Candle · he had · that · he lit it

łôa · łoodzék · lôoch'i · hunịn · u t'áát · ge,
everything · was shiny · just like it · they said · it inside · way,

a yę · lêech'i · u-t'áát · hutl'áá cho. · Eyet · jí
that · just like · it inside · all all over. · That · in

Ts'aw · Cho · Aan · jí, · tth'ayu · hutl'äw · daję, · tth'äy.
Frog · Big · Den · in, · straight down · it went down · the bottom, · they say.

Chu · ts'ịn · hetę · e-yu · hutl'äw · daję nịn,
Water · to · sitting · there · going down · the bottom this,

Dajun · Ts'aw · Cho · An · ech'i. · Eyet · jí · tthayudo,
This · Frog · Big · Den · is. · That · happen · straight down,

daję. · Chu · ts'ín · daję · hééch'i?
it went down. · Water · to · went down · is (I guess)?

Etsi · intát · huninę, · u'an.
My grandfather · inside · saw, · there den.

Tl'a kú.
The End.

Adaalàl Kwàch'e Kwadą̂y (It is spring time long ago)

ENGLISH INTERPRETATION

They say frogs lived at Eagle Rock. They call it Big Frog Den.

When my mother told me the story about this, she said a Big Frog lived inside the den. Actually, it was nobody's business that they were living there. Some people came by raft, and they said, "Let's kill them, let's kill them, let's kill all the frogs."

The people came with rafts. Some of the people started to climb toward the frog den. Some of the people stayed on the boat. And some of the people climbed up to the Big Frog Den.

They carried wood with them. They all climbed up toward the frog's den. As they came closer to the den, suddenly the frog blew his breath at them, Khuu! As he did, the frog blew the people down the hill and into the water. The frogs killed all the people. They killed the ones on the boat, too.

From that time the frogs all came down to the riverbank. Every one of them left that site. Because they killed people, that's the reason they left, never to be seen again and never to return to Eagle Rock.

My grandfather saw inside the cave after the frog left the cave, I guess. He tells a story about when one day he was hunting porcupine. He followed the porcupine into the cave. He lit a candle that he was carrying. Inside the cave when he lit the candle it was really bright like that [pointing to tin foil] all over the place. Like crystal inside, I guess.

This was the den of the Big Frog. Then the cave went straight down, maybe it went toward the water, I guess. That's what my grandfather saw on the inside of the cave.

The End.

facing Ts'aw Cho An (Big Frog Den) at Eagle Rock. People say that you are not to make a sound while passing this place or the Frog's spirit will take you.

above Ts'aw (wood frog).

Ługûn—Lugóon—Sophie Smarch

Sophie Smarch, or Ługûn (Inland Tlingit) or Lugóon (Coastal Tlingit), was born on Teslin Lake at the B.C.–Yukon border in 1930 to Annie Maryann Morris of the Yanyèdí Clan, whose mother's people came from Juneau, and father Frank Morris, whose people were Inland Tlingit of the Ishkìtàn Clan. Sophie learned the traditional ways of her Tlingit ancestors—how to hunt, fish, trap and preserve the bounty of the land to make a good life. Her father's mother lived to be 116 and passed down many survival lessons, especially the importance of sharing. Sophie was proud to be a Tlingit woman and a hunter, and held deep knowledge of her traditions and language. Her children all went to residential school, where they suffered many abusive practices unknown to Sophie at the time. Sophie lived and worked in Whitehorse for many years, continuing her family's tradition of passing down wisdom through storytelling. In recent years she recorded many of her stories in Tlingit on YouTube as a legacy for future generations. Sophie passed away in 2020.[10]

Nindal Kwädīndür
(I'm going to tell you a story)

XÓOTX X'AYAAKUWDLIGADI SHAAWÁT (THE WOMAN WHO SAID SOMETHING TO OFFEND THE BEARS)

Told by Ługûn—Lugóon—Sophie Smarch*

Axh toowu yak'é · yei yagée kat, · i.în · shkakwkhwałnîk.
I am happy · on this day, · to you · I will tell a story.

Ch'âkw, · ch'âkw, · asâyi · a kat xhat seiwaxh'akw, · tlêkw.
Long ago, · long ago, · its name · I forgot, · berries.

A áwé â k̂eixh hîn wát. · Kanat'a áwé · à kanat'êtch,
They grow there river delta. · It's blueberries · that grow there,

àxh du.în · ch'i tlákw. · Sheyadihên.
people pick them · all the time. · There's lots.

A tlènaxh shàwat áwé, · tidên khumduwak'ít, · nèł niyàdé dê
It was one woman, · they picked lots, · to home now

yû.á, · de xânà · áyá. · Tlâkw yà ana.át.
they said, · now evening · it is. · Quickly they walked.

Wé tlenáxh shàwát, · s'îk gande nagùdi · kâ áwé yan · kamdliyás'.
That one woman, · bear droppings · on she · stepped.

Du tlêighu · łdakát yan · kamjixhén · du jinákh.
Her berries · all out · dumped out · from her.

Ghâxh, · gushé · yà yu wayankhêini. · "Jâdê," yû dàyadukhá,
She was crying, · I don't know · what all she was saying. · "Be quiet now," they told her,

łighas · yaxh khuxhêyana · khânîch. · Wé à tlénx' i à · yàde yakhałît.
taboo like · she would · talk. · The big ones · she swore at.

Dèxwâ, ch'a at.â · wé du tlêghu kax · akawaxhiji yé. · "Tlâkw de"
Later, she just sat · her berries out · she spilled at. · "Hurry now"

ch'a ghà yû dàyadukhá. · Du nakh awa.àt, · yàkwdé nèłde axh àwa.àt.
in vain they told her. · They left her, · into the boat, to home, they went.

Ghâxh, · tsas du ît xh'amduwatán, · yê dàyadukhá,
She was crying, · then someone spoke to her, · they said to her,

"Mà sáwé î ghâxh?" · "Axh tlèghu · axh jinákh · yexh kamjixhen."
"Why are you crying?" · "From me · from me · out it spilled."

*Told in the Tlingit language by Ługûn—Lugóon—Sophie Smarch, who recorded this story with Joe Binger in 2015.[9] In the Tlingit way, according to the older Elders, people are not supposed to talk directly about grizzly bears, so when the narrator mentions "the big ones," she is talking about grizzly bears in a respectful way. This story is also known as "The Woman Who Married the Bear." Teslin Tlingit Elder Bessie Cooley transcribed and translated the Tlingit version for this publication and provided the English interpretation.

"G̲hàyatî. · I jiyís · àxh yêkh khwasanî," · yû dàyadukhá.
"It's okay. · For you · I will pick it up," · she was told.

Àxh łdakát · du tlêkw yî,adi · tle shwahík tsú.
From then all · her berry pails · were full again.

Łdakát wé tlêkw · wush kàde yê mdudzinì.
All the berries · she put together.

Dèxwâ · àxh wudihân · we g̲hàxh shût àyi yé.
Later · she stood up from · where she sat crying.

Wé tlêkw àxh amsi.în (pail). · Tle daa yamkhududlighát
The berries she picked up (pail). · And she forgot

wé at tlénx' · ashji.în · yà.anasín · à wé du tlêghu.
the big one · with her · was carrying · the one her berries.

Gushé, · nàłée áwé · at has wu.àdi yé. · Yâx' xi wa.át.
I don't know, · it was long ways · they travelled to. · Here it got dark.

Wé khâ yè ashdàyakhá, · "Ch'a yàx' dê hà gaxhê." · "Gúk." At wudishî.
The man told her, · "Just here now let's camp." · "Okay." She helped him.

Wé hàw · wush kâdé. · Uhân tsu · hàw · tuł'îx'i tsas · às yík daxh tu
The boughs · piled up. · Us too · boughs · we break only · from spruce trees

ł'îx' nijin · kînà dáxh. · Tle · ash yís · x'ânt unûkch · wé khâ.
would break · from up high. · And · at/with her · mad he would get · that man.

"Tlèl a yaxh · áwé yê dà.iné, yisikû gí?" · "Mànaxh sáwé?" · yû adàkhá.
"Not right · it is you do, do you know?" · "Why is that?" · she told him.

"Ch'a wé tl'átgi ka · hàwu áwé yak'ê." · Ach áwé wé · tl'atgi kax
"Just the ground on · boughs are good." · That is why the · ground off

ayamsihâyi · hàw axh yê daxh adàné. · K'idên · amłiyéxh · wé à has
he gathered · boughs he picked up. · Good/well · he fixed up · the place they

wagha xhêyi yé. · Tle a katsewaxh'ák, · wé ch'a tlèxh · àn agûgu · khâ.
will camp. · And she forgot, · the for good land · he knows · man.

above Kanat'a (blueberries).

Dèshgi, dèshgi, dèshgi, · ch'ayàk'udé áwé · dleit yei wùni.

Later, later, later, · suddenly it was · it snowed.

"Gûk, · nèłde de · naxh tu.àt," · yû ashdakhá. · Tle àn wùgùt.

"Okay, · to home now · let's go," · he told her. · And she went with him.

Yà has na.át. · Yà has na.át. · Gushéi mâ kunałî

They walked. · They walked. · I don't know how far

at has wu.ât sáwé, · hít amsitîn, · nùw hit áwé · yû dusâgin ch'âkw.

they walked when, · she saw a house, · it was a fort house · they called it long ago.

Wé às kê dułyéxhch, · wé hít tleł tsu · xh'a.ât aka ti tsu.

The trees they built, · the house didn't even · have a door in it.

A shakîde · dzèt · at shudustànch, · axh kè a átchjin.

To the top · ladder · was leaned against it, · they used to climb up it.

We ch'âkw · xha khustîyin · ach áwé yê hít · dulyéxhin.

Long ago · it existed · that's why the house · how they'd build.

A yîx' nagêch. · Khushtuyêxh tsu tlêł xh'awûl a yí yê tîxh

It was big inside. · No matter if there was no door

tsu tâkw kanaxh · a yî khundu.éch. · Dèshgi, dèshgi

to winter over · they lived in it. · Finally, finally

tleł tsu awuskú · mâyikuwât'sa · khaa xhù yû yatì, · ch'a yâk'uda áwé

not too she knew · how long · them among she was it was, · suddenly

a xhax'êw · tsas kèmdzigít wé shâwat. · Mâsê shdênt

they were sleeping · when she awoke the woman. · How around her

khudatîs' wé nèł yì. · Dàsáwé wé nèł yî, · tle mâsa kûgéi,

she looked in the room. · Here in the room, · as big as it is,

at tlénx' · at x'éx'w. · Chush dà yâ anałghín tliyàde · k'idên.

the big ones · were sleeping. · She looked all around her · good.

Yàx' áwé, · ch'a yàdachûn · shamdzitâ tle tâch · uwajákh.

And then, · she just rolled over · and she fell · asleep.

A kat sèwaxh'ákw. · Yàx' · áwé · gán ghà · akghwa.ât,

She forgot about it. · Here · it is · wood for · they will go,

gán shuwaxîx. · Tle hú tsu khûn wùgùt.

wood was all gone. · And she too went with them.

Wé hîn yík, · tle tsas wé · hîn tâ daxh · áwé gán · yê dà duné.

At the river, · only the · underwater from · it is · they took.

Tle tsas · we hintâ daxh à · yê has adàné · wé khu.û.

And only · the underwater ones · they took · those people.

Mâ sakw shê · yû adà tuwatî. · (Wé du âyi khu.á dâk)

How is that · she wondered. · (The hers though back/inland)

Ch'âl dax wudzi xuxgu · daxh alît · wush kâdé.

Willows those dry ones · she threw · in a pile.

Du gáni · tle shxh'anà · daxh du tsèxht.

Her wood · out of their way · them they kicked.

"Tlel ayaxh · áwé · yè dà iné," · wé du xhúxh. · A jît ghâxh wé du gáni

"Not right · it is · you are doing it," · that her husband. · Over it she cried her wood

àde dàduné yé. · Tlel tsu · du îxh · khuwaxìx, · wé gán du yà.

how they were treating it. · Not to · to her · paid attention, · the wood they packed.

A wé du àyi · tle wûsh kat awul.àtch khûn. · Nagútch wé neilde.

That her own · she would put with them. · She would go home.

Wé du gáni gândé · du lît. · Ch'a.àn, · khûxh dashî tsu.

That her wood outside · they threw. · Even so, · she helped them too.

Deixwáa · xànà · nel · awa.at. · We tliyà · gukshutû · shâwát shàn

Finally · evening · home · they came. · The over there · corner · woman old

ax' kindachûn · unúkch · tle ch'a àde · tsu natêch.

there up straight · would sit up · and then just · sleep again.

Ch'i tlakw · wugûdi · tle a xh'êxh datánch. · Da x'ûn wu xhiyi sá

Always · when she would leave · she would speak to her. · After how many days

tsu · gán gháa · àwáat. · Shâwat yê asdàkhá · dúshá ên,

again · wood for · they went. · Woman told her · with her head,

"I.îx · a áwé · àxh · khukamdik'ît · gán ghâ." · A xhant uwagút.

"With you · it is · from · everyone is gone · wood for." · She came to her.

"I.ît khadashît áyá · i xwaxhûxh. · At tlenx' áwé imsinêxh,

"To help you is · why I called you. · The big ones it is that saved you,

yisikû gí? · Xhat tsu · yè xhat wùnî. · Ach áyá

do you know? · Me too, · that happened to me. · That's why

yéi khâ xhût xhát kamdlishât. · I tawàsagûwu · i.îdekh · khwadashî.

like people among I am trapped. · If you want · to you · I will help.

Xhwasikû mâ sá · a shuyadà · yà akhgwa.ât · wé jun. · Wé kha tuwu

I know how · around · they will go · that dream. · A person's mind

ke dut'îch." · Yu adàkha, · "Nas'k yagì · yidadi daxh · àghâ

they find." · She told her, · "Three days · from now · then

yandekh gwanî · i.ádi i jiyis." · Á áwe tlel tsu… · à khutuwu yé.

be ready · your things for you." · It wasn't even… · where we live.

Ach áwé xhât xuk, · tleł tsu à dus.êxh wé xhât xùk.

That's why fish dry, · not even cook any that fish dry.

Tle ch'a yê has a xhânìch. · Du âyi · khu.a at'ushnîch.

Just like that they'd eat it. · Hers · though she roasted.

Dèxwâ nas'gi à yagî, · tsu àwa.ât tsu gán ghâ. · Àghâ áwé ashwûxùxh,

Finally on the third day, · again they went wood for. · That's when she called her,

"I àt yaxh áyá xhát kàwahâ, · i àt yaxh. · Iguayaxhx'wán,

"Like your paternal aunt I am, · like your paternal aunt. · Encouragement and support,

shghîsnèxh. · Yâdu àde yàghisgit ye," · yû. · "Yidat ghunayê yegûdî,

save yourself. · Here is what you will do," · like that. · "Now, if you start walking,

yaghîghákh. · Iguà.axhx'wán. · Yâdu áyá · àdekh ghîsgîdi yé.

you will make it. · Encouragement and support. · Here is · what you will do.

I yik has ikakwghwakê, · ayi.àdi ya hîn · khudaxh · i xhènáxh

They will track you, · it is there this water · too much · to you

yà has na.adi · yû at tlénx' · we hîn · i xhusyik àyaxh kasaxá

they are catching up · the big ones · the water · your tracks into pour

àxh kê tleł · i xènáxh has wugha.àt,

from there · they won't catch up to you,

hîn khudaxh kakwgwagè has du xh'anà. · Yè áyá · i ît xwadishî,

water too much will be in their way. · This is how · to you I help,

yà dáxh gagu · tlâkw, · kha ch'a tleł · kóogéiyi · yaa neegúdi.

from here go · quickly, · and don't · carelessly · you travel.

Xûn àde wuduwanugu ye, · àde áwé yàghî gût,

North wind the way is blowing, · that's the way you will go,

tleł tsu gunêde yù igûtdakh. · Kha xhandékh ghî gût.

don't change direction. · You will come to people.

Mànx'ís gushúkh tàt ikgwaxhî · khushtuyexh tsu tàt yaa

Maybe nine nights you will camp · no matter too night you

nigoodi łíł ch'a kùgê yû i.gutákh, · kha ch'a tleyê yan hán ch' tlakhw," · yû

walk don't any old way you walk, · stop. Stand still all the time," · she

ashdakha wé shàwat shân. · Tle axh'ayexh, · mà nagût sáwé · àwa. áxh

told her, that woman old. · Just like she told her, · as she walked along · she heard

akayêk wé xûts a jín dàt. · Wé hîn àde asdàkhá yaxh amsinî.

the noise of the bear's paws. · The water as she was told to she did.

Dàsáwé tsu â tlèn · yan ûwadà. · A t'ênaxh kèjixíx,

Here there a big lake · flowed there. · She ran behind it,

khushtuyéxh tsu · mâ kunaɬiye yêdesá. · Wé shâwat shàn
no matter too · how far to. · The woman old

áwé yê · asdakhá yàdu · xhât xùk · ghanida shât, yû.
it is like this · told her here · fish dry · pop in your mouth, like so.

Oooh wé xweitl yaxh · shtidanoogu, · xhât xùk áyá, · yè ashdakhá.
Oooh that tired like · she felt, · fish dry this is, · she told her.

Dêshgi kêmjixíx, · keimjixíx, nàɬee · at ùwagûdi yé · tât uwa.àt giwa tle
Still she ran, · she ran, long ways · she got to · night they arrived maybe

nèɬ ùwanúk, · tle tâch ùwajakh. · Ts'ùtàt axh kê anagut, tsu.
she sat inside, · and fell asleep. · Morning waking up again.

Kêmjixíx, · dèshgi, dêshgi, · tleiɬ tsu dâsa ùwátî. · Mânagut sá ts'as,
She ran, · still, still · not too anything she took. · When she walked so far,

khâ àn.îti àwat'î. · Ahhh axh tlâ has du àn.îti yê yatî yàdu.
she found a campsite. · Ahhh my mothers, their campsite it is here.

Tle àxh yaxh yà wagut du tûwu ɬitsîn wé àn.éeti, · àn.îti uwat'îyi.
She walked away her spirit was strong, · as she had found a camp.

Dêshgi, dêshgi, · dàx'ûn à · tledê xânà, · khâ se awa.áxh.
Still, still, · the fourth · almost evening, · she heard voices.

Tle tsas akamdlixhîtl', · às gêt uwanúk. · Màsakshe yekhw
She just got scared, · she sat against a tree trunk. · What will I

khwakhâ tleɬ.shakde · xhat yaghaxh dutîn, · ɬdakát yûtuwatánk.
say, maybe not · they will recognize me, · she was thinking every which way.

Tle tâch uwajákh, · asiyekh ch'a yèsu khî.á yànagút, · tsas hâw ghà
And she fell asleep, · the next day at daybreak she was walking, · and boughs for

at awa.àt · wé shâ. · Dà sáyá tsú yé . . . · "Aaay khuxhwat'î, · àshakshe?
they walked · those women. · What the . . . · "Aaay, I found someone, · I wonder who?

Tle hàt yi.á." · Du xhant kha ɬuwagúkh. · Yìwayât · ɬyûdutínxhi
All of you, come." · To her they ran. · Long time · they didn't recognize her

tléɬ tsu k'idên shûɬtíni. · Yá du shaxhâwu · kha dàsá wuɬich'éxhw.
not too well she look after herself. · That her hair · and everything were dirty.

Tleil tsu dàsá uyâ · ch'a.àn áwé · du xháni has khîn.
She didn't look like anything · even so · with her they sat.

"Shyidzikû gi, · mâsá khiyanûk, k'idên gi i.tî?"
"Do you know who you are, · what are you doing, are you okay?"

Khà xhût amdligîn, · "À, axh yû xh'atángi · tleɬ khutxhwaghix',
She looked around at them, · "Yes. My language · not I lost,

xhát áyá, xhát." · Du sàyi · akat xhat sèwaxh'ákw, · shdisâkw.

me, this me." · Her name · I forgot, · she introduced herself.

Tlâkw áwé · wèdu has · ka i îsh tin · yûdu has,

Quickly it is · over there · with your dad · they who are over there,

Àde · jimduwatân. · Tle ash dêkî wé · du tlâ, · kha du îsh,

Over there · led somebody by the hand. · And that · her mother · and her father

du îk' has, · du shátxhi has · ayamduwatín.

her brothers, · her older sisters · they recognized her.

Ye áwé · kàwagê wé shkłlnîk. · Yàx' áwé du îsh · kha du tlâ,

That is · the size the/that story. · Here her father · and her mother,

"Tea yê gaxhtusanî · shułtî áyá khâ xhexh at gaxtûtî. · I yitde yis áyá

"Tea we will do · it is people we will feed. · It is for you

wùsh kâde at kamtuwajéł. · Hà ch'a a yànaxh áwé · wûk'ê yîdat yidisêkw.

we gathered things. · But it is better · now you're alive.

Ha tleil tsu · has a kuwa.àkhw · wé yûxh'atánk · ach áwé

And not even · they tried · a speech · that's why

tea yei gaxhtusanî i jîyís. · Ûwayâ · gunalchîsh · yû x'eiyatûkhàyi

tea we will do for you. · It's like · thank you · we are saying

yáxh áyá." · Łdakat yède · yan has amsinî · ajîyis.

like it is." · Every way · they finished it · for it.

Khà xhêxh has at wûtî · tleił tsu àsá wudu.îx.

They fed the people · not to anyone they invite.

Ghûch kha · Yêł kha · łdakat · wùshxhût akhîn.

Wolf people and · Crow people · all · together they sat.

K'idein atxha khâ xhêxh has àwatî. · Tle àxh has wudlitsûw we àndé.

Good food they fed people. · From there they moved to town.

Tle ch'a àxh · has du xhan · naxh nèł · uwagút wé khuwusgîdi has du sîk'.

And from there · with them · into home · came the once was lost their daughter.

Yei áwé · kaawagê wé shkłlnîk.

That is · the size/length of the story.

Gunalchîsh · axh xèt · yinsa.àxhi.

Thank you · my voice · you listened to.

ENGLISH INTERPRETATION

I am happy on this day. I will tell you a story.

Long ago, long ago, I have forgotten the name of the berries. It grew at river delta. Blueberries grew there. People picked them from there all the time. There was lots. There was one woman. They had pick lots. And homeward now they said, it is evening now. They were travelling fast. That one woman stepped on bear droppings. She lost all of her berries, all spilled. She was crying, I don't know what all she was saying. They told her to be quiet. She was saying things that are taboo. She swore at the big ones.

Later, she just sat where she spilled her berries. In vain they tried to tell her to hurry. They left her and went home in the boat. She was crying. Then someone spoke to her and said, "Why are you crying?" "My berries spilled." "It's okay, I will pick it up for you," she was told. And her berry pail was full again. All the berries were gathered up together.

Eventually she stood up from where she sat crying. She picked up the pail of berries. And she forgot it was the big one that was helping her carry her berries.

I don't know, it was long ways where they travelled to. Here it got dark. The man told her, "Let's just camp here." "Okay." She helped him gather up boughs.

Us too, when we broke spruce boughs, we would break them from up high in the trees.

And the man would get mad at her, "Do you know you are not doing that right?"

"Why is that?" She told him the ground boughs are the good ones. That is why he picked up the boughs she had gathered off the ground. He fixed it up really good where they were going to camp. And she forgot the man knew the good land.

Later, later, later, suddenly it snowed. "Okay. Let's go home now," he told her. And she went with him. They walked and walked. I don't know how far they walked when she saw a house. Long ago they called it a fort house. They built it of trees and it didn't even have a door. They leaned a ladder to climb up. It existed long ago. That's how they built houses like that. It was big inside. It didn't matter if there was no door, over the winter people lived in it.

Finally, finally, she didn't know how long she was among them. Suddenly, they were sleeping and the woman woke up. She looked around in the house. Here, the big ones were sleeping in large room. She looked all around her really good. Then she just rolled over and fell asleep.

She forgot all about it. Then they were going for firewood. The firewood was all gone and she went with them too. At the river, they were getting underwater wood. The people got only the underwater ones. She wondered why. Her inland willows that were dry she threw in a pile, but they kicked them out of their way.

above Hàw (boughs).

"You are not doing the firewood right," her husband told her. She cried because of how they were treating her wood. They ignored her; they were packing wood. She would put hers together and go home with them. They threw her wood outside. Even so, she helped them too. Finally they came home in the evening.

Over in the corner there was an old woman who would rouse herself and then sleep again. She always spoke to her when she would leave. And for many days they went for firewood again. The woman motioned with her head, "Everyone is gone from you for firewood." She came to her. "I called you so I could help you. Do you know that it is the big ones who saved you? It happened to me too, that's why I am trapped among them. If you like, I will help you. I know how you will walk around in the dream. A person finds their mind." She told her, "Three days from now, get your things ready for you." It was not like where we live. Dry fish, they don't cook any dry fish. They ate it as is but she roasted hers.

Finally, on the third day, they went for firewood again. That's when the old lady called to her, "I am like your paternal aunt, like your paternal aunt." Encouragement and support, "Save yourself. Here is what you will do," like that. "Now if you start walking, you will make it." Encouragement and support. "Here is what you will do. They will track you. If the big ones are catching up, pour that water in your tracks. From there they will not catch up to you. There will be too much water in their way. This is how I have helped you. Leave quickly from here and don't go carelessly. You travel the way the north wind is blowing. That's the way you go. Don't change direction. You will come to people. Maybe you will camp nine nights. No matter two night, don't walk carelessly. Stop and stand still all the time," the old woman told her.

Just like the woman told her, as she walked along she heard the sounds of bear paws. She did what the woman told her to do with the water. Here there was a big lake flowed there. She ran behind it, no matter how far. The old woman told her, "Here you put the dry fish in your mouth like so." Oooh, she felt that tired. "It is dry fish," she told her.

Still she ran and ran. She ran a long ways. It was night and she fell asleep. In the morning, waking up again, she ran and didn't take anything. When she walked so far, she found a campsite. Ahhh, my mothers, their campsite is here. She walked away. Her spirit was strong as she had found a camp. Eventually on the fourth day, as evening was nearing, she heard voices and she got scared. She sat against a tree.

"What will I say? Maybe they won't recognize me." She was thinking every which way. Then she fell asleep. The next day, she was walking again at daybreak. The women were out gathering boughs. What? "Aaay, I found someone. I wonder who? All of you, come." They came running to her. They didn't recognize her for a long time. She hadn't looked after herself too well. Her hair and everything were dirty. She didn't look like anything; even so, they sat with her. "Do you know who you are? What are you doing? Are you okay?" She looked around at them, "Yes, but I have not lost my language. This is me, me." I forgot her name. She introduced herself. "Quickly, your dad is over there." Somebody led her by the hand to her mother, her father, her brothers, her older sisters. They recognized her. That is the length of the story.

Here her father and her mother said, "We will do a tea in appreciation and feed the people. We gathered things for you. Well, it is better now, you're alive," and they didn't even make a speech. "That's why we will do a tea for you. It is like we are saying thank you." They finished it for her in every way. They fed people. Everybody was invited.

Wolf people and Crow people and Ravens all sat together to eat. They fed them really good food. They moved to town from there, and from then their daughter that was lost moved into their home with them. That is the length of the story.

Thank you all for listening to me.

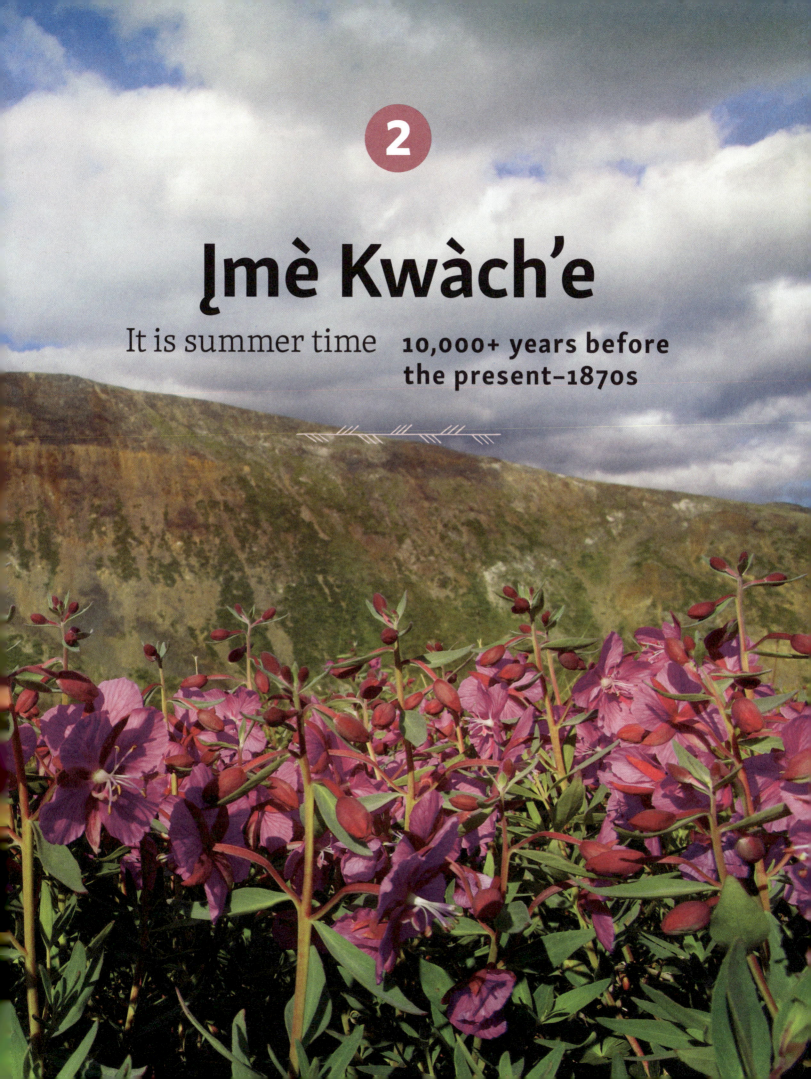

Įmè Kwàch'e

It is summer time   **10,000+ years before the present–1870s**

Long time ago, Mom said this
whole place, it's covered with ocean.

GLADYS HUEBSCHWERLEN[1]

overleaf Fireweed in full bloom at Primrose Mountain.

facing Phlox in midsummer.

SUMMER IS THE TIME of near-twenty-four-hour daylight and warm sunny days—a happy time of growth and abundance, with family gatherings, feasting and celebrations. Skies in the Yukon are mostly blue, with occasional storms. Flowers and trees bloom, migratory birds return by the thousands, animals bear their young, and people come together to harvest fish, berries and roots. Food is plentiful and the days are long, so there is time to relax and enjoy the gifts of this land.

Our kwadą̂y kwadań (long ago people) lived as "part of the land and part of the water."[2] For thousands of years they were completely self-sufficient, thriving on their own resources, technologies, beliefs and life ways, travelling on their seasonal rounds to gather food and other essential items. They traded with other Indigenous peoples as part of a complex network that circulated goods throughout the northwest. Through stories passed down to us we know that our ancestors lived a good life in this land.

Ch'e'a Mą—May Hume

Ch'e'a Mą—May Hume of the Crow Clan was born in 1928 on Scotty Island near Carcross. Her mother, Kàdùhikh—K'ałgwach—K'odetéena—Kitty Smith, was related to Marsh Lake and Dalton Post people. May's father, Kanéł—Billy Smith, was related to Tagish people including Keish—Skookum Jim. May grew up with her parents and siblings, trapping, hunting and mining for gold in various locations throughout the southern Yukon. The family spoke Southern Tutchone, Tlingit and some Kaska as they travelled between Whitehorse, Marsh Lake, Teslin and other areas. May learned many traditional stories from her mother, Kitty, who was a renowned storyteller, and her father, Billy, who was a widely respected leader. She spent some years outside the Yukon in the Charles Camsell Hospital in Edmonton, receiving treatment for tuberculosis, and later worked on Vancouver Island. May returned to Whitehorse for her later years and enjoyed sharing her knowledge with her children, grandchildren and great-grandchildren until her passing in March 2020.[4]

CROW STEALS LIGHT

Told by **Ch'e'a Mą—May Hume**[3]

There's no end to it, you could go days and days and days, different things the Crow did and everything. One time he, well, they didn't have sun. They said there was no sun. But there was Crow that time and everybody was used to just dark, eh, pitch-dark. And here, people play around night time, you know. And he told them, he said, "Gee!" He said, "You guys go to sleep now." He say, "I get tired, you guys play around so much all the time." He say, "I'll make light on you guys, you don't stop." And so, they don't believe him, eh? But before he got the light, he heard about that sun's daughter that have the sun and the star and the moon.

And so he went to it, eh? He went there. And he turned to be this thing here, this little, this little branch, this little branch, eh? And when they get fresh water for that girl, it's just young girl. Young girl, they used to drink fresh water in the morning, eh? For some reason it was like that. So he was this here little needle, see? And then here her mother gave her that drink of water. That man that owns the sun, that's his daughter, eh. So she drank that water, and here she felt something went down in her throat and she—choking sound—"Eww," she say, "I swallow something." And her mom say, "Gee, can't be!" Said, "Because I just got that water, it's clean." And anyway, not very long, and here that girl, she's getting big, here she's pregnant! And so his wife said, "I don't know, no man come around, how that girl get pregnant, eh?" So they don't know.

And then pretty soon, here now it's baby's time to be born. Next that baby can't be born. And they are rich people, too, that one, eh. And they put everything, nice fancy blanket underneath him. Oh, just every kind of blanket, nice. No, he still can't be born because, you know, like, he thinks, "What about poor people?" You know when poor people they have their baby, they not going to be born on top of nice thing all the time, eh? So he think to himself, "I want to be born on squirrel nest."

That's what everybody was born on, Native, squirrel nest, you know. You get all the squirrel nest and you stack it up, eh. And you put that underneath that woman when she's going to have a baby, cover it up with material. And the baby is born on that soft. On that soft squirrel nest grass, eh.

So anyway, they go to this medicine woman and they ask her, "How come that baby can't be born?" She say, "Because you put too much fancy stuff on that thing, that's why that baby don't want to be born." He say, "Try squirrel nest." So they did. Ugh! Right away that little Crow was born, eh. Then he was a little Crow then.

He was human but they call him Crow, eh? He turn to anything. Then he, not even very long, very soon he's born, you know. Here he just wink his eye, his little eye, just black like little crow. And here he wink his eye at . . . his grandma. His grandma says, "Ahhh, look it," he say, "that little baby," he said, "he just wink at me," he said. He got little crow eye, little black eye. Not very long, here that little Crow started grow already. Then not very long after, here that little Crow already started get big, he started talk. Anyways, how smart. Because he want to get that sun, eh.

His grandfather been have that sun inside little box. Sun got its own box and moon and stars. Oh, he cry for that box, eh. That sun and the moon. They tell him, "No, you can't have it," they tell him. Oh, he cry and cry. And that grandfather said, "Oh," he say, "let him play around with it." He said, "He can't lose it, it's inside the house." So they let him have it, eh. Ugh! He open that box like that. Just light shining, he close it, eh. Then next, he hide it away. Oh! He lost that thing. Now, next he start crying for moon, so same thing, they give it to him again. So he play with that, play around with that. Then here, he lost that one again. Now just stars left. So he cry for that one, so they give him that one again, eh. So he got it all now, see. As soon as he got all that stars, moon and sun, then he just fly from there. Gock! He's gone. He got that stuff what he been come to get, eh?

So then he get back to that place where he left first time, where he tell them people to sleep, "I might make light on you." So he come back there again and he try to sleep. And here, they play around again, night time. "Go. Watch yourself," he said. "I'm gonna make light in the sky and light and a night time, and now it's going to be day and night," he say that. They tell him, "Hahahaha." They laugh at him. So here he throw the moon up, he throw the sun up. Both, sun and moon, both

above When Crow threw the
moon into the sky.

same time, up. And here, daylight, just like this, eh? Some of them they got scare, you know? They just lay down in the bush, and that's the one that turn to animals. Like, we were all humans one time, eh. And the ones that got scared, they ran, some of them ran into the water and they turn to be everything that's living thing in the water. And then some of them run up on a tree and it's all that living things on a tree. And some of them flew and them are the living things in the sky. And then the ones that just didn't go nowhere, they just stood one place, them are human.

So that's how they say, you know, that they say that Crow created sun and moon and stars and created all living things on earth, eh? And that was supposed to be the story of that Crow, when they say how he made sun and moon, eh? That's the way it was told to me, anyway.

BIG RAFT STORY

Told by **Gladys Huebschwerlen**[5]

Long time ago. Yeah, when I was small then. We walking on a old trail, turned out to be game trail. Moose and bear and caribou all in that trail. And I find wood, great big wood, about pretty near twice as long as this table. But big one, it's got all kinds of funny face in it. I don't know how it got there. It was about the size of a totem pole. But it's got all funny face in it. I still don't know how it got there.

Not too far away, I find an elephant tusk. And I was riding it, I pretend I was riding a horse. Mom gets mad at me, she always call me a tomboy. And I didn't know that was elephant tusk. Later, Mommy tell me, "You know that big stick you was riding and you said it was a horse?" I tell her, "Yeah." She said that was an elephant tusk. I tell her, "How... did it get there?"

And then about another hundred miles or so, I don't know how far it is, I couldn't tell you how far apart. Way up on top of mountain, find a big raft, big, huge raft. About pretty near same wide as this house. Here, only longer. They joined it longer, longer. Way up on top of the mountain. Logs, big logs. For string they use willow string or roots. 'Cause I tore it apart, it was just mushy, it's been laying there so long...

Klukwan, yeah, toward that place. My daddy kicked it one time and he said, "Get... out of the way!" He say. And I jump on it, and I say, "Oh!" I said, "There's one here look like you!" I say. Then he say, "Oh, get out of here!" He say, kicked it. I asked him, "How this get here? It's all got funny face in it." He said, "Oh, some crazy Indian build it around here some- place," he said. As far as I know, it's still there, 'cause who in the world gonna pack that out? No colour on it now. Just all rotten, just peeling away, just rotting away.

Long time ago, Mom said this whole place, it's covered with ocean. Mom told me that. That's how come that raft was there, on top of that mountain. And that is how that elephant tusk got there and this big, huge, stick got there. That's what Mommy told me. That's what her mom tell her. Her mom, mom-mom or something like that. This whole place was, was burnt, everything was burnt long time ago, too. This whole area, this whole place. How that went now? Water come first... fire come first... I don't remember. Yeah, that's how that elephant tusk got there. 'Cause that got that far, was floating around all over the place, I guess.

Gladys Huebschwerlen
Gladys was born on August 14, 1928, to the Burns family at Marsh Lake. She was Tagish Kwan of the Wolf Clan. As a child she heard the stories of her ancestors told in Southern Tutchone by her mother and father, although she herself did not speak the language in later life. She married George Huebschwerlen and together they raised five children. They made their home at Robinson, where Gladys always kept busy tanning moosehides and sewing mittens, hats and moccasins for her family. She also made dolls clothed in traditional outfits, which she called her babies, and sold them to customers from around the world. She loved to bake and kept her family and friends well fed with fresh bread, buns and Sunday pan- cakes. Gladys and George lived a traditional lifestyle, travelling and hunting up and down the Dempster Highway every year. They broke many trails together for weeks at a time, thoroughly enjoying life on the land. Gladys passed away in 2006.[6]

Ronald Bill

Ronald Bill of the Crow Clan was born in 1936 at his parents' camp at Fifty-Two Mile on the Old Dawson Trail. His mother was Annie McGundy from Big Salmon, and his father was David Bill from Champagne. They lived on the land hunting and gathering until Ronald was nine, when they moved to Whitehorse. They made their home in a tent on the east bank of the Yukon River while his father worked on the White Pass docks. As a young boy, Ronald witnessed the arrival of the U.S. Army in 1942, but soon after he was sent to Choutla Residential School when his father died. He left school at age sixteen and joined the Canadian Army, serving in Canada, the United States and Germany. After leaving the army, Ronald trained as a draftsman and carpenter, then returned to Whitehorse to build homes for the Whitehorse Indian Band. He served on the Band Council for many years. He married Rose Charlie and they had seven children and later many grandchildren. Ronald passed away in 2015.[8]

Nindal Kwädīndür
(I'm going to tell you a story)

CANNIBAL LAKE STORY

Told by **Ronald Bill**[7]

They tell me stories about all these summer areas . . . Coghlan Lake through there . . . I tell you that there is lots of copper . . . they stick out. They say wolverine climb up there for people . . . so kill people. He slides things so people trip into them . . .

They call . . . this lake Cannibal Blood Lake . . . this, Cone Hill. There is a lake there. It is red there, red rock there. A long time ago there were cannibals . . . and they were following these groups of people so they made a slide right down to the lake. They get water from the lake and they made ice on the hill there . . . and these people, they stick out a whole bunch of sharp sticks on the bottom . . . These people were coming down and they started following these guys down the mountain, and here they all slide right into the sticks and they kill them right there. They killed a whole bunch of them. They say it is blood, the blood of those people.

DOUBLE WINTER STORY

Told by **Kashgêk'**—Johnnie Smith[9]

Kashgêk'—Johnnie Smith

Kashgêk'—Johnnie Smith was born near the Marsh Lake dam in 1922. His parents were Kàdùhikh—K'ałgwach— K'odetéena—Kitty Smith and Kanéł—Billy Smith. His father was a nephew of Keish—Skookum Jim. As a child, Johnnie travelled with his family throughout the southern Yukon, hunting, trapping and gold mining. He learned the traditional languages, drumming and stories of his parents and continued to share those with audiences to the end of his life. He served as Chief of the Kwanlin Dün First Nation for three terms between 1969 and 1988. Johnnie Smith died in 2010.[10]

So he [a long-ago man] talked there. He tell people, "From here three years," he say. "Three winter," he say. "You watch this next winter." He said, "Ducks, geese, everything goin' to come in. Ducks, swan, everything gonna fly into here." He said, "Three winter, next one." He say, "Put a lotta grub." He say, "Make sure you kill lots of game. Make sure you put lotta dry meat. Put lotta things what you need." They listen to him, he talking. He said, "When ducks and all come in," he said, "north wind gonna start again. North wind gonna come." He said, "Just quick and the ducks is gonna try to fly back—they all gonna froze."

"Swan, they fly back—they all gonna froze," he said. "All the birds come in gonna froze off." That man—he warn 'em. "Lake," he said, "gonna froze to the bottom." And deepest lake, that's where they fish at, I guess. He said, "Gonna go back winter time, another six months again it be two winter. And you people, you gonna eat your own grandchild." He said, "You gonna be starvation. You people, people, some of 'em gonna turn to cannibal. Your own people, they're kill one another, eat themselves. They don't care, they're gonna go like that." That's what he tell people, that man.

I couldn't tell you how many years ago but my dad, his mother, were just little kids that time, little kids. They walk around, that happened that winter, that double winter. That eatin' people, passed my dad's mother, his kids, you know. And my daddy's mother, spring time coming again so they start digging bear roots. Get hungry, start eatin' that. But five of them eater, man-eaters, they come on top of the hill, over on top of the hill. They didn't see that kids down at bottom and behind a bank. And lucky they didn't hear it. I think if they eat up my daddy's mother and mother get eat up, I wouldn't be here I don't think. Telling this story.

So that's a really true story what happened. Right there they went past, that man-eaters, they went down to that camp and they eat up people. That's what the man saying. That man, he left for good—he didn't come down in here, he gone. He warn people what's gonna happen. And that's what happen.

People got hard time, they said. They go look for lake, poke chisel, you know. They poke down, make a ladder. Go down like a ladder, like down, right down 'til hit the mud. I guess some places were fish that deep water—that's where they fish. So that's a . . . true story there.

Conshua—Rachael Dawson

Conshua—Rachael Dawson (née Baum) was born in 1904 at Fort Selkirk. She was of the Gaanaxteidí Clan. Her mother was Mary Campbell, a Tlingit woman, and her father, William Baum, was also of Tlingit descent. Rachael grew up at Fort Selkirk speaking several languages—including Tlingit and Northern and Southern Tutchone—and hearing the stories of her ancestors. She married George Dawson from Tàa'än Män (Lake Laberge) in 1923. They moved to Whitehorse where they raised their family. Rachael was a renowned storyteller, sewer, culture bearer, community leader and matriarch to a large family of children, grandchildren and great-grandchildren who continue to preserve her rich legacy of stories, cultural traditions and community service to this day. Rachael passed away in 1976.[12]

Nindal Kwädīndür
(I'm going to tell you a story)

THE FIRST POTLATCH

Told by **Conshua—Rachael Dawson**[11]

The first potlatch started with Crow girl down in Haines. She find little worm out in the woods and she keep it and it grow. She nurse it too, they say, with her breast. And it grow big. And pretty soon it was dangerous. It started to be big and danger when she's going to let it go. She talk to it too, and it understand her. She always go down there in the house (where she keep it), and it started to smell funny.

So her brother said, "Gee, people start to notice our house. Every time my sister open the cellar it start to smell awful. She don't let nobody go down there, too. Smell bad."

That snake, I guess he pee too, just like people.

"Every time she open cellar door I always notice it, and she close it quick." When she go down there he listen to it. And she talk, she talk to herself down there. Then he said to his five brothers, "She must got something down there. A person can't be like that. I can't go down to the cellar talk to myself for a long time."

His older brother said, "Why can't we fool her, let her go away someplace?"

"She never go away," they say. "She stay home all time."

She watch that snake, see. One day her younger brother say, "Tomorrow you go down there, see Grandma. See if she want anything done."

Her grandmother was sewing gopher skin. Must be from Yukon, I guess. This happen down in Haines, Alaska, this story. Her stitches are fine, too. Got to be just fine when you sew gopher skin, so it don't pull apart. So she's doing that, helping her grandmother.

"Here, I can't see," she said. "I'll take it home with me," she tell her grandma.

"No, I got to guide you. I want it done well. I don't want it done just any way."

So she want to go home, she want to go home. Her grandma said, "What you got at home anyway? You never come see me or never do anything around here for me for a long time. What happen to you?"

She said, "Nothing. I just don't want to go round," she said.

While she sew that thing, the boys look down [the cellar] and they see two shiny eyes, you know. Snake eye! So they go down there and they look at it. It move around so they get ready.

"I'm going to let it out," he say.

The youngest brother, he say, "You stand this side, you stand here." The cellar open and it crawl up. As soon as he get there they make stick like that [forked] and they poke his neck. His older brother kill it. That thing scream—it make funny noise—it scream, they say. She hear it, that girl.

"Oh," she said, "my son, ah hyeet." She run home and, sure enough, he come out of the cellar and he's dead. She go on top of him and she hold him, she cry.

Then she said, "You people, you take first button blanket you got around here. You wrap it up good. You make a box for it, put it in there and you bury it good." She said, "The reason why I raise this thing is because when somebody go to Inside"—they call it Inside here, this Yukon—"when somebody go Inside they never come back. They always get killed, something like that. They said lot of our friends got killed. They never come back. So I raise this thing. I talk to him. He know you people were his uncle. I know because when I go down to see him, he understand me." She cry. She said, "I want you people to make a potlatch for him."

That's how potlatch started, you see, first time. That Indian lady, Crow lady first started.

"You invite all the Wolf people," she said, "and you make party for him." So they did. And that song she made, that's the one those Indians sing.

"I hear my son. I hear my son cry." She finish that song like that. When they make party, she think about him, I guess she sing that song. When they make party, she sing it and she say, "All you Crow people, Wolf people, you got to use that song." That's what she tell them after.

above Arctic ground squirrels, often referred to as gophers, were snared for both food and fur.

above These terraced ridges at present-day Tàa'än Män (Lake Laberge) mark the shorelines of the ancient post-glacial lake.

"MYTHS" OR MEMORIES?

Myths are often considered to be untrue or fanciful stories, and in the past our ancient stories were sometimes dismissed as having no value. Today our oral traditions are being re-examined as valuable evidence of our ancestors' observations of many happenings and changes in this land over time.

Many of the older stories told by Kwanlin Dün Elders parallel scientific evidence. One example is the oral tradition that describes a huge barrier between winter and summer worlds, which may refer to ice age glaciers eleven thousand years ago. During the last glaciation, the vast Laurentide ice sheet lay over much of Canada, while the Cordilleran ice sheet covered the Rocky Mountains and Pacific coast regions. These ice sheets eventually merged at the height of the Wisconsinan glacial period and effectively blocked any access south from the unglaciated regions of central and northern Yukon and Alaska.

The winter barrier to another world has been described by many of our people. Tagish and Inland Tlingit people told anthropologist Catharine

McClellan of another world on "the other side of the horizon where the sky and the water meet." They said, "Sometimes the sky lifts up from the water long enough for humans to go through."[13] As Elder Angela Sidney described it,

> One time the sky used to come right down to salt water. Here the animals lived on the winter side. It was cold!... So they went to a meeting, all the animals: they are going to try to poke a hole through the sky. They are on the winter side and they are going to poke a hole through the sky so they have summer time, too. Summer is on the other side... Those two worlds were side by side—winter on one side, summer on the other. On one side were winter animals—on the other, summer animals. They broke the sky down, and after that, it went up.[14]

Elders also told McClellan stories of a great flood and of Crow or another animal helping to remake the world after that.[15] Many Yukon First Nations people have heard these stories from their parents and grandparents or had sites pointed out by older people where long ago peoples' rafts from the great flood ran aground.

The whole Takhini River valley, including Haines Junction, was under water when melting glaciers produced Glacial Lake Champagne thousands of years ago. When ice receded in the Coast Mountains and Big Salmon Range, Glacial Lake Laberge covered what is now Whitehorse. This occurred about nine thousand years ago, and this area was under about two hundred feet (sixty-five metres) of water at that time.[16]

This could have been the great flood related in our traditional stories, where Crow remakes the world after the great flood. The Crow story cycle is part of "Earth-Diver" myths that are common throughout northwestern North America. When the Earth-Diver helper brings up earth from below the water, as Seagull does in Louie Smith's story in Chapter 1, the Creator or Crow, depending on different versions of the story, spreads the earth out in the four directions or outward in all directions at the same time. In later episodes, Crow teams up with Esuya (Beaverman), the smartest man in the world, and they travel around fixing the world for humans. They do this by

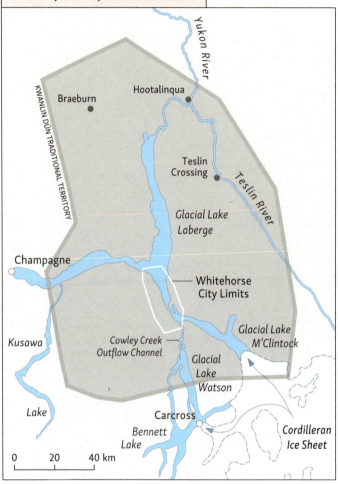

GLACIAL LAKES IN WHITEHORSE REGION, CA. 13,000 YEARS AGO

above As the ice began to melt 10,000 to 14,000 years ago, huge lakes were formed. One of the earliest was Lake McIntyre, which filled the valley to a level 120 metres higher than present-day Łu Zil Män (Fish Lake). Tàa'än Män (Lake Laberge) began to form about the same time. As more ice melted, an immense body of water kept growing until it eventually extended north beyond present-day Lake Laberge, west to Champagne and south to join post-glacial Lake M'Clintock, which covered present-day Tàkwädàdhà (Marsh Lake). As glaciers melted further, glacial Lake Champagne receded and Lake M'Clintock grew to encompass both Marsh and Tagish Lakes.

getting rid of cannibals and making the giant animals shrink to the small size they are today.

Our Elders' stories often describe giant animals that lived in past times, and some of our traditional place names describe places where giant animals or cannibals used to live. Evidence from archaeological sites indicates ancient people did hunt mammoths, horse and bison and shared this vast area with giant beavers and bears. All those animals went extinct many generations ago, but oral traditions about them persist to this day. Louie Smith tells the story of Thäy T'äw (Haeckel Hill) as a place where a large golden eagle once preyed on people:

> That one up there, that's the Eagle Nest Mountain... that Haeckel Hill, they call it. And long time ago, what the Indian people tell a story about it... There's the great big eagle up there, years ago, it's awful bad, and mean, he gotta eat something. And he, if somebody making noise, somebody walking through here, on the trail, he got a good eyes, he could see them from top of hill, and he get him just like a rabbit, pick him up, but it's a big one. Killed a lot of Indian people, long time ago... That's why they call that Thäy T'äw... That's a golden eagle nest. That's what that meant. Thäy T'äw.[17]

How was the disappearance of these giant animals explained by people of earlier times? Many ancient stories tell how Crow, Esuya (Beaverman), Two Brothers or other heroes teamed up and travelled around the Yukon making the world right for humans. When they came upon giant animals or cannibals, they made the giant animals small and killed the cannibals.[18]

These stories were important to our ancestors and they are still part of our lives today. They explain the world as it once was according to our oral traditions. Today there are new influences, such as Christianity and science, that provide other explanations about how the world came to be the way

above Thäy (golden eagle).

facing The giant beaver was the size of a black bear and weighed about 200 kilograms.

it is now. Yet when we look at our First Nations oral traditions, there are many examples that appear to have direct connections to current archaeological, geological and paleontological evidence. Great floods and giant animals are just a couple of the themes that echo through our stories, providing glimpses of our ancestors' first-hand experiences with the changing world around them.

LIFE IMAGINED: THE WAYS OF KWADĄY KWADAŃ, OUR LONG AGO PEOPLE

The stories below are fictionalized accounts set in the eras before written historical records were compiled in the Kwanlin region.[19] They draw on archaeological, geological and paleontological evidence, along with oral traditions, to create an idea of what life may have been like for our people in the distant past. They are set in locations corresponding to the archaeological and geological evidence of the southwest Yukon. Fictional names are based on the landscape and resources available to ancient peoples in that time. Very little is known for certain about these ancient times, and our understanding changes when new archaelogical and paleontological discoveries are made.

Bison Hunting Man

NEAR BEAVER CREEK, CIRCA FOURTEEN THOUSAND YEARS AGO

Bison Hunting Man was sitting on a hill overlooking a creek, working on a stone spear point. Taking a break from stone knapping, he scanned the valley for signs of bison or elk. The landscape was a vast dry grassland and Bison Hunting Man could see across great distances. It was a warm day, the time when the bison were calving. New grass was growing for the calves. The nights no longer were freezing and would stay that way for another four moon cycles. Life was good. There were many more bison than people, so the people never went hungry. Bison Hunting Man and his family had come to this place for a short hunting trip, as his father had done before him. After a few days they would travel back toward the west to the main camp.

Hare Snaring Woman came walking up from the creek where she had checked her snares. As she returned to camp to prepare the hares for an evening meal she smiled, knowing she had caught enough for food to last well into the next day.

Bison Hunting Man's thoughts turned to the stories of long ago when his people had followed the huge bison herds and the elk to the edge of the world. Ice and snow stretched beyond as far as the eye could see, and strong winds blew in icy blasts. The weather had warmed little by little through the years as the ice fields melted and slowly moved farther away from Bison Hunting Man's camp.

Since there was lots of food, Bison Hunting Man did not have to hunt for a while. After some further deliberation, he made up his mind to travel to the southeast, down the valley. Just then, Fast-running Man came sprinting into the camp. He was very excited and told of a big gathering and feast at the main camp at Swan Point, where the swans gather in the spring and fall.

above This spear point was recovered below cabin foundations at Canyon City. Campfire charcoal associated with the point was dated to approximately 2,500 years ago.

The people there had killed a mammoth and its calf. It was a big happening since females stayed in herds and it was difficult to separate cows from the herd to kill. After the kill the Swan Point people sent runners out to all the surrounding camps to invite people for the feast and to witness the event. The news excited Bison Hunting Man and he called his wife and family together. They would leave right away! His exploration to the southeast would have to wait for another time, but Bison Hunting Man told his wife that he would travel to see the White Winter World within the year.

Little John Archaeological Site—Beaver Creek

Based on archaeological evidence, some of the first people entered the south-central Yukon in the Beaver Creek area about fourteen thousand years ago. The area then was a vast grassland that supported large herds of bison and elk. This was the time before forests spread into the region. Food was plentiful and life was probably quite good for the people.

They likely stayed mainly around the Tanana River valley and made seasonal trips to outlying areas. The Little John archaeological site near Beaver Creek is one location of a seasonal camp from fourteen thousand years ago. That site and the Britannia Creek site on the Yukon River are among the earliest human occupations in the central Yukon. Farther north at the Bluefish Caves near Old Crow, archaeologists have found knife marks on animal bones that date to twenty-four thousand years ago.

above Remnant grasslands in the Takhini Valley and Kusawa Lake area are ecologically similar to the steppe tundra that was widespread in Beringia (a vast northern region that included the Yukon, Alaska and eastern Russia). During the ice ages, mammoths and steppe bison roamed terrain like this.

At the Britannia Creek site on the Yukon River, the water would have been flowing wide and fast fourteen thousand years ago, with huge ice sheets to the southwest rapidly melting. There would have been no fish yet, since the river had only recently formed and was full of silt from the glaciers. It would be a while before the river cleared of silt and salmon could navigate the river. There were still woolly mammoths roaming the North. People were killing them for food and for tools from the bones and ivory. Perhaps they used the hides for clothing. The huge leg and rib bones may have provided structural supports for domed shelters covered by animal skins.

Bison in Kwanlin Dün Traditional Territory

Bison first appeared in North America around 160,000 years ago, after crossing the Bering Land Bridge from Asia. They are one of several large mammal species in the Yukon that survived the extinctions at the end of the ice age, some twelve thousand years ago. Nearly 80 percent of the ice age fossils found in the territory are from the steppe bison, the ancestors of today's bison. In the Yukon, bison continued to live alongside elk, moose, caribou and people for several thousand years.

One dramatic find occurred in the Versluce Meadows area of Porter Creek, Whitehorse, in 2012 when a man excavating for his basement found a number of large bones. Paleontologists recognized that these bones came from an ancient bison. They carried out a full-scale excavation that led to the recovery of a nearly complete skeleton almost five thousand years old.

Parts of an ancient bison skull found along the shore of Fish Lake were dated at 3,800 years old. In 2014, bones found on the shore of Fish Lake demonstrated that people hunted and processed bison at their camp more than a thousand years ago. Additional discoveries of ancient bison bones and skulls have been made at Policeman's Point, Rivendell Farm, Franklin Lake, Schwatka Lake and Riverdale. The most recent bison remains—four hundred years old—were found at Annie Ned Creek. For unknown reasons the species likely died out in most of the Yukon at around this time. The bison in the southern Yukon today were reintroduced in 1986.

Łu Zil Män—Fish Lake Archaeological Site

Fish Lake is named Łu Zil Män in the Southern Tutchone language, after the whitefish that spawn there in the fall. According to Elder Jessie Scarff it was also called Dis Hini—Moon Lake in the Tlingit language, because people used to set their nets for trout on Fox Point according to the phases of the moon.[20]

The moon, that's . . . how you set your net at Fish Lake. I was taught that . . . back in 1942, when I first got married. My aunt Jenny Lebarge is telling me. That's this Fish Lake was actually,

above Today's bison are closely related to ancient steppe bison, illustrated here.

facing top Bison skull found at Versluce Meadows. Bison first appeared in North America around 160,000 years ago.

facing bottom Elder Jessie Scarff (*arm raised*) explains traditional land use and trails at Fish Lake camp, 1993.

the Indians believed was run by the moon, because when, when you go set your net, you go which way the moon is . . . That's why my aunt Jenny Lebarge told me that Fish Lake was run by the moon. That's the old-timer's belief and I quite believe it too because I tried different ways. I could go up here when there's a full moon. I know exactly where to set my net, over here or across that side. Or over, out a little ways, and things like that. I always get the fish.[21]

In the past, many families fished Łu Zil Män in summer and winter. They trapped and hunted in the surrounding alpine country in the fall and winter. In summer, many people remember Fish Lake as the site of gatherings and potlatches. In 1993 the importance of Fish Lake in the history of Kwanlin Dün led to a partnership between Yukon government archaeologists and Kwanlin Dün First Nation to explore and further document First Nation history in the area and evidence of the more distant past.

A total of fifteen archaeological sites were recorded as a result of the project, representing occupations of Fish Lake dating from historic times back to the end of the last ice age. The oldest sites appear to be on the mountaintops around the lake, suggesting that people were here soon after the glacial ice retreated. Water levels in Fish Lake were much higher than at

present. The beige/grey shale bedrock of the Fish Lake area was used by all the past inhabitants, giving the stone tools found in the ancient sites their distinctive appearance. By far the largest site was the traditional fish camp, which occupies most of the north end of the lake, extending over two kilometres along the shore. Based on the types of stone tools recovered here, people have been using this camp location for at least five thousand years. Recent shoreline finds at this site provided evidence of bison hunting at the camp approximately one thousand years ago.[22]

Archaeology in the McIntyre Creek Area

In 2010, Kwanlin Dün First Nation and the Yukon government partnered in exploratory excavations at several sites in the McIntyre Creek area in Whitehorse. In addition to trying to better understand the unusual archaeology of this area of Whitehorse, the project was organized to provide a crew of KDFN, Ta'an Kwäch'än and other Yukon university students with opportunities to participate and learn more about Yukon archaeology.

facing top Elders socialize around a fire at the Fish Lake Gathering, a community consultation held in 2018. *Left to right:* Norma Shorty, Irma Scarff, May Bill and Jacine Fox.

facing bottom Flakes of shale, a stone used by our ancestors for toolmaking, found along the shores of Łu Zil Män (Fish Lake).

above Aerial view of Fox Point and the north end of Łu Zil Män (Fish Lake).

left Looking south at Łu Zil Män (Fish Lake).

Archaeologists working in the McIntyre Creek area since the 1980s
have identified thirty archaeological sites in the lower reaches of the creek
valley. Most intriguing about these discoveries is that the majority of sites
relate to a specific period of Yukon history predating five thousand years
ago. A very distinctive stone tool technology is characteristic of this period:
spears, knives and other implements were made by using highly uniform
small stone slivers, called microblades, to form the cutting and piercing
edges of antler and wooden tools.

Why sites predating five thousand years ago concentrate around
McIntyre Creek is not well understood. Archaeologists speculate this may
relate to different subsistence patterns: people of this time may have been
hunting elk and bison, and as a result their camps were situated in places
that later inhabitants did not use as intensively. McIntyre Creek is a natural
corridor between the Yukon River and the alpine regions surrounding Fish
Lake, and this may have been a migration route for bison and elk moving
between their summer and winter ranges.

Work at one of the McIntyre Creek sites was resumed by Yukon College
in 2013 to provide continued opportunities for Yukon students to learn
about archaeology.

facing Several significant
archaeological sites are located
on Kwanlin Dün lands in the
Michie Lake area.

Obsidian Trading Man

NEAR BEAVER CREEK, CIRCA 11,500 YEARS AGO

Obsidian Trading Man, Hide Tanning Woman and their extended family returned to their summer camp at Beaver Creek, joining the rest of their band after a trip to Hoodoo Mountain that lasted a whole moon cycle. It was summer but quite cool... not like the stories his Elders told of warmer times. They had taken their time, exploring and hunting, and then climbing up Hoodoo Mountain to the source of obsidian. People used obsidian for spear and dart points, knives and tools. Obsidian Trading Man's ancestors had discovered the obsidian at Hoodoo Mountain long ago, and his people had been coming here to collect it when obsidian was not available from elsewhere.[23] At Hoodoo Mountain, Obsidian Trading Man had taken his time knapping the obsidian into points and blades. This way he would have less to carry back with him, and he would be ready to trade at any time if the opportunity arose.

It had been a successful trip and now Obsidian Trading Man was looking forward to travelling to the west to trade with the people living on the Tanana River. He felt it was better not to wait too long. Not only did he want to trade, he also wanted to see family and friends. After only a week at the Beaver Creek camp, the band packed up. Unfortunately, Obsidian Trading Man misplaced a couple of the obsidian points, never to be seen again. The band started their long walk toward the west.

Travel to the Tanana River took half a moon cycle. Along the way they stopped at other people's camps to spend a day or two visiting and getting the latest news. At most camps there was somebody connected to them— family members married into the group, a trading or hunting partner and old friends. Trading was on Obsidian Trading Man's mind, and when his group stopped in a camp where the people had many mammoth-ivory tools, he was very pleased. This ivory was not from mammoth kills but from ancient mammoth bodies appearing out of riverbanks. While the two groups exchanged conversation and ate bison, Obsidian Trading Man began trading with Broken Mammoth Man. He received four pieces of ivory for two pieces of obsidian. Both were happy with their deal. Broken Mammoth Man could easily find more mammoth ivory along the rivers, but he would have had to travel to Wiki Peak in southern Alaska to get obsidian.

After some pleasant days, Obsidian Trading Man and his band continued their journey. On a cool evening they walked into the Upward Sun River camp. There was sadness in the air. Obsidian Trading Man's cousin Salmon Woman had lost her baby girl, who had only lived one moon cycle. It must have been a bad summer for newborns, since her husband's other wife, Berry Gathering Woman, had earlier given birth to a stillborn girl. Salmon Woman's husband, Wealth Man, was in deep sorrow. Both his wives had

lost their infant girls. There would be a potlatch and the babies would be buried in the ground inside their home.

At the potlatch, Berry Gathering Woman's brother gave antler foreshafts and stone projectile points for the burial of his niece. Obsidian Trading Man gave obsidian from Hoodoo Mountain to Salmon Woman for the burial of his niece. The two grieving women sprinkled red ochre over the infants and wrapped them in hide. Red ochre was sprinkled in the grave. Wealth Man sadly buried his children. After the burial, everyone sat together and ate salmon.

Some days later, Obsidian Trading Man and his band departed from the Upward Sun River camp and headed back to the east. When they got to their camp at Beaver Creek, Obsidian Trading Man thought about spending more time in the Hoodoo Mountain area. There was lots of game and he would be closer to the obsidian. As the summer days passed, people came from the Tanana River area and told of more sadness at the Upward Sun River camp. Salmon Woman's three-year-old son had also died. They had cremated the boy and then abandoned the site forever. Obsidian Trading Man wished for Salmon Woman to have more babies.

The following year, Obsidian Trading Man moved closer to Hoodoo Mountain and found a nice camp about halfway to the destination. Obsidian Trading Man lived a long life and had many children and grandchildren. His descendants would continue to move toward the southeast, following animals and exploring new areas.

left top and bottom *Left top:* This multi-edged scraper was made ca. AD 1400. It was found in the M'Clintock River area near White-horse, as was the point (*left bottom*). Both tools are made from obsidian (volcanic glass) derived from a site 375 kilometres away, at Mount Edziza, near Telegraph Creek, BC.

right An archaeology crew digs test pits at Michie Lake, 2010.

Upward Sun River Archaeological Site

The Upward Sun River site on the Tanana River in Alaska was the location of infant cremations and burials 11,500 years ago. In the burial sites, archaeologists also found antler foreshafts decorated with a repeating "X" motif, some of the oldest art found in North America. Obsidian found in the adjacent camp area was analyzed as originating from the Hoodoo Mountain source located just to the west of Haines Junction. The Hoodoo Mountain obsidian indicates people at that time were highly mobile and accustomed to travelling great distances.

People who camped and travelled in the Haines Junction area in those times would have been using higher ground than people today due to the presence of Glacial Lake Champagne, which filled the whole valley between present-day Whitehorse and Haines Junction with hundreds of feet of water. Scientific estimates vary as to the date, but most agree that

OBSIDIAN SOURCES AND DISTRIBUTION IN THE YUKON, CA. 11,000–200 YEARS AGO

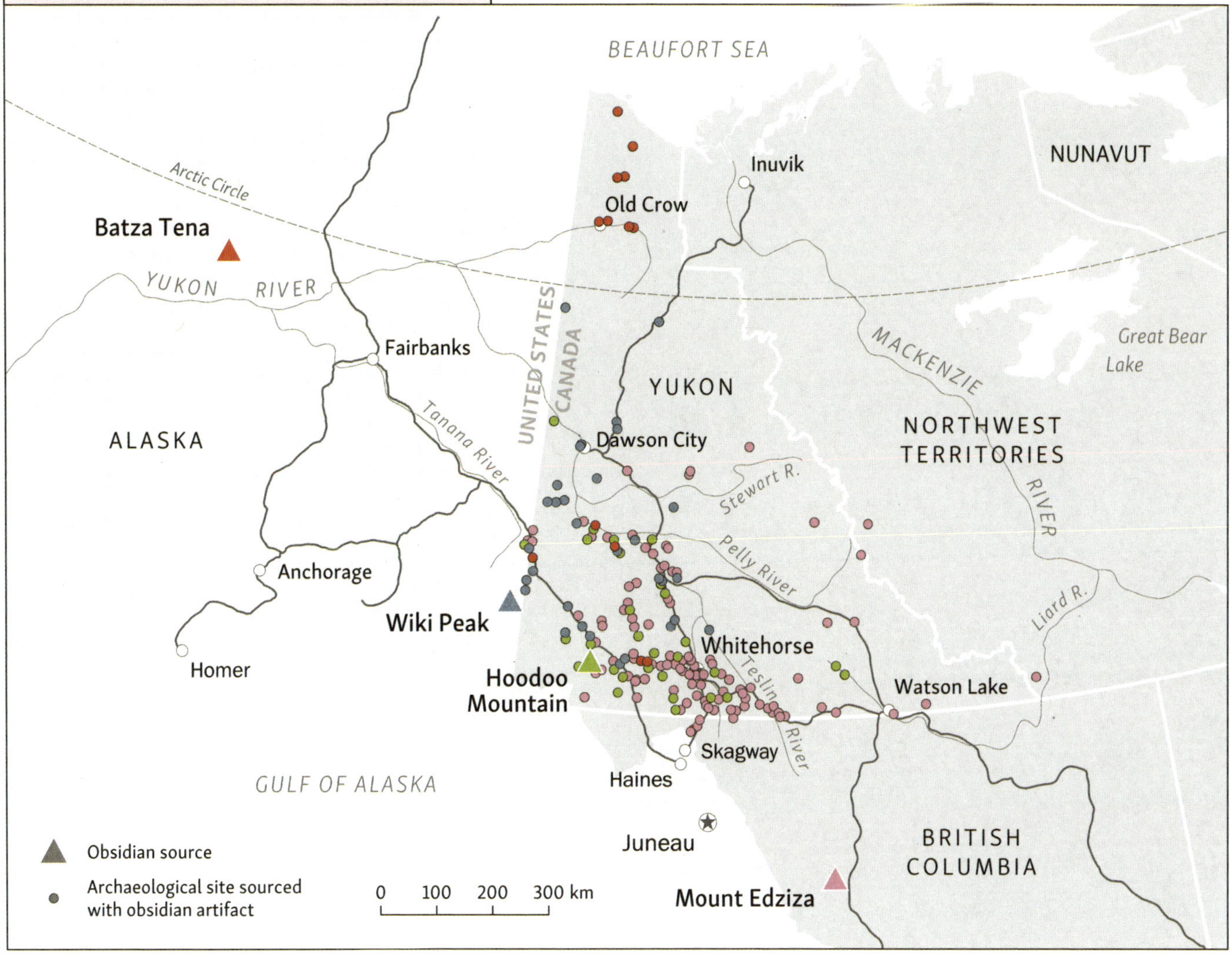

BEAUFORT SEA

NUNAVUT

Inuvik

Old Crow

Batza Tena

YUKON RIVER

Arctic Circle

Fairbanks

ALASKA

Tanana River

YUKON

MACKENZIE RIVER

Great Bear Lake

NORTHWEST TERRITORIES

Dawson City

Stewart R.

Anchorage

Pelly River

Liard R.

Wiki Peak

Whitehorse

Watson Lake

Hoodoo Mountain

Teslin River

Homer

Skagway

GULF OF ALASKA

Haines

▲ Obsidian source

● Archaeological site sourced with obsidian artifact

0   100   200   300 km

Juneau

BRITISH COLUMBIA

Mount Edziza

this lake drained sometime between 7,200 and 10,000 years ago. Artifacts more than 8,000 years old have been found above the old Glacial Lake Champagne shoreline, but none have surfaced below the old shore-line that date to before 8,400 years ago. This means that people did not live in the valley floor until after 8,400 years ago, but they did live at higher elevations before that time.[24]

Obsidian

Obsidian is volcanic glass. It is extremely sharp, is easy to work and makes wonderful projectile points, knives and tools. Obsidian is formed as an extrusive igneous rock, and each volcano has its own chemical makeup. When a piece of obsidian is found, its chemical composition is analyzed to determine its original source, providing clues to the travel and trading patterns of early peoples.[25]

above Obsidian from several sources in northern B.C., Yukon and Alaska was traded widely across the northwest from 10,000 years ago until traders brought metal tools in the late 1700s.

Swan Woman and Atlatl Man

TAKHINI RIVER NEAR KUSAWA LAKE, CIRCA SEVEN
THOUSAND YEARS AGO

Swan Woman sat on the hill at her group's summer camp overlooking the rushing river below. She was with her children and extended family members. She had just returned from checking her gopher snares. It had been a good day and she had a bag full of gophers. Now there was more food, and skins to make blankets.

All of the men, including Swan Woman's husband, Atlatl Man, had gone up in the mountains to the ice patches to hunt caribou. Swan Woman looked up toward the hill where her husband was hunting. She could not see his hunting group yet. She stared at the side of the hill, seeing an old shoreline from the time of the flood. The old people told of how Crow remade the world after the flood, and people saved themselves by building rafts. There was still an old raft across the valley on the side of the mountain.

Swan Woman and the other women and children would soon go berry picking. Each woman would pack a caribou hide, which they would combine together to make small temporary shelters. They would also bring knives and skinning tools to skin and cut up the caribou after the men finished their work on the carcasses. Once packed, the group would move up the side of the mountain to where the men had hunted and set up the temporary camps.

The caribou liked the ice patches, where they cooled off in summer, escaping the swarms of bugs. There they were predictable in their habits, and it was easier for the hunters to find them. Atlatl Man, together with his brother, his sister's husband, a nephew and some men from camps to the west, settled down behind the crest of the slope. The wind came from the southwest and the caribou were upwind. They would not smell the men hidden downwind behind the slope. Two of the older hunters, who could no longer throw the atlatl darts with much force, crept around to the far side of the ice patch. They then began to walk across the ice toward the caribou, driving the nervous animals toward the hunters concealed behind the slope.

The men got their atlatls ready to throw and made sure the spare darts were handy. Atlatl Man was the most experienced hunter, and he would signal to the others when to jump up, run toward the herd and launch their spears. He signalled to his nephew to stay close to him. Then he leaped up and rushed out. Atlatl Man launched his spear toward the centre of the herd and quickly loaded another dart and launched it. The other men rushed out and launched their spears. The caribou were surprised by the sudden appearance of the hunters and turned to run down the mountain.

Atlatl Man's nephew threw his spear toward the fleeing caribou but it fell short and slid down the slope into the snow.

The hunters found four caribou lying on the ice. One was dead, hit in the heart. The other three were wounded and the hunters quickly cut their throats. Once the caribou were dead, the hunters examined them to see who was successful at hitting their targets. One caribou had two darts in it and the others had one dart each. Each dart was unique in how it was made and in the type of stone point that was used so that each hunter could recognize his dart. All the men had hit a caribou except one man from the west and Atlatl Man's nephew. Only Atlatl Man was quick enough to launch two darts while the caribou were in range. Working as a team was important, and nobody boasted at getting more caribou than others or criticized hunters for missing. Yet secretly, each successful hunter was pleased, and those who missed were embarrassed. Atlatl Man teased his nephew about missing, suggesting he throw earlier before the caribou fled. He sent his nephew down to find his missing dart, but it was buried in the snow and could not be found.

The men began butchering the animals. Soon their wives, children and old people would move closer to their site to set up camp. It would be a good night. They thought about how Crow and Esuya (Beaverman) had made the world better for humans!

The Ice Patches

Ice patches are accumulations of snow that develop over long periods of time but are not yet thick enough to become a glacier. If an ice patch grows to twenty-five to thirty metres thick, it will generally be heavy enough to begin moving, and then it becomes a glacier. Glaciers can move from nine

top, bottom right Caribou seek refuge from biting insects in the cool of the Friday Creek Ice Patch, as they have for millennia.

bottom left Many layers of ancient caribou dung are visible along the melting edge of the Friday Creek Ice Patch. As the ice melts, tools made by our ancestors are revealed.

metres to almost a kilometre per year. Over time an artifact could be lost in ice or destroyed by glacier movement. Ice patches do not move, so items that were lost in the ice patches stay in place over thousands of years. As temperatures increase or moisture decreases over time, ice patches begin melting or evaporating. In the Yukon, climate change has caused ice patches to melt rapidly in recent decades, revealing artifacts that have been in cold storage for thousands of years.[26]

Atlatl Hunting

Archaeologists have found projectile points, atlatl darts and arrows dating to 7,700 years ago in the ice patches located in the Whitehorse-Kusawa area. Atlatl darts found to date in Yukon are almost all tipped with stone points. There is a range of stone point types: stemmed, unstemmed (with various base configurations), side-notched. Each would be recognizable by their makers. These artifacts most likely were lost accidently, as described in "Swan Woman and Atlatl Man." Stone hunting blinds have been found in the area, which likely were used to hunt sheep. There is no evidence that caribou were driven toward the blinds. Caribou fences identified throughout the Yukon were used for hunting caribou.

Ashfall Woman

KWANLIN AREA, CIRCA 1,170 YEARS AGO

Ashfall Woman and her band had recently returned to their lands after living for several years in an area that took more than a month of walking to reach. Ashfall Woman remembered the winter day, before her first child had been born, when the people had heard a distant noise like thunder. Soon a layer of ash began to rain down, covering everything.

The people did not know what had happened, but the ash caused many problems. When they melted snow for water, it was too silty to drink. They had to cut holes in the ice to get drinking water and to catch fish. Luckily they already had their caches of food for the winter. Many animals were sickened by the ash and easier to hunt, so the people still had plenty of meat. But when spring came, very few animals survived because all their food was covered with ash. There were hardly any fish left in the lakes because the silty water suffocated them. Once their food caches were empty, the people realized they would have to leave their homeland to find a new place to live.

As they began their travels in search of a new place to live, they heard the ash fall had been even heavier to the west, so they could only go south.

top left This barbed atlatl point made from an antler was recovered from the Texas Gulch Ice Patch.

top right An atlatl dart point with the base missing (*above*) and a scraper.

above KDFN youth Aurora Hardy poses in the remains of a hunting blind used by our ancestors to hunt caribou, Alligator Lake Ice Patch, 2017.

left Evidence of ashfall is visible in many places along rivers and roads, as seen here on the Teslin River, 2020.

right A side-notched atlatl dart point rests on caribou dung that has melted out of the Granger Ice Patch. The point has traces of red ochre near where it was tied with sinew onto the wooden dart shaft.

Life was difficult, however, as they came to new territories where people were already living; the land could not easily support all the new arrivals. Some people kept going farther south. Some people stayed, and families joined together to share the work, but there was always a shortage of food. Over the years, Ashfall Woman heard stories about some relatives who had travelled to very distant lands in the south.

Ashfall Woman and her people missed Kwanlin, however, and began to think about going back. Every year they explored farther to the northwest to see if the land was recovering. After her first child had children of her own, people saw plants were growing again, and gophers and other small animals had returned. The world was fixing itself.

One summer, people came from the northwest to Ashfall Woman's camp, looking for others who had survived the ash. They said their people had gone to the north and west, to the land we now call Alaska, when the ash fell. In those lands they met people who talked a little differently, yet they could undertand each other well enough to trade and marry. The knowledge of how to make bows and arrows and how to work copper nuggets by heating and hammering was passed from group to group, along with the finished tools. Double spiral copper daggers were especially prized and usually only owned by the headmen. Sources of copper nuggets in the Burwash Uplands and near the head of the White River were jealously guarded, and competition for the trade in this new material became fierce. At the same time, the bow and arrow transformed how men hunted and how they conducted warfare.

Ashfall Woman finally returned to Kwanlin when her grandchildren had their children. Ashfall Woman and the other Kwanlin Elders were happy to be home with the familiar lakes, rivers and hills. She saw large pockets of ash buried along the riverbanks and among the roots of fallen trees, but the land and the animals had recovered and food was no longer scarce. By this time, however, they no longer heard any news about their relatives and friends who had continued on to the distant south.

Oral Traditions about the Ash Falls

There are several Yukon First Nations stories about the Sun burning the world. Tagish and Inland Tlingit stories tell about one of the Sun's daughters marrying a human. Others recount stories of the Sun himself marrying a woman. When the people were unfaithful, he angrily burned them all up except for one hero who escaped.[27]

Volcanic Ash Falls

About AD 800, the eruption of Mount Bona and Mount Churchill, forty kilometres west of the Yukon–Alaska border near Beaver Creek, spread ash throughout the southern Yukon. The White River ash originated from the Mount Churchill eruption. It covered about 340,000 square kilometres of land. This layer of ash is visible in cutbanks beside the Klondike and Alaska Highways and along the Yukon and Teslin Rivers, and in many other locations north of Whitehorse.

An earlier eruption occurred about 1,950 years ago and covered the area north of Mount Churchill with ash. The two massive volcanic eruptions displaced any nearby survivors. The air became unbreathable, forcing people and animals to flee to the southeast. The caribou that returned to the southern Yukon in later years were genetically distinct from their predecessors. The ash fall layers are useful markers for determining the age of archaeological sites and artifacts in this region.

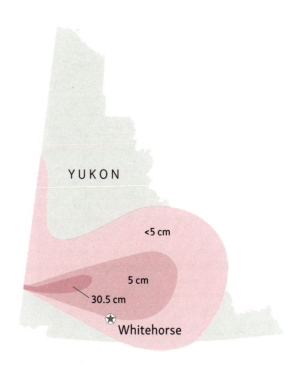

above Depth of White River ash deposits, ca. AD 800.

New Tools

After the time of the White River ash fall, our ancestors started hunting with the bow and arrow, a more effective hunting tool than the atlatl. Evidence of this appears in the ice patches, and the spread of this technology can be traced across North America starting around that time. Our ancestors also began producing ornaments and objects, including sophisticated double spiral copper daggers. Perhaps people west and north of the White River ash fall fled westward and met Denali people, who taught them new metalworking processes. When these people returned to their own lands many decades later, they may have taught other people those skills.

Native copper is hard but does not break like stone or antler when struck, so it was a material that was unlike any known by Yukon people of the past millennium. When copper is struck repeatedly, instead of breaking, it deforms. Continuous hammering and heating will flatten a copper nugget

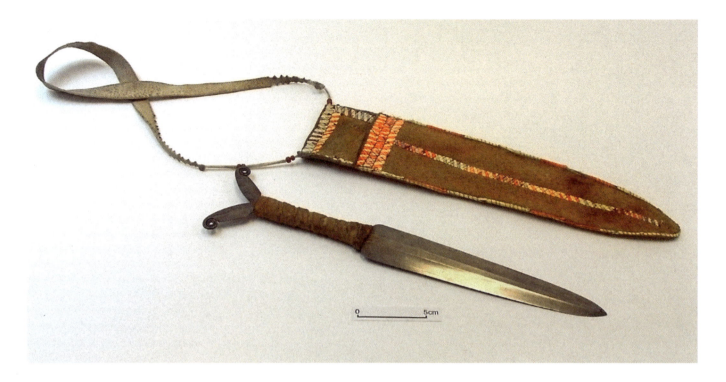

above Copper knife made by unidentified Athapaskan craftsman, ca. 1800s.

into small sheets, which in turn can be folded together with other sheets to form a larger object. Additional hammering and heating will combine the sheets, and with grinding and polishing the final shape and metallic shine of a dagger or arrow point, or another object, can be achieved. Because of copper's unique properties, people attributed special power to the copper and to objects that were made with it.

Greedy Man

NAALIN-SWAN LAKE AREAS, CIRCA TWO HUNDRED YEARS AGO

Greedy Man was sitting beside a fire near his caribou skin shelter, making snowshoes for the coming winter, when he heard people approaching. He saw six Chilkats walking down the trail. They were returning from trading with the people of the Fort Selkirk area, and they were packing big loads of fur. Greedy Man was envious of their riches and planned to steal the furs through trickery.

Greedy Man acted friendly and invited the Tlingit traders inside his house to rest and warm up. He told them there was not enough room inside the shelter for their furs and to leave them outside. He said he would get food from his cache and went outside. Instead he got poles to block the entrance, threw a basket of pitch over the skin shelter and set it on fire. When the Chilkats realized what was happening they tried to get through the doorway, but Greedy Man stabbed them with a spear as they tried to get out. All the Chilkats died, and Greedy Man was rich with furs.

Greedy Man boasted of his newfound wealth, and soon his people realized something very bad had happened. He had always been lazy and poor,

above Tàa'än Män (Lake Laberge).

but now he was rich. As the winter passed, Chilkat people in Klukwan told stories about six of their traders who had not returned home. The Chilkats thought that a large group of people must have ambushed and killed them for their furs. When the Lake Laberge people heard these stories, they realized that Greedy Man must have killed the six Chilkats. The Laberge people feared the Klukwan people would want to take revenge on their group. They decided they would hide when the Chilkats came back to the area.

In Klukwan the Chilkats heard stories of a poor man from Naalin area who suddenly got rich. They thought one man could not kill six Chilkats, so he must have had help from other people. The Chilkats decided to retaliate against all the people of the area. They determined that whenever they went on their seasonal trading trips to the north, they would look for the killer and his accomplices. When the Laberge people realized that the Chilkats were looking for them, they were even more frightened and started hiding in the bush and concealing all signs of their presence. They no longer built fires for fear of signalling their location to the Chilkat traders.

Every year the Chilkats looked for the killers, but they never saw any people in the Kusawa-Laberge area. Then one fall day a Chilkat trading group camped at Naalin (Lookout Mountain, where signal fires were built). Early that morning a Chilkat Elder climbed to the top of the hill to look for

signs of people. The Laberge people had camped near the shore of Swan Lake. Someone from the Swan Lake camp was cold and thought it was safe to build a fire. The Elder saw the smoke. The Chilkats planned to attack in the middle of that night when everyone was still asleep. They spent the day preparing and started their march late at night. The Chilkat medicine man used his power to find the trail to the camp and to ensure everybody was asleep.

At the camp a family slave was out checking his rabbit snare line. He took a shortcut and did not see the approaching Chilkats. Ya je hen was a coastal woman married into the Laberge people. She woke up early, and when she went outside to pee she spotted the Chilkats. The Chilkats began their attack. At the same time the slave returned and ran to Ya je hen, leading her away to hide in a bear cave. Everybody else was still asleep. The Chilkats killed every man, woman and child in the camp. After the attack the Chilkats noticed the tracks left by the slave and Ya je hen. They followed them to the cave. Ya je hen spoke in Tlingit to them, telling of her coastal family connections. They decided to spare her and the slave because he had helped her to escape.

When other Laberge people heard of the attack, they were horrified. Nobody went to the Swan Lake camp anymore. They thought the Chilkats were bad for killing everybody because of one greedy man. As time passed, the Tagish Kwan people and people from Hutshi started moving to Lake Laberge and filled the void left by the Lake Laberge people who were killed. This event was so horrible that few people ever spoke of the Naalin War after that time.[28]

Conflict and Resolution

Trade was very important, so Athapaskan people always tried to avoid war. At times when it was necessary, the usual tactic was to attack when the odds were totally in the attackers' favour. In the Naalin War, the Coastal Tlingit adopted the same strategy of attacking early in the morning, when everyone was asleep, and killing every man, woman and child to prevent retaliation. Young women might be spared and taken as a wife or slave by the victors. While many Elders know about the Naalin War, most do not like to talk about it, as it is a sad story.[29]

Most wars were between people from different language groups, but sometimes conflicts occurred between people who spoke the same language. The Coastal Tlingit and the Inland Tlingit and Athapaskans fought many times. The Coastal Tlingit, though powerful, did not always win. The attackers' tactic was to scout the enemy camp before the attack and signal other members of their group by mimicking owl hoots. For that reason, many First Nations people feel nervous when hearing owls hoot. Owls bring bad news, such as news of death or injury. There are some stories about smart people who recognized owl hoots as human voices and were able to prevent an attack.[30]

Elder Violet Storer remembered her mother, Jenny Lebarge, telling stories about Naalin (Lookout Mountain):

> The people used to have someone living there ... many, many years ago before the white man came to this country, the Yukon. And they used to make smoke signals from there when the people came from Alaska. They could see as far as Kusawa Lake, and Champagne, and Marsh Lake and Lake Laberge area. And when there is someone coming from Alaska, they could see smoke coming from the camps, and the guy on this Naalin Mountain would give signals so that the people from Marsh Lake, and from Champagne, and from Lake Laberge could see this smoke signals, then they knew the Tlingit were coming over from Alaska. Sometimes they used to come over fighting until they started trading for furs and stuff like that. They brought some of their food over and traded with the Indians here, at the Yukon Flats.[31]

facing Naalin (Lookout Mountain).

above Jikakw—Violet Storer (*left*) and Gus'dutéen—Frances Woolsey visit traditional sites in the Takhini River valley with Naalin (Lookout Mountain) in the background, 1988.

Lucky Hunting Man

KWANLIN AREA, CIRCA 1816

The winter had been long and hard—everyone was looking forward to the coming spring. The snow started melting and the animals were giving birth to young ones. Then a steady and strong cold north wind started to blow. Nobody was concerned as the north wind often blew in the spring. But this time it blew for days, and dark clouds came over the land. It got colder and began snowing. It snowed for so many days it covered the whole land. All the rivers and lakes froze over. It was so cold that the ice was too thick for setting fishnets. All the newborn animals froze and many other animals died of starvation, since the summer food was covered by deep snow.

People had used up all their winter food caches, and there had not been time to replenish supplies before the unexpected snows. Nobody knew why this was happening. People were very worried. Lucky Hunting Man and his family were scared, but he was determined to find game for his people. He prayed to his spirit guide and went to the medicine man to ask for extra help. Lucky Hunting Man went out hunting but came back empty-handed after five days.

All the men in the camp went out hunting as often as they could but were only able to find small game, which was not enough to feed all the people. Women cleared the snow and built fires, thawing the ground so they could dig for roots. People made very watery soup from whatever food they could gather. It was not enough. People were starving—the old and the frail were dying. People were desperate. Hunting parties returned empty-handed most times, and the hunters were getting weak. Any extra food went to them since they needed strength to find game so all could live.

One day Lucky Hunting Man led a small party to a new area in the hills. They found a feeble older caribou and killed it. Lucky Hunting Man supervised the handling of the meat. He told the other hunters to make soup from the meat, then to drink only a bit at a time to regain their strength and get used to food again. After a day of sipping soup and resting, Lucky Hunting Man took two men from his group and made a skin sled. Now they could bring some of the meat back down the hill to the camp. They left one hunter to guard the meat and cut it into smaller pieces to carry more easily. At the camp, everyone was excited about the arrival of the hunters with fresh meat, but they were so weakened they could hardly stand. Lucky Hunting Man made soup for everyone, telling them to drink it slowly to regain their strength before having more. He went to all the homes and gradually the people started to revive, except for a few Elders and very young ones.

As the band recovered, Lucky Hunting Man took several hunters and returned to the kill site. The hunters at the site were stronger, and Lucky Hunting Man told them to start hauling meat to the camp. He went out hunting again with another man. Lucky Hunting Man proved his name again when they got two more caribou. As a result, his people were able to survive through the summer and subsequent winter.

This was known as "the year of no summer or double winter," and many people died. The people of Lucky Hunting Man's camp also heard about Gáta'ada of the Crow people, who hunted when his people were starving.

99

Gáta'ada killed a moose and brought it back to his people, where he first made soup and fed the people. Gáta'ada saved the people of Aishihik in this way.

Mount Tambora Volcanic Eruption

On April 5, 1815, Mount Tambora (located in present-day Indonesia) erupted, sending a cloud of ash around the world. This eruption lasted for many days and killed as many as a hundred thousand people in Indonesia. As a result, the winter of 1815–1816 was the second coldest since 1400, and the following decade was the coldest in recorded history. Worldwide, tens of thousands died because of cold temperatures and failed crops.

The oral history of "the double winter" and the hunter Gáta'ada is one of the first instances in which an identifiable person can be traced to a date-able event in Yukon history. Gáta'ada is the ancestor of Chief Albert Isaac of Aishihik, and all Tutchone people named Isaac trace their roots to him. His story was told by Mary Jacquot of Burwash.[32]

Our Tagish Kwan Elders also remember stories of this time when people had to move away to escape the food shortages and other hardships caused by the Mount Tambora eruption, often described as a time of double winter. Ida Calmegane remembered her grandmother Maria Johns talking about that time: "You know, Grandma said it was five Grandmas ago when she said we had two winters in one year… She said five Grandmas ago, and it would have been six with her because she was a Grandma then, too, when she told us that story. She said a whole bunch of people followed the caribou down [south]."[33]

Musket Trading Man and Embroidery Girl

KWANLIN AREA, CIRCA 1830S TO 1860S

The Tlingit arrived from the coast earlier in the spring than usual, and this time they brought many strange new things. Musket Trading Man was curious about these goods, but Embroidery Girl was even more curious. She was shown tiny shiny beads that were unlike the silverberry seeds and dyed porcupine quills that she used on her clothing and bags, and not even like the shell beads that the Tlingit had brought before. These were tiny smooth beads like obsidian but in many different colours, including vibrant blues. Embroidery Girl and all the Kwanlin women were fascinated by the beads and soon learned to sew with them.

The Tlingit showed the men a new thing called a musket. They set up a block of wood, then pointed the musket at it, telling the people to watch. Suddenly, a loud bang—like a crack of lightning! Women screamed and children ran away crying. The Kwanlin men startled and jumped, then stood silently, looking at the block of wood on the ground. The Tlingit were very

pleased with the effect of their demonstration. Their headman spoke up: "You can have one musket for only five beaver furs." That was a good deal! So Musket Trading Man paid five furs and became the first musket owner in the Kwanlin area. Two other men bought muskets as well.

There were still many traditional items to trade, along with the new goods. Kwanlin people had superior tanned moose and caribou skins, expertly sewn hide clothing, and exquisite furs to trade for hooligan oil, dentalia shells, seaweed and other coastal products. Sometimes they exchanged dolls, pendants and bone skinning knives. Decorated arm bands and a copper dagger might be offered for fancy wooden tea boxes and maybe sometimes a metal coin from far-off China. The Tlingit had many other new and useful goods—steel files, axes, knives, pots, frying pans and calico cloth.

After a week of trading, telling stories and feasting, the Tlingit left with all the inland goods they treasured—beautiful furs and strong hides. They were very pleased that the muskets had earned so many beaver furs. Kwanlin people were also happy: they had new goods that nobody else had in their area. Musket Trading Man kept some of these items for his band and took some to people in the east and to the north to trade for more furs. With increasing demand, the price for muskets went up. Soon inland trappers had to pile beaver pelts as high as a standing musket to make a trade. That was a lot of beaver pelts!

When Kwanlin people asked the Tlingit people where they got these new things, they replied: "From Cloud People." Kwanlin people wondered if and when K'ǔ Ch'an (Cloud People) would come to their area. What new things would they bring, and what would happen in trading with them? Almost as soon as the Tlingit brought the new trade items, inland people started getting sick with frightening new diseases that killed whole families and bands within a short time. People wondered if this was a warning about more dangers coming with K'ǔ Ch'an.

left A beaded bag with a medicine wheel and feather pattern, made by Edith Baker.

centre Beaded fireweed on Judy Gingell's hide commissioner's dress (see p. 241). Judy's mother, Elder Annie Smith, and her daughters (Judy's sisters) Dianne Smith and Lesley Smith MacDiarmid, as well as Elder Irene Smith, made the dress for Judy's first Commissioner's Ball in Dawson City after her appointment as commissioner, 1995.

right Beaded flowers on the vamp of a child's moccasin, made by Betsy Smith.

Beads and the Evolution of Design

When Tlingit traders in the early 1800s first brought glass beads, silk thread and cloth, Interior women rapidly adopted the new materials for their clothing manufacture. The Northern Tutchone and Hän people saw the first examples of beaded floral designs on trading trips to Fort Yukon, in northern Alaska. When the people returned to their homes in southern Yukon, they started to bead in that style, now identified as Upper Yukon River Style. Within a generation it was common to see new designs using glass beads, such as beautiful beaded flowers on baby belts, carrying bags, straps and a new style of hide jacket. By the time Lieutenant Frederick Schwatka of the U.S. Army explored the Yukon River in the summer of 1883, floral beading styles were firmly established in the region.[34]

Tanned Hide Winter Clothing

When Tlingit traders brought factory-made cloth to trade, inland people started to trade furs for new lightweight cloth garments. There was great prestige in wearing the new style of clothing. Within one generation, most people wore pants, shirts and hats made in far-off factories in Europe or southern regions of North America. Schwatka noted that almost all First Nations people were wearing manufactured clothing when he rafted down the Yukon River in 1883.[35]

Inland people did not abandon their winter hide clothing, however, and they rarely traded it. Athapaskan winter clothing was far superior for the cold inland winters to anything that the Tlingit or white traders had at the time, and perhaps to almost anything available today. The winter leggings and tunic consisted of two caribou hides with the fur left on and the tanned hide facing outside. Doubling the fur meant twice the insulation that a caribou in the wild has. As a result, people dressed in this clothing were, in essence, wearing a warm house! In the 1790s, Alexander Mackenzie observed this style of winter garment among the Chipewyan: "This dress is worn single or double, but always in the winter, with the hair within and without. Thus arrayed a Chepewyan will lay himself down on the ice in the middle of a lake, and repose in comfort; although he will sometimes find a difficulty in the morning to disencumber himself from the snow drifted on him during the night."[36] Imagine trying to do that today with our modern clothing! Inland people continued to wear home-tanned skin clothing into the early 1900s, and well beyond that for footwear, hats and mitts.

Coming of K'ŭ Ch'an (Cloud People)

The Russian American Company had been trading in coastal Alaska since the mid-1760s. In 1799 they established a permanent post at Sitka. Their relationship with the Coastal Tlingit was often strained, but over time the two groups developed protocols to promote lucrative trade for both sides. The Tlingit brought highly prized furs to the Russians, acquired from Interior Yukon people, and obtained manufactured goods to carry back to their inland trading partners. The Tlingit people also brought stories about K'ŭ Ch'an, Cloud People, strangers from far away who came in big ships with billowing white sails. The name "K'ŭ Ch'an" came from the Southern Tutchone words "k'u," which means "clouds," and "ch'än" or "ch'in," which means "people from."

By the 1830s, glass beads, muskets, knives, axes and other trade items were commonly exchanged goods in the central Yukon. When Hudson's Bay Company trader Robert Campbell first explored the Pelly River in 1843, and later carried on down to the Yukon River, he reported that people in that area already had European manufactured goods. Campbell noted that they used Hudson's Bay Company glass beads and guns, which they obtained through trade with Tutchone and Gwich'in middlemen from the Peel River post. From the Tlingit they obtained knives, axes, pots, blankets, and cloth that the coastal people acquired from Russian, American and Hudson's Bay Company traders on the coast. Campbell also heard that inland people purchased guns from the Tlingit for "five made beavers each." Campbell observed only four muskets among the Fort Selkirk people, which included twenty-four men. Later, as muskets became more popular, prices soared. Campbell established Fort Selkirk at the confluence of the Pelly and Yukon Rivers in 1848. In 1852, the Chilkat Tlingit from Klukwan pillaged the post and drove Campbell out because he was interfering with their trade monopoly in the region.[37]

When Coastal Tlingit first had contact with white people, they were exposed to many new diseases for which they had no immunity. Later, when they traded with inland people who had not yet had direct contact, they passed on many of those diseases. Tutchone people also suffered numerous epidemics as a result of visiting Hudson's Bay trading posts along the Mackenzie and Yukon Rivers, or dealing with other people who had visited the trading posts. As many as twenty-four epidemics decimated inland people between 1848 and 1907.[38]

facing This octopus bag, made in the early 1900s by a wife of Kashxóot—Jim Boss, incorporates Tlingit-style seaweed and floral designs.

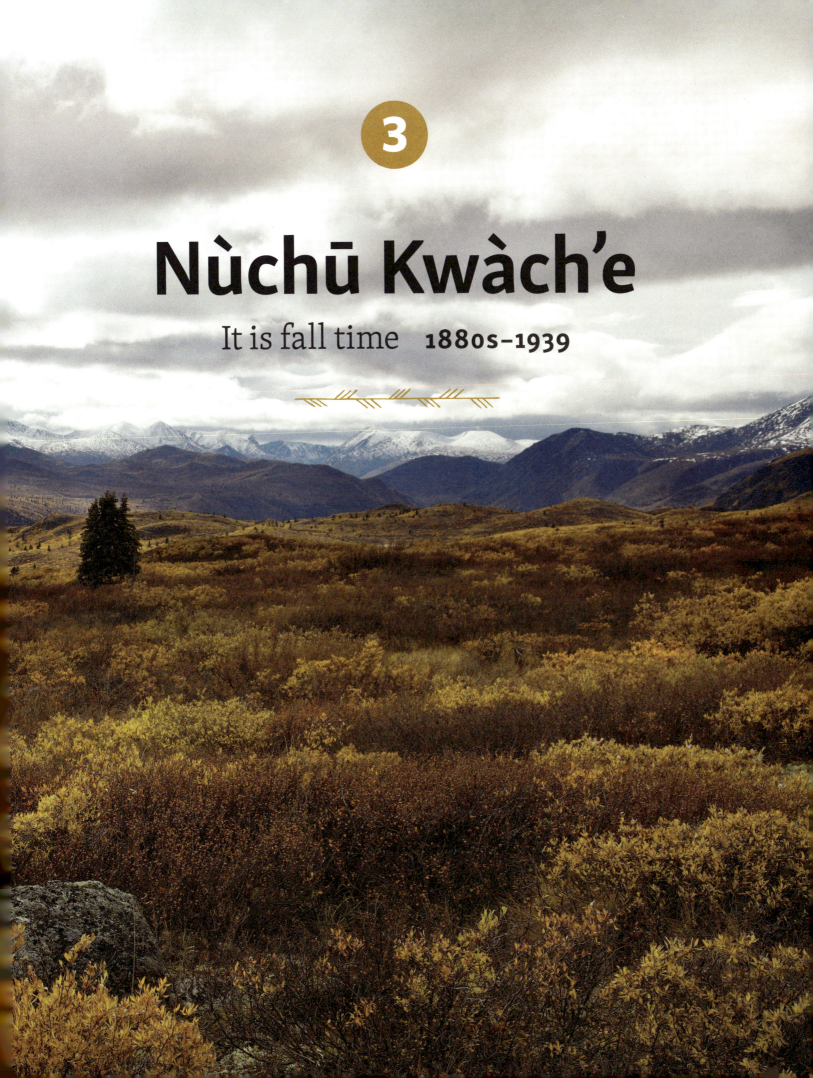

3

Nùchū Kwàch'e

It is fall time   1880s–1939

> Yeah, I know about the Miles Canyon and Whitehorse
> Rapids. My grandmother told me about it. We use
> to come and fish, gaff salmon and spear salmon there,
> in the rapids area, when they come close to shore.
>
> **RONALD BILL**[1]

overleaf Fall in the alpine, KDFN Traditional Territory.

facing Cow moose and calf in fall.

FALL IS A TIME of transformation, with big winds blowing in from the coast and from the north, leaves turning gold and dropping, salmon spawning and dying, swans and geese and cranes flying south for the winter, animals on the move or denning up for winter. The colder weather and shorter days signal the urgency for people to prepare for winter, too. Creeks and rivers begin to freeze over, mountaintops are covered with snow and change is felt everywhere.

The years from the 1800s to World War II brought major changes for Kwanlin Dün. Tlingit traders brought intriguing new goods from K'ǔ Ch'an (Cloud People)—Russians, Spanish, British and Americans who sailed into coastal Alaska. For decades the Tlingit had maintained control over the coastal mountain passes, but new diseases carried by K'ǔ Ch'an swept across the region in waves of epidemics, devastating entire communities along the coast and in the interior.

By the mid-1800s, Hudson's Bay Company traders crossed the mountains from the Mackenzie Valley to the Yukon. American military commanders negotiated with Tlingit leaders to open the Chilkoot Pass to prospectors in 1880. Our Kwanlin Dün ancestors began to meet a few K'ǔ Ch'an travelling in our lands, but continued their lifeways without interference. Everything changed in 1897 when thousands of stampeders rushed through our lands to Dawson City. Most soon left, but new transportation and government organizations remained. The White Pass & Yukon Railway, riverboats and the town of Whitehorse encroached on our lands. Our people maintained traditional activities while incorporating wage labour into seasonal rounds. As the decades rolled on through the Great Depression, Kwanlin Dün made a good living by trapping, fishing, hunting and gathering, with seasonal work for the railroad, steamboats and wood camp operators. Our Elders tell of these times, from memories passed down from their parents and grandparents.

Lucy Wren

Kų' Eyû—Ghùch Tlâ (Wolf
Mother)—Lucy Wren was a
member of the Dak̲l'awedí Clan,
born in Carcross in 1917. Her
mother was Nadagáat—Susie
Joseph and her father was
Káa Goox̲ Éesh—Billy Atlin.
She grew up speaking Tlingit,
Southern Tutchone and Tagish,
and she heard the stories of her
people in all those languages
from her earliest years. She
was renowned as one of the
last fluent speakers of the
Tagish language. She worked
for over a decade as a Native
Language Instructor in the
Carcross public school, helping children to learn her language. She also contributed her
knowledge to many linguistic
and heritage projects, including archaeological research in
the southern Yukon. Lucy Wren
passed away in 2008.[3]

Nindal Kwädīndür
(I'm going to tell you a story)

RABBIT BOY

Told by **Kų' Eyû—Ghùch Tlâ—Lucy Wren**[2]

Long time ago my grandma used to tell me no rabbit, you know... She
say long time before her they say no rabbit, just moose and sheep and
caribou and things. Gopher, you know, summer time... and then this
woman, she single woman and she got no husband. She got no kids
and... everybody moved camp. They just give her... any little thing...
just like they're stingy to her... Everybody moved camp and then her,
she says she going to camp there one more night and she's got something to do. I guess she's making a skin toboggan, eh. She want to sew it
one corner, I guess, and after she finished sewing she figures she's goin'
to follow them tomorrow, that woman... fall time, I guess, it's cold...

She hear baby cry in the bush. Up there in the bush somewhere. She
listens, she listens, she really [hears] baby, she hear him cry so she get
up and then she went back there. That baby just laying on the ground,
just kicking up like that and crying, and it's a boy. Boy, she just pick
him up and everything, and then she take him home and she raise him
since then. She make clothes for him and everything. She take him to
those womans got babies, ah. So they can feed him for her so she can
follow those people. She catch up to them.

And that boy grow fast, you know. And... when he grow big, maybe
about seventeen or twenty years old, I guess, he live with his mom. He
kill caribou. He kill moose. He kill everything for his mom. Dry meat,
he make dry meat, help his mom. Because the way they treat that
woman they didn't like it, ah... just like they throw things to dog...
That's why... she find that son...

That woman she fix skin, everything, you know. Pretty soon he tell
his mom, "I here, I come here to see you. I'm gonna go get rabbit. I'm
going to rabbit's mother and I'm gonna go get rabbit... You're not going
be hungry." So he tell his mom, "All that caribou skin clean, you sew
them together," he said, "like blanket, ah. Big blanket, big blanket."
And he said, "I'm goin' to build big brush camp, ah," and he put that
blanket there, and he tell his mom, "I'm going go to sleep. Five days I'm
going to sleep and don't wake me up or don't let nobody wake me up. I
don't want no noise." He say, "I'm going to sleep. I'm to go get rabbit for
you now so you don't get hungry." So he went and five days he sleep
then and never move. She get worry about her son sleep so long, ah. So

above A rabbit snare set during a youth culture camp at Jackson Lake Healing Camp, 2018.

she just make fire all the time. And then five days' time that blanket, that caribou skin, is getting big all the time, you know. Skin getting big inside where that boy sleep, ah.

Pretty soon, five days' time, that whole blanket start move around, eh. Oh, pretty soon she see that white little thing run out underneath— this rabbit. And then that boy, he wake up and he throw that blanket off. All rabbit just good like that all over in the bush, eh.

He tell his mom, "Go set snare around the camp there. Before five days you set snare for rabbit." He show his mom which way to set the snare and which way to make it, eh. So that's what she did. Boy, "Quaw! Quaw! Quaw!" all over through his snare—rabbit. Boy, she take those rabbit off and then she tell her son, "Holy," she say, "I can't eat that much rabbit," she said, and then too much rabbit, you know. And that boy tell her, "Well, take off your snare. You goin' have snare there." So she took off her snare and she got lots of rabbit. And that rabbit, just like tame rabbit, they got thick skin, ah. They use it for mitts, for anything, the skin, they tan it and things like that.

And pretty soon about one year, one year after, I guess, he tell his mom, "I'm going to go back where I belong. I gotta go back to my country." He said, "That's why I bring rabbit for you, so you can live on it, so you don't get hungry." They said he tell his mom, that boy, and they said he went back and he went home.

They said that highest mountain, that's the one they see his track, eh, high mountain like that, the track come up and they said all at once disappeared. Don't find his track no more, that's where he went in the mountain. That's where he come, he was from. And that's all I know about that rabbit . . . Since then been rabbit all over, they say. And that's where rabbit go when no rabbit for five years. Five years the rabbit come back again. They say that's where they go, to the mother, Rabbit Mother. And then in five years' time they rabbit all come back again.

OUR ELDERS SAY...

Our Tagish Kwan Ancestors

Carcross/Tagish Elder Angela Sidney told many of the stories about the ancestors of Tagish Kwan, beginning with the histories of her clan—the Deishitaan (Crow) on her mother's side and the Dakl'awedí (Wolf) on her father's side. Her Deishitaan ancestors included three or possibly four Coastal Tlingit sisters who married men in the interior as trade grew between coastal and inland people throughout the 1800s. One married to a Tagish man, a second to a man from Teslin Lake, another to a Tahltan man and perhaps a fourth to a Pelly River man.[4] One of the descendants of the woman who came to Tagish was Saike who was Angela Sidney's maternal grandmother.

CH'ÓONEHTE' MÁ—STÓOW— ANGELA SIDNEY Tagish women married to all parts of the Yukon... my father's sister Tashooch Kláa married Gunaaták, Marsh Lake Chief; Jimmy Kane's mother married to Champagne; Tatl'erma, Kitty Smith's [Kàdùhikh— K'ałgwach—K'odetéena] mother, married to Dalton Post; Jenny Dickson married to Ross River; Tagish Jim's mother's sister married to Mandassa, Laberge Chief.[5]

In the late 1800s, Gunaaták' of the Gaanax̱teidí (Crow) Clan was the Marsh Lake Chief— also known as Marsh Lake Chief Jackie. He and his first wife had nine children: Jenny Erikson, Bessie Burns, Sadie Baker, Mary Billy, Susie (Saih kie), Slim Jim, Joe Jackie, Jackie MacIntosh and Tagish Jim. These are the ancestors of many Kwanlin Dün today.[6]

Mandassa (also spelled Mundessa), who came from Hutchi, married a Tagish woman named Klondé, and they settled at Tàa'än Män (Lake Laberge). They also had a large family, including Maggie, who later married Henry Broeren; Jenny, who married Dawson Jim (later known as Jim Dawson); and Jim Boss, who married three times (Kathleen, Maude and Annie) and had several children. Many of their descendants are part of Kwanlin Dün First Nation today, while others are part of the Ta'an Kwäch'än Council.

Ida Calmegane heard many of the stories about the Tagish Kwan from her mother, Angela Sidney, her grandma Maria Johns and other Elders through the years: "Well, the Tagish Kwan people used to live across the river and some over on this side of the river [Tagish River at present-day Tagish]." Other Tagish Kwan lived all the way down the Yukon River.

above The wife and son of Tagish Chief Kuck-shaw travel during the gold rush era, ca. 1897.

**KAAX' ANSHÉE—LA.OOS TLÁA—
IDA CALMEGANE** You know Roddy
Blackjack and Clyde Blackjack and the
Skookums... and I'm sure there must be
other people. They just stayed down there
in Carmacks. And they [Tagish Kwan]
even went up to Ross River... Dorothy
John and her sister... [and] Ladues...
There's even Tagish Kwan people living
in Telegraph [Creek]... they spread out
all over... Lake Laberge was [home to]
Frances's grandmother and them, Jenny
Lebarge. They have a big family, too.
There's Violet [Storer] and Polly [Irvine]
and Amy [Cletheroe] and they all have
big families... That was Tagish Kwan
country all over... It only became Kwanlin Dün after the Second World War. That
was all Tagish country right down to
Carmacks...

[In Fort McMurray, Alberta,] this
one old man came up to us and start
talking. He talk to us in Tagish, Dän K'é
language... He said, "You know long
time ago," he said, "we followed the caribou down here. My ancestors followed
the caribou down here, we lived way up
north in the cold country... We had to
eat, so we followed the caribou because
there was nothing up there. So that's how
we still talk the language." [Other Tagish
Kwan people went] to Fort Nelson, Uncle
Johnny [Johns] met them. And you know
where you can get a really good reading
about all of the country is William Ogilvie, when he was making a map of the
Alaska and Yukon boundaries and B.C.
When they were mining down in the
Bonanza Creek in Yukon, those people in
Alaska were packing for the gold miners.
In one of those books, William Ogilvie
said that the Alaskan people put their

above Tàa'än Män people meet
with white traders at the upper
end of Tàa'än Män (Lake Laberge),
1894.

packs down when they got on top of the
Chilkoot. The boss asked them why did
they do that. "Well," they said, "this is
Tagish Kwan country, we're not supposed
to be working in Tagish Kwan country...
unless we get permission."

So Marsh Lake was a main fishing
part for the Tagish Kwan people...
Everybody that lived here in Tagish used
to go to Marsh Lake and they fished in
that river, M'Clintock River. The salmon
used to come up there all the time in the
summer time. But after they put that
dam in in Whitehorse, the fish had a hard
time to come up. They made a jumping
place for them, you remember?... Yeah, I
think that's when it all affected the fish
and the people.

When my sister [Mable] was born,
they were fishing there at Marsh Lake,
at that river [M'Clintock]... about
1924... The fishing was really strong
then because she was born in September.
September 9, her birthday. The people,
when they used to fish like that, all the
guys would be fishing and stuff, and the

young boys, the young kids would pack the fish to the fish house. All the women would be cutting the fish and they put it up for smoke. And when in the fall, when they're going to split up, they divide the fish up to everybody. 'Cause the whole community, it was a community project... My family was there, Grandpa and them... Tagish and Marsh Lake and all around Laberge.[7]

Other people have shared stories about the Tagish Kwan too. Mike Smith noted, "We are on Tagish Kwan land [in McIntyre], but that is different than Kwanlin Dün First Nation." He stated that Indian Affairs created Reserve No. 8 at Lot 226—the Old Village—and moved Indian people from all over the Yukon there. The traditional Tagish Kwan settlements were at Laberge, Hootalinqua and Marsh Lake. Dianne Smith said it's important to remember the linkages between people from different communities who are Tagish Kwan. Her grandfather Billy Smith was the first Chief of Whitehorse Indian Band in the 1950s, but his "true brothers" were Patsy Henderson and Dawson Charlie from Tagish.[8] ◉ ◉ ◉

◇◇◇◇◇◇◇◇◇◇◇◇◇◇◇◇◇◇

Our People Fished at Kwanlin and Chūlin

RONALD BILL Yeah, I know about the Miles Canyon and Whitehorse Rapids [Kwanlin and Chūlin in Southern Tutchone]. My grandmother told me about it. We use to come and fish, gaff salmon and spear salmon there, in the rapids area, when they come close to shore.

They go up the river, and they use to hunt across the river, where Riverdale is. They get moose there. Moose, and people use to live there. They dry fish. We use to go all over the place... People fished along where the rapids [were] one time. Where fish swim close to shore when the swift water. Indians use to spear them there. Grandma told me stories about people drying fish up the bank up by where the rapids. They spear these fish when they come close to shore. And then they dry them along the shore. There's also trout and grayling that goes up the Yukon River... Right below the canyon, they use to fish right down to the island. There's islands right below the bluff... Spear and nets. They use to make nets... and they had fishnets because they use to get it from coast. People use to come over from coast, I guess they had contact with white man a long time.[9]

VIOLET STORER In my mother's time, she told me that about Miles Canyon. People use to do the same thing, they use to float down, all the way down to Lake Laberge, or maybe down to Hootalinqua. They used boats, rafts. How they use to get through the canyon was by pulling... empty boat. They pull the boat through by rope, I guess, or whatever, skin-rope or whatever they make. They pull the boat through. With whatever they had. But with raft they couldn't do it because there's a big... I don't know what you call those things by the canyon there, whirlpool. That killed a lot of white people, and their boats went down there...

The Indians knew about that, so what they do was to just string the boat on to the other side... This here, the whirlpool,

facing top Stampeders in an empty scow shoot the high-water rapids at Kwanlin (Miles Canyon), 1899.

facing bottom First Nations men skin a moose on the bank of Chu Nįį Kwan (Yukon River) near Whitehorse, 1909.

Natives. Skinning Moose
White Horse Y.T.

on the opposite side, down … you know where the canyon bridge is, like this, there's a big eddy there. That's where the whirlpool is. So anyways, they use to pack all the stuff over, from the canyon right down to the rapids. They pack it down and take the stuff … and they keep on going. Some of them settle here and some of them they settle down in Lake Laberge. All the way down. To Lower Laberge to Hootalinqua. That's how they use to travel. If they want to come back, they have to use the poles. I seen my dad do it. I guess it's quite hard, especially if your boat was loaded. I use to see my mom sometimes get off the boat and help pull along the shore way … You don't call that hard time … them days.[10] ◉ ◉ ◉

K'ŭ Ch'an (Cloud People): Strangers with Different Ways

ÁYENJIÁTÀ—LOUIE SMITH When my dad tell me a story about how white people travel on this Yukon River, they use to pull a boat from Dawson City or either farther down, the place they call Forty Mile. My dad was pretty young then, he says first time he ever see white people, down below Whitehorse, the place they call... it use to be city dump, right above McIntyre Creek. He said first time he see white people with bunch of whiskers, figure they got no mouth... About four, five of them going to Bennett, B.C., they got big boat... they were talking about canyon. They try hire my grandpa, and my grandpa don't know... what these white people talking about. All they do is just move his mouth. They show him money. He got an idea, he know guy want pay him but...

My grandma talk to him, she say, "Don't go with him because you don't know those people, see. You don't know what they, what they going to do to you," so he didn't go with them. They go alone. They must have pull the boat across the canyon. They must have went through there before. They're going back to outside.

Pretty hard to get to Skagway, Alaska, from Dawson City in those days. So when this Canyon City was here, maybe way long before Canyon City too, that time when they're pulling that boat up the stream, up the Yukon River. That's what I hear. My dad tell me many stories about this. He said he was over in Canyon City too. I believe this is '98.[11]

RONALD BILL The only thing I can remember about this... is what people told a long time ago. My grandmother... she was about twelve years old when she first see white man. She said these white people gave them pilot bread. They said you [put] butter on, and the butter tasted bad so they wiped it off with a stick, cleaned the butter off and eat the pilot bread. They didn't like the taste of the butter.[12]

VIOLET STORER And my grandmother, I guess, was living along the river . . . maybe where the hospital is . . . She said sometimes Uncle Charlie and my mom used to run down to . . . where the camps are, white people? So . . . this white guy says, "Come here, come here." So Uncle Charlie ran out, and, "We're gonna give you something. Tell your mommy to put lots of water in a pot, put this stuff in there, with dried apple, eh? It's good for you, put some fig in, some sugar, something like that."

So Uncle Charlie took that, and then he [the white man] gave them some bacon, "You cook that, and then have some eggs or something with it." So he took it. It was a great big piece, I guess. So just before they got it home, my mom said to him, "You can't take that home, it's bear meat, and we're not allowed to eat bear meat." And my uncle says, "What are we going to do with it? Throw it in the river?" "No." She dug a hole in the ground. They buried that bacon. They buried it. Said, "Don't you tell Mom, don't you tell my Mom, it's bad luck if you eat it."

So they left that and they took the apple home. So she [their mother] said, "What are you doing with those things? You shouldn't take things from those white people." And if you could understand Indian, it's more comical if you say it in Indian. And he couldn't tell my grandmother.

"Just where did you get that stuff from?" "Those people over there." "What people?" "The kind that put that stuff on bread . . . you know? The kind that put butter on bread." "Oh, you meet those people that come from Outside." "Yeah." "That white skin?" "Yes." "You shouldn't

go there, they might take you away someplace, you know."

So Uncle Charles says, "This guy told, 'Put it in a pot, and boil it.'" So that's what she did. She put it in a pot, on the campfire, eh? . . . She put the whole thing in there. So, a little while, and things start moving, eh? Start moving around. "Why did you get, it's coming alive, oh boy." She took it off, because it was going like this, you know? And she told those kids, "You should never [indiscernible], it's going to kill us."

And she just threw it in the river, pot and all. She killed it. She never forgot that, you know? . . . And, I guess, Grandma told, "Never do that again, never take things from those people." But the best part, I like, is that they're explaining who gave it, and they say, "They put butter on bread."[13]

HOODLUA—KITTY SMITH Just like this story too. That's about Miles Canyon. That's way before that Whitehorse start . . . When white people come right here, they go down by raft. My grandfather told me that one. Hootalinqua Johnny. When he tell story about that.

That's the time Dawson City strike. They always get a job. They all stay in Whitehorse, in shipyard, and this side, and where we stay now. From here right down and up to above the hospital, up to hill, rapids, right there most of the people stay because . . . [the rapids] Indian way they call it the-ton-glu [phonetic transcription, language unknown] water run into bunch of rocks. Indian way they used to say it . . .

People, they go to work, packing stuff. Helping white man. White man hire them. Even women. Packing groceries

for white man over to this side. They pack them over. From then on they make a little raft [?], walk down … and Indians … guide them down the river. Cross Lake Laberge. Spring time, lake froze yet, my grandfather, Hootalinqua, get dog team … they take them to other end of Laberge. They say rich people. They pay hundred dollars for one way then. They take it back to Lower Laberge and then come back again. Take another load down. They make raft and go again …

That time my grandfather said he see lot of white man drowning. They're sticking out that far he said. He try stay on top that ice. Nobody think about it there. Leave him behind. Take off. They don't try to help them. Which one rich people, that's all they take.[14]

VIOLET STORER I wanted to mention something about my grandfather [Tom Smith] … My mother told me about the days of '98 when she could just remember when she was just a small child. She said that everybody lived at the rapids. That's where most people use to live because they use to gaff salmon there in the summer time, all the way down to Lake Laberge. They always use to fish, I guess for salmon. Their favourite place was the rapids because they can gaff the salmon there and just make their own net with sinew to get the salmon.

And meanwhile she says the white people start coming in, and they couldn't understand what was happening. A lot of them go drown in that Miles Canyon in this whirlpool. My granddad and some other Native people went up and talk to them. Try and talk to them. No one could speak English, so they try to tell them not to go down there with their family, and they refused. They waved … away … Sometime they get into a whirlpool, and they all disappear.

So they finally caught on, some people … My grandfather says they'll take the boat through for them. They take the rope and tie it to the boat, and I guess they use hand motion … just so the white man would understand what the Indian's trying to tell them. They finally caught on so he hauled the boat through the canyon by rope. They pay him when he gotten over here by the … Robert Campbell

above Newcomers often wrecked their boats in unsuccessful attempts to shoot the rapids. Our people rescued many of them, or, in some sad cases, retrieved and buried their bodies.

facing This chart shows Chūlin (Whitehorse Rapids), ca. 1898. They were submerged in Lake Schwatka, the reservoir created by the damming of Chu Nįį Kwan (Yukon River) in 1958. Chu Nįį Kwan means "shining water" in Southern Tutchone and describes the part of the Yukon River in the immediate Whitehorse area.

Bridge. He stop there, they reload again, they pay him some money. They don't know what money is, they rather have food. They don't know what money is, so my granddad says he'd rather have something to eat. Show them how, and this way they get flour, sugar, and they still don't know what it is.

White man showed them to drink tea, that's how they got started. Making tea, making bread, bannock, I guess. The main one was tea, molasses, and I guess maybe porridge, I don't know. Anyway, that's how they learn from the stampeders.

The saddest part is he had a job burying the drowned people from the canyon. He had to bury them, my granddaddy and some other people ... They put crosses ... All the way from here down to Lake Laberge you see little crosses here and there. Right now some of them must have fell over ... She [my mother] told me one thing where he had, he tried very hard to take the family through. They refuses, this woman refuses to go. He said, "You come with me ..." She said, "No, no, no ... I'm going." She said her, her husband, three kids, and they all got drowned. You know where they bury them all? Over here ... right beside there. All their graves had five little crosses, and now I don't know what happened to them. Lost forever, I guess. That's what happen as far as I know.[15]

CH'E'A MĄ—MAY HUME [My mom Kitty] married Canyon Johnnie, then ... she meet all ... her relatives, her Grandmother on this side and all her cousins ... and that's how she used to know ... that Whitehorse Rapids. That's where that Whitehorse Billy and ... Florence

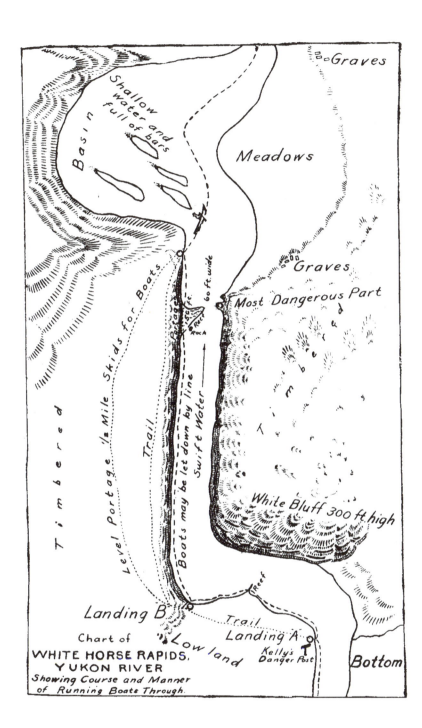

MacIntosh, her grandfather ... him and Whitehorse Billy used to own that part ... where the old canyon, just the end of the canyon, you know where that camp is ... Robert Service [campground], right there, that. It's kind of pointed like that

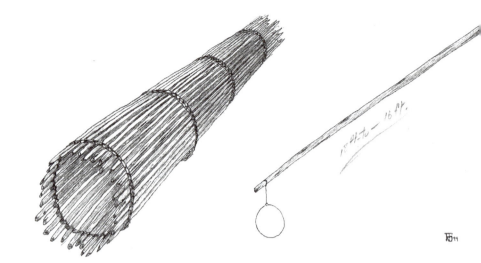

and then there's the big rock sticking out... used to be eddy behind it... that's where they used to gaff their salmon, eh... and then it comes around the bend and then it goes into shallow water on this side, they used to have the fish traps there, she said. That Lily Kane's dad... that's Frank Slim's dad, I am talking about. I think his name, Hutchi, Hutchi Slim, yeah, and them old people, eh... that's where they fish and everybody come from every place. They put up their share of salmon and everything. And Marsh Lake, up M'Clintock, fish used to go up that way, eh. And the Marsh Lake people, that's where they stayed and did their fishing there too [at] Whitehorse Rapids... Mom showed us that place, eh, where she used to fish when she was married to Canyon Johnnie, that time she was young... and she told us how people used to live all behind, you know where that canyon is now? They said that used to be full of people there, eh... all used to be cache and camp there, they said. And they used to have a house up there. There's quite a few people used to have house there. Then they don't want it there, the government don't want it there 'cause water running down dirty, they say that, I guess, eh? Native don't make it dirty water. You know they never even pour... anything you wash it, anything, they don't throw it into the water. They throw it into the bush and the water they say go through sand, it makes it back anyways, eh, but it's clean by that time. That's the way Native all say that... and nothing was thrown into the water because that water is life, in the water, eh, life is fish. Fish and everything lives in the water, eh. [Annie Smith] and I

guess a lot of them was born there, eh because that, that used to be village, the Indian used to stay there, eh, put up their grub. Then from there people go, after you put up fish, then you do your moose meat... then gophers and pick your berries. And berries, they used to preserve them when we did it with my mom when I was raising up... you wash the moose stomach, you soak that 'til it is just clean, just white you got to bleach it, in the water, running water, eh. Then you dry it and then when it comes to berry picking time, then they soak it, eh [and store berries in it].[16] ◉ ◉ ◉

Clash of Cultures

CH'E'A MĄ—MAY HUME You know that, that first people that got hung in Dawson City? Them were my great-uncles, my mom's mother brother were two of them. And one was a first cousin, and they hung one cousin and one of my mother's mother brother... And then there was the third boy, he was too young to be hung. They kill white man, up here by Marsh Lake, coming up off the canyon somewheres.

What happen is, I guess these white people, they camp around and they been left this thing in the camp. I guess . . . that thing they burn gold with it [arsenic], you know, they put it in there, I guess, and you burn your rocks down and you put it in there. And I guess it's poison and it's apparently, it's white, eh? And so these people found this camp and they found that can and they thought it baking powder. Them days they were already using flour and baking powder. And they didn't have no baking powder, so they thought it was baking powder. So they cook that bannock with that, eh. And this is been happen before they kill, I guess a year or so before the killing. Not even that, maybe just shortly before that.

And then they cook that bannock and it rise and everything, eh. And then, so then they thought they don't wanna eat it to be safe. They gave it to a dog and the dog eat it and everything, you know?

And he was okay, and I guess they waited maybe twenty minutes or so and nothing happen to that dog so they thought, well, it's safe then. So they make tea, they have tea all ready and they eat bannock and tea. And here, they all got poison right there, eh? Only about two safe out of it, I guess. And that was the relatives of that boys.

And so they held it against them prospectors. Only when people started getting sick, they said, and that dog start showing sick, too. And so they all got poison, eh?

And they died, they all died, eh. And so and that's why, and I guess when they were hunting there and they saw this boat coming. Already there was Whitehorse then, eh. Little bit, Whitehorse. There's policeman up here too, everything then, eh.

Then they see that white man going with a boat. And that oldest cousin, they

above The Nantuck brothers of Tàkwädàdhà (Marsh Lake) stand in shackles beside Corporal Rudd of the North West Mounted Police (*far right*) at Tagish Police Post, 1898. The brothers killed two white prospectors to avenge the death of some of their relatives, who died from eating arsenic that they found at an abandoned prospector's camp and mistook for baking powder. After their trial at Dawson, Jim and Dawson Nantuck were hanged in August 1899, while Frank and Joe died of tuberculosis in prison. The case was shocking to both our Tagish ancestors and white newcomers at the time, illustrating the misunderstandings and deep cultural conflicts that arose during the gold rush.

said, "Let's kill 'em," he said, "that's the same people that been kill our relatives and poison them off." Them other two, my grandmother's brothers, they said, "No, we don't have to do that, we don't want to do that." And that other one said, the other cousin said ... he was raised up here, see? And then the other ones, they were raised amongst the Tlingit and stuff like that, eh. And he said, "Oh, I should think you're not my cousin, you're chicken because you were raised in a different part of the country. You don't got no Indian blood in you!" So what they said, "Okay, then!"

So they shot, they shot them guys, eh. And I guess one of them guys got shot through here, but he recognise them boys. They're just right there, eh. Anyways, when they shot, he fall down too, he dead. But there was wound just through his arm, right here. That boat kept on floating down the river. After he

get long ways, I guess, then he paddle good. He come right to Whitehorse, right here. So then he report it. The three of them, he recognise them good, he know it, eh.

And so then they come back there, they said, to that place. And they told 'em what they did. And then, uh, that's when my mom, I think she was about five or six then. She said [she] remember her mom and they heard the news that them boys are gonna get hung. They wait one year, eh, before they hang them. And so they send my mom, my grandmother, they living in Haines. So her cousins, they come and get her, hey, and they told her that, "Your brothers, they're gonna get hang and your mom wants you for support, eh." So she came up and left her daughter over there, my mom, with her dad, um, not her dad, but her ... his sisters like and the grandmother ... And she came back to Yukon, back here.

left Kàdùhikh—K'aɬgwach—K'odetéena—Kitty Smith as a young woman at Shäwshe (Southern Tutchone) or Neskatahin (Tlingit) (Dalton Post), ca. 1910.

right Four Yukon leaders pose in a Whitehorse studio, ca. 1908. *Left to right*: Gold Commissioner George Mackenzie, Kashxóot—Chief Jim Boss, Keish Skookum Jim and Anglican priest Reverend W.G. Blackwell. Chief Jim Boss and Skookum Jim combined traditional activities with new entrepreneurial opportunities after the gold rush and worked with lawyers, government officials and clergy to raise concerns about issues affecting their people.

facing This letter by Kashxóot—Chief Jim Boss of Tàa'än Män, sent by a Whitehorse lawyer in 1902, is now recognized as the start of Yukon First Nations land claims. The second page listed populations of some of the larger First Nations camps in the southern Yukon.

And then the boys, they got hung, two of them and that youngest one, they send him out. Nobody ever know whatever happen to him. 'Cause how they gonna know that? Natives don't know how to go and . . .

And then my mom says she thinks she was about five or six then, eh. 'Cause she remember good. But that was the last she saw her mother. Her mother died shortly after she was up here, maybe, she stayed like for the summer, eh. And then she didn't live very long, she died up here. And so that's the only way we could find out how old my mom was when she died . . ., my mom died five years ago and I wanna know how old she was when she died, eh.

She said she remember her mom good 'cause she used to go out, do saps and dig bear roots and pick berries and stuff like that, eh. She said she knows her mom good. We figure she must've be hundred, over hundred and ten at least. She lived a long life and then and she was just strong like me yet. She walk around right to the end. And she never lost her mind or anything. She tell stories about all, everything, eh.

My mom was Kitty Smith [Kàdùhikh—K'aɬgwach—K'odetéena], she married my dad, Billy Smith [Kanéɬ].[17] ◉ ◉ ◉

Wood Camps and Steamboats

RONALD BILL [My mom and dad] used to go from, from Bend . . . up to Tanana Reef. We never went down to Carmacks, but when I was small . . . they went down to Selkirk, and then they come back to Carmacks, and all this, they'd ride up to Tanana Reef . . . they'd keep moving up . . . Wherever there was work, I guess they'd go there . . . There was wood camps all the way along there . . . down Whistle Bend, there was another one there, and then Lake Laberge. And there were way down the other end, Laberge, and then Tanana Reef, that's where we stayed there for quite a while. Tanana Reef. Big Salmon, eh? Big Salmon, and then, just below Big Salmon, there's a bar or wood camp, they called it . . . And then Carmacks and Little Salmon, Little Salmon and Minto and all this places.[18]

HOODLUA—KITTY SMITH That's the time [1930s] lot of people stay on this side [east side of river]. All kinds of them. Down here, too. See that Marwell area? Right down to cliff [opposite Marwell]. Right to there. Nothing but tents. Tents everywhere. That's the time we're cutting wood back there . . . where that village is, right behind there, where that big rock go through. See that sidehill on this side. Right on top there, we start cutting wood . . . we use to hunt gopher there with my grandmother.

. . . George Ryder, that's the one we're cutting wood for. Gordon Ryder, Lloyd Ryder daddy? That was a long time ago. Lloyd, Gordon Ryder they was about . . . I don't know how old they, ten . . . they were just kids yet.[19]

TL'UA—JOHNNY MCGUNDY Oh yes, cut wood for the steamboat, in the summer time. Lower Laberge, we used to cut wood for the steamboat . . . in Carmacks and . . . [leave it right beside the river] . . . They paid us right there . . . Bob Price wood camp . . . they paid for it . . . groceries. In the fall, go up on the mountain and dry meat.[20]

EFFIE CAMPBELL North, I think. From Big Salmon, north, go up the mountain. Don't know what they call this mountain. And, for living, my dad cut wood . . . Me and my sister would help him all the time, cutting wood all winter long . . . just all time, just work

top Frank Slim with nearly a tonne of mail in his canoe, early spring 1937. He was working for Klondike Airways but it was too early in the season for floatplanes to land on the river—so Frank paddled the mail from Whitehorse to Dawson City, through ice floes on Tàgä Shäw (Yukon River).

bottom In 1937, Frank Slim surrendered his Indian Status so he could obtain a river pilot's licence. For many years he captained the Taylor & Drury supply vessel *Yukon Rose* (pictured here ca. 1936–1937), and in 1960 he piloted the SS *Keno* on her last voyage to Dawson City.

facing top Steamboats pass the busy Whitehorse riverfront, June 9, 1901.

facing bottom First Nations families lived and worked at wood camps all along Tàgä Shäw (Yukon River) during the steamboat era.

Indians Waiting To Load Firewood On Steamer - Yukon River - Y.T. July - 1900

all the time ... [When riverboats come] sometimes we go there and put a load of wood in, eh? Buy some things.[21]

LILY KANE Frank Slim, that's my brother. Yeah, he go to work, ah. I don't know, been go to work but I don't know how old he is, about fifteen year old. He stay in town. Works around some place, I guess. After a while he get on the boat, I guess. Yeah, he work on the boat every spring [for Taylor & Drury].

Yeah, first time. He was a captain [on the *Yukon Rose*].

Yeah, after he get in, you know that Taylor & Drury boat he drowned [sank] down in Laberge? After that he changed to a big boat, eh. That's the last boat, he take it down to Dawson. That's the one, Dawson, they got it [ss *Keno*].

... Oh yeah, been ride that ... picnic boat used to be, they got scow, I guess. Goes around Laberge and go back. People dance inside. It's nice to ride. Boat just like sail.[22] ◉ ◉ ◉

◇◇◇◇◇◇◇◇◇◇◇

Fox Farming

VIOLET STORER All I know about the fox farm is the one that use to be across the river. Old Dan Snow use to look after one time, Mom said.[23] I just go by what my parents tell me. You know where that great big Mormon church is over there across the river? That's where the fox farm use to be right there. That old Dan Snow [Dan Snure] use to look after it. Taylor & Drury use to be in charge of that. In fact, that old house that he use to live in is still standing there. That big old log place there? That's old Taylor & Drury house. Those people that lived there use to look after fox over there. It was a great big place.[24]

HOODLUA—KITTY SMITH Long time ago, when they want to know about this fox ranch, they had one in Mason's Landing, too. Mason's Landing. That's where they had one a long time ago too. Where the road go to Livingstone. Right there. That one too, the same way, they hire Indian to feed them and watch it for these white people. They don't know who's that. They get pay good for that, they had to watch them. They go big farm there too. Mason's Landing . . . my grandmother said she's seen something there, they don't know what it was. They seen something back in the bush. Some kind of animal. They don't know what was that. Been eating rabbit. That's how they find out. Long time ago rabbit, when they set rabbit snare, they don't use wire. Nothing. They use little twine. Twine? They got little knot right here and they put windfall, pole, put it on, put that snare right on rabbit trail. Soon rabbit get catch, pole right here, this thing unsnap and get hung up. Something like that. Fishing line, yeah. Early days, they use babiche. Babiche, snowshoes babiche. They use to have fox farm in there. Aunty Mrs. Ladue. Don't know her name, I think it's Jenny. Her mother, she hunt rabbit. And my grandmother, Alice Cody sister, her name is Sen-nah-neh, she got no English name. She hunt rabbit with her. They kill lot of rabbit, they go along the snares, to feed those fox. Pretty soon, something been eat it. They dig all the snare up, not one rabbit. Pretty soon she look back and she seen something's leg, lift his head up, she said. His head, just his head. He look just like a horse head. That was that one eating that rabbit. She say she see it, she start to run, her. Mrs. Ladue mother, her she just stand there, she got stunned. She run down to Hootalinqua, she drag him. Nobody know what was that.[25] ◉ ◉ ◉

◇◇◇◇◇◇◇◇◇◇◇◇◇◇◇◇◇◇◇◇◇◇◇◇◇◇◇

Trapping: "An Interesting Life"

LILY KANE Yeah, we trapping. My daddy is trapping lynx on the side of mountain. I always walk with him, take dog, yeah. We got dog team. Catch lynx. Always go with my dad. Hunt rats, winter time, in the spring time, in March, I guess that's the time we hunt rats, trapping . . . Yeah, lake, around lake other side mountain, M'Clintock Lake.[26]

RONALD BILL A long time ago . . . almost year-round. Hunting and fishing and trapping. We use to make a lot of money in fur trapping.

Now fur don't worth anything. We use to travel by dog team in the winter and pack up our stuff in the summer. We use to pack up the dogs. It was an interesting life, but when we came out of the bush, they put us on the reserve and things like that and spoilt the nature of the Indians.[27]

DON MCKAY Father and Mother used to trap around Fish Lake, up to the Ibex then down through south end of Fish Lake and back. They had cabins, one in the Ibex and one cabin at Louise Lake, and they would travel from cabin to cabin. And depending on how much time and supplies they had, they would start at one section, starting early in the winter and trapping season, and work their way up.[28]

TL'UA—JOHN MCGUNDY [Those days a] .22 [was] seven dollars; shells, thirty-five cents, something like that. Everything cheap. He [Uncle Frankie Jim] used to tell me about they go trapping, they take twenty dollar worth of grocery, it last them till Christmas. Fall time, October month, eh. Bunch of fur, come in, Christmas, sell the fur then. Twenty dollars, big load I guess. Everything cheap those days. Dollar-seventy five for jean. Everything cheap. You get the silver, grey [fox] seventeen hundred dollars, something like that. Black fox I think almost thousand bucks. Yeah, Indian had lot of money. Like, Harry Cooper [who used to be the local Whitehorse magistrate], he telling me, white people get tough time, Depression. But Indian well off, he said. Because trapping, eh, and fish in the summer time.[29]

POLLY IRVINE No, my dad was trapping on those mountains [Teslin River], I guess. I don't know where he go... My dad say, trap the mountains, they had quite a few fox. Red fox... wintertime for fur... Only one person live out there [Fish Lake] was David Jackson. He became my brother-in-law after... They just trap there in wintertime... [then they go] back to Carcross. We came back and made a home at McRae. Little old cabin down there where we live. Oh yes, he [my dad] did quite a bit [of living off the land.] Well, that's the first year we came over from Hootalink [Hootalinqua or Teslin River], Winter Crossing, they call it. That's the first place we stop... [at] Wigan [McRae], from there he trap around. And then years later, there's no more fur, he said, so he went to work around town here.[30]

ŁUGÛN—LUGÓON—SOPHIE SMARCH
And also, our people has been spoiled by breaking down fur prices, like, our Native people used to live real good from trapping. We used to get lots of money for a pelt. Used to get sometimes $1,500 for a red fox, and $2,500 for a black fox. Cross fox you could get up to $3,000 for it. And the lynx and everything else used to be worth killing. We used to kill them and live off it. But today, the prices are so bad, people don't even bother with hunting or trapping anymore. Trapping and going out hunting, it just, do away with it, because it's not worth it.[31] ◉ ◉ ◉

above Mrs. Slim Jim holds Lily Kane, near Tàa'än Män (Lake Laberge).

PLACE NAMES AND HERITAGE ROUTES IN THE KDFN TRADITIONAL TERRITORY

Legend:
- ⊗ Gathering place
- — — Heritage route
- ▲ Mountain

Scale: 0 — 15 — 30 km

Place names within the KDFN Traditional Territory originate from the Southern Tutchone language. Other place names indicated with an asterisks symbol (*) are of Tagish origin.

Place names and labels on map:

Dambäl
Daghal Shäw Män
Kwejel Män
Ts'al Shäw Ay
Hudìnlin
Ji Thi Th'an Dhäl ▲
TÀGÀ SHÄW
Gyu Shäw Chù
Du Chù
Kursi Män
Thay T'aw Män
Titl'ät
Tl'ukshän Män
Dhäl Ts'ala
Tà'òla Män
Tli Yel Ätan
TÀÀ'AN
Chu Yàna Män
Kwätan'aya Män
T'äw Tà'är
Dèlin
Chusay Män
Tali Män
Sua Nàgan
Nètdinlin
Tsawadenji Chù
Kwätan'aya Dhal ▲
Män Néju
Nambür ▲
Dhal Anu ▲
The A' ▲
Chänkua
Lür Dàyhèl
Naalin Dhä ▲
Nàkhu Chù
Tl'äw Kwäshän
Tajenà Tlura Män
Dasetay Män
Du Chù
Sha Dhäla
Kàkwäts'änägru ▲
Thay T'äw ▲
Chù
Gà Dhäl ▲
Whitehorse
The May ▲
Kwanlin
Łu Zil Män
Sima ▲
Gyù Chùa
Nekhù
CHU NJI KWAN
Desgwa'age Méne*
Jekudìtleda
Tékhaaje*
Tàkwädàdha
Tló Kaa Dzéle* ▲
Nekhù Män
Dahmbet Setaa*
Tagish
Lúu Chó Méne*
Äthèkal ▲
Taagish Tóoe*
Todezáané* ⊗
MEN CHO*
Nústséhé Méne*

KWANLIN DÜN TRADITIONAL TERRITORY

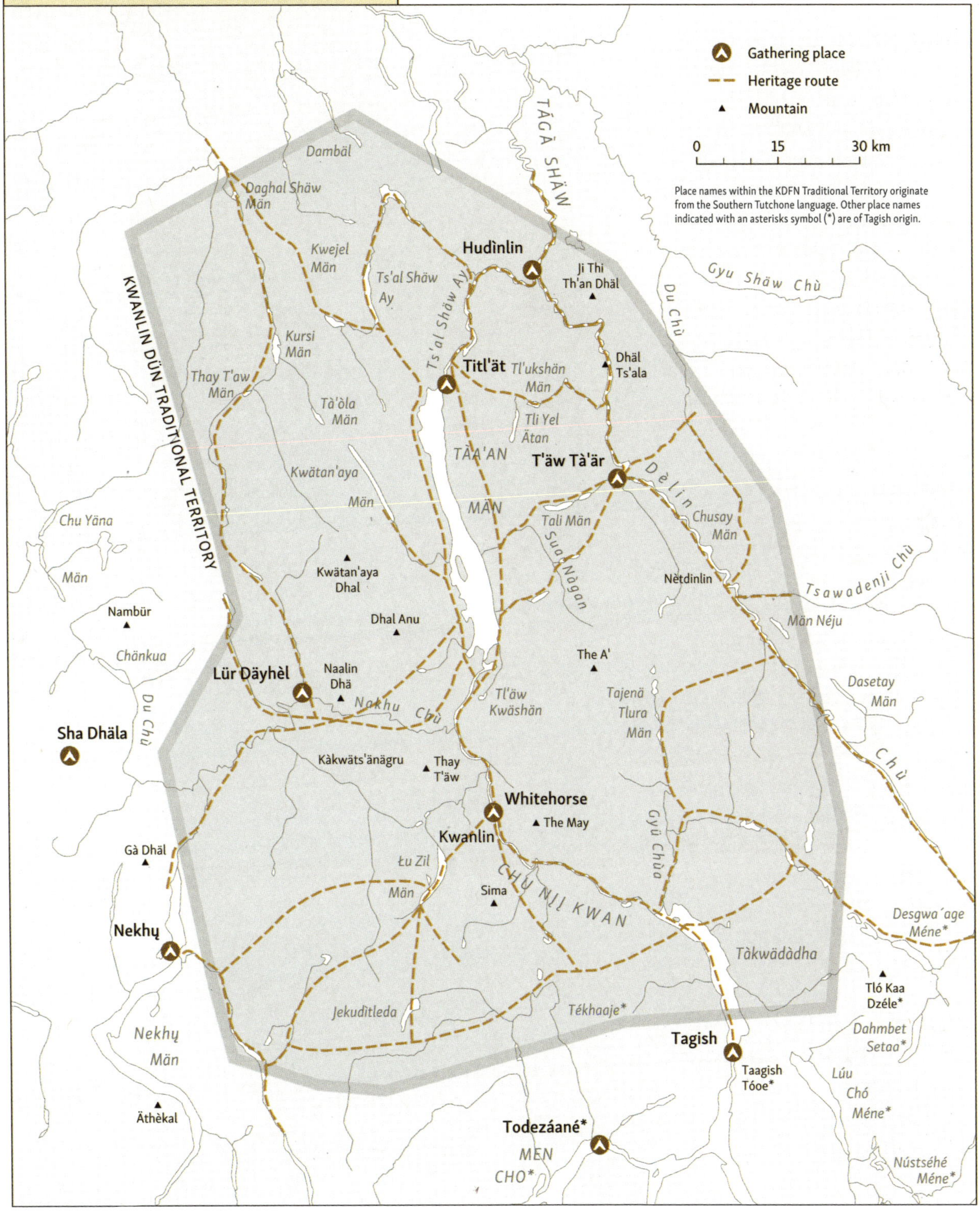

MAP DISCLAIMER: Work to document place names and routes in KDFN Traditional Territory is ongoing. This map is not intended to be a comprehensive inventory of all First Nations traditional places and routes within the area. It should be noted that these traditional places and routes continue to have significance for First Nations people today.

facing K'ah'aata'—John Joe (*far left*) and Frank Slim (*far right*) on an outfitting trip with clients from Seattle, ca. 1940s.

Shich'ulee Maa—Julia Joe
K'ah'aata'—John Joe

Shich'ulee Maa (Expecting Mother)—Julia Joe of the Dakl'ushaa/Wolf Clan and K'ah'aata' (Pointing Arrows Father)—John Joe of the Gaanaxteidí/Crow were an extraordinary couple who lived at Marsh Lake and Whitehorse for more than seven decades. They combined their traditional hunting, fishing and gathering life on the land with wage employment to make a good living for their large family, extending their generosity to other families in times of need. Over the years they witnessed many changes that had huge impacts on their lives and the lands they called home.

Julia was born in 1907 to Seki Jackie, daughter of Gunaaták', Marsh Lake Chief Jackie. Following her mother's line, Julia was of the Tagish Kwan Wolf Clan. Her father was a white man. Julia was born in Whitehorse at the old campsite on the east bank of the river where Whitehorse General Hospital is located today. Her mother later married Henri "Shorty" Roils,[32] but died soon after when Julia was only five. Seki is buried at the gravesite behind Whitehorse General Hospital.

Julia's Aunty Jenny Flynn looked after her for several years. Jenny and Shorty Roils were a couple. He was a citizen of France. Before he left the Yukon to fight in World War I, he convinced Bishop Stringer to allow Julia to attend Chooutla School in Carcross, although she was not technically eligible as a non-Status child. Julia stayed there until she was twenty, learning to read and write, and studying the Bible, which remained a lifelong interest for her.

John Joe was from the Hootchi Chief family, born in 1873. He moved to the Whitehorse area around the time of the gold rush via the Takhini and Yukon Rivers, over to the Teslin and Livingstone area where he trapped for a few years. He moved to Marsh Lake in 1900. His first wife was Louise Dawson, and they had three sons before she and the youngest son died in an epidemic. Their oldest son, Jeff Sheldon, continued to be close to the Joe family after John Joe remarried.

As was done in those days, the Elders decided that Julia and John would be a good couple, but he waited for her to finish school before they married. Julia and John built a house at Marsh Lake, which served as their main home for them and their ten children. They also had a house in Whitehorse, a cabin at Yard Limits on Miles Canyon, and cabins on the upper Lewes (Yukon) River and on their traplines.

The whole family worked very hard throughout the year, following an intensive round of seasonal activities. In the spring they hunted geese and ducks on the lake. In summer they set nets and traps for king salmon on the M'Clintock River. They caught pike and trout in Marsh Lake with nets year-round. The pike were dried to provide food for their large dog teams, which provided transportation on their traplines in winter. Both Julia and John had boats, which John built himself for fishing on the lake.

The family ran traplines for wolf, fox, lynx, beaver and muskrats. John trapped as many as three hundred rats a night. Daughter Virginia took her holidays from her job at the laundry in town to trap rats, which were worth a lot of money in the 1950s. Squirrel camp was up what is now the M'Clintock Valley River Road. The pelts were sometimes worth thirty-five cents. Country foods included gophers, grouse and beaver. Gopher brains were a delicacy that resembled cream, and beaver tail was cooked over the campfire.

The Joe family did not hunt caribou because local herds were depleted by prospectors during gold rush years and later by the U.S. Army during construction of the Alaska Highway. They did not hunt bear either, believing that they were kin, like brothers and sisters.

Before the Whitehorse power dam was built in the 1950s, the M'Clintock River would be red with spawning king salmon. Families from Lake Laberge and Carcross came to harvest fish there alongside Marsh Lake relatives. The first year after the dam was completed there was no fish ladder,

so the salmon were blocked from migrating upstream. John Joe and other First Nations people carried some of the big salmon in gunnysacks up above the dam so they could continue upriver to spawn, but the run was never the same again. The M'Clintock fishery had often yielded three hundred salmon a day during peak runs in mid-August. After the run was destroyed, John Joe took his family to the Teslin River to fish at Johnsons Crossing, with permission of the people there.

Humpback whitefish were harvested in October in the marshy bays along the Lewes River where they spawned. The Joe kids, with their Suits family cousins who lived nearby, went with John on a big raft to run the nets. It had an outboard motor but John preferred the boys to pole the raft to save on gas. The Joes' granddaughter Pat Joe set net there in the fall up until 2004, catching humpback whitefish and distributing them to Elders. Ta'an people and others would ask the Joe family for permission to set nets in Marsh Lake. It was a way to show respect and continues to this day.

top Shich'ulee Maa—Julia Joe with K'ah'aata'—John Joe.

centre Shich'ulee Maa—Julia Joe and granddaughter Tammy Joe beside one of the boats that Julia and her husband, K'ah'aata'—John Joe, built for their subsistence and commercial fishery at Tàkwädàdhà (Marsh Lake), ca. 1960s.

bottom The Joe family home at Tàkwädàdhà (Marsh Lake).

John Joe was a renowned big-game guide and outfitter, with clients from all over North America and Europe. He had packhorses for the hunts, which meant the family had to plant and harvest hay for them. Men from the Burns and Shakoon families worked as guides with him, and sometimes they all worked with Johnny Johns from Carcross, too.

During the building of the Alaska Highway there was a big demand for hide products. Julia and her girls made many items to sell to American soldiers and other workers. John built a road with his sons and some of their cousins from their homestead on Marsh Lake to the new highway. Mink farming was another way that the Joe family supported themselves. Remains of the cages can still be seen around the old Marsh Lake homestead. At Shorty Ville, near the Marsh Lake dam, the Joes and the Shortys cut wood for the steamboats, which provided more income until the steamboats stopped running in the 1950s.

During tough times, when some families were unable to harvest enough food to make it through the winter, they would come to Julia and John Joe's home for help. John began calling it "Hungry Town." They always gave what they could and are still remembered today for their generosity and good humour. John Joe died in 1985 at the age of 112. Julia lived to be 93 and passed away in 2000.[33]

OUR ELDERS SAY...

Taylor & Drury: Traders in Town

RONALD BILL We were going to build a house, but I guess my dad died, changes things. My mom got married to Ole Wickstrom there, the guy that built that road. Yeah, he had a wood business...there, a huge contract, him and another guy. They were working night and day, [Ole and] Bob Porsild...

My mom, she sewed quite a bit...She make moccasins and mukluks and all these things, and she sell them at a good price...Yeah, and here they make a good living. I know some of those women... you get your squirrels that you're trapping...you get one pelt, a squirrel, for $1.85. And I know, when I work, I work... for the army. I got $1.05 for one-hour work. And these people, they can kill five or six squirrels, so they make more money...[take their furs] to T & D's [Taylor & Drury's store] and they buy 'em...

Cash, cash...They were very good. They had all these, like, Hootalinqua, and Big Salmon, Carmacks, all these. They establish a...fur trading place, post, T & D's, eh? My grandpa named his sons after them. Taylor and Drury [McGundy]...I guess they were pretty popular with the people...Hauling freight, even in winter time, they'd get freight to these place. Yeah, so they were pretty busy. They had a boat too, that *Neecheah*...They go to Teslin.[34]

RENEE PETER We go around for some meat. We got fresh meat again, like that, in winter time. Go hunting, furs, like that, then they get something to white man. They kill fur. Taylor & Drury, Charlie Taylor and them, that time, them they buying fur, too. Fall time, we get enough grub, they give you charge up [credit]. After that, you pay it back with fur. The way they got it. You got nothing, anytime, summer time. After that, Charlie Taylor and them, you go to them, they give you lots of grub. Sometime you pay them back again.

Good people, you know. That's the one there. If you got nothing to go out with to hunt fur, they give you tent, stove, trap, everything. They put out trap, everything. For Indian people, they go out. That's what they making money from, Indian people, eh. But they look after Indian people pretty well. They look after Indian people well. They're like that, that's how Charlie Taylor, I just think about it yet. I just think about Charlie Taylor yet. If we got nothing, we stay down in Carmacks. Grub too high,

above Cars line the street in front of the Taylor & Drury store, Whitehorse, ca. 1920s.

so you put down what you want, send it to Charlie Taylor in Whitehorse. He send it on freight. Come with freight. Where you stay, come right there. Good people, those people there. They got no son that's why. Just one son he got, Charlie Taylor.

Yeah, Charlie Taylor said he give the house [on east bank of river across from Whitehorse] to Harry Silverfox, they stay there. They use to live across there. Other side [east] of Whitehorse. Like that, they look after Indian people, they worry, you know, those people there. Now we lost them, we lost everything. Different people, all of them.[35]

HOODLUA—KITTY SMITH & DONSALÄ—FRED SMITH

KITTY: Then before dark, Daddy come up Whitehorse. They come in to... they come in to, they come in to doctor. Man got shot in the leg. That's the time I told you Daddy play gambling this side. See where that house up there, way up, right there. We stay in Shipyard, us. All night we hear them gamble going on there. Harry Silverfox in there. Big Salmon George and my grandfather, my daddy, my Uncle Joe Ladue, my Uncle Taylor McGundy. All of them there. From Ross River. They play gamble for five days steady. Night and day.

Yeah. He... been... Harry Silverfox. You know Billy Johnny mother, I mean dad and his mother. He has been dealing with that Taylor & Drury since long time. He hunt fur for him. He sell fur to him, all that. When Taylor & Drury, they move to other side. They start shoemaking... first time Taylor & Drury, when they first came to Whitehorse, they started making shoes. You know, shoes wear out, they repair it. When they started making

that shoemaking, and they make enough. Then they open store. Start to buy fur. Grandpa said. Grandpa Hootalinqua Johnny. Shotgun, I don't know how big shotgun. You know really long. You know how they buy that? They pile up fur beside it. When same high that shotgun, then they give them shotgun. That's how they do it.

FRED: That's how they cheat. Oh boy!

KITTY: Trade, they call that. Then Harry Silverfox see that Taylor & Drury, they got open store on other side [west]. They move across. They open their own store. They get their own house. That's the time Harry Silverfox been trapping for him for so many years. Nice friend to him. Then he give him that house. He give him that land, everything. That's what I heard anyways.

That's how he stay there, Harry Silverfox. He own that house because it was given to him. Taylor & Drury, both of them, two different. Taylor's different and Drury different. That's how my dad

above Hootalinqua Johnny, grandfather of Hoodlua—Kitty Smith, with his wives, Alice Cody (*left*) and Nelly Johnny, ca. late 1920s.

got name, too. Drury, they say, another man. Taylor, he's another man. See? Taylor & Drury, store there too, two company. That's how they start that store. And use to be first time they started buying fur, my grandmother said over from across they stay, Taylor & Drury boat go down this way, all around Teslin, right around Hootalinqua, from there up the Teslin River. Every camp, Indian camp, they stop there. They buy fur and they carry bunch of groceries, too. Right in there, they just buy groceries and they buy fur same time. Then they go to another place, they keep doing that right up to Teslin, all the way Teslin, too. They buy fur from there, same time they deliver groceries, too.[36] ◉ ◉ ◉

Living on the Edge of Town

RONALD BILL We travelled into Whitehorse from Little Salmon area in 1938–1939 when [White Pass & Yukon Railway] give him [my dad] a job... Loading the boats... There were a lot of workers... I was pretty young... [We lived] across the river. Straight across from the Cultural Centre... Yeah, there was a road that went right through to Livingstone, to that Livingstone Creek. Yeah. Crossing, Winter Crossing... we lived in a tent frame... [He had a little boat to go across the river to work]... There's some people across there, they had boats too... There was Charlie Johnson, Johnson Sam and my uncle, Emma and George, they stay there... Silverfox... There was a lot of people there... T & D gave them a house. They had those houses before, so they gave it to them. I don't know if they sell it to them, for eighteen dollars or something like that... Some [other families] had houses...

My brother was working then. He started pretty young. I was nine, and he was about fourteen I guess, he started working... [My mom]... she sew. They get this moosehide and they make moccasins and they sell them, eh? So they had a lot of things going. They sell, they get good money there. It was more cheap then, you get groceries for thirty-six dollars, in a big pile there... [Mom and I went berry picking]... We fished there too, in the creek. Fishing, grouse... when I got older, I used to go when I got out of school, sixteen year old, I used to walk around way back. My stepdad taught me, "Is that your track way back there?" I'd tell him, "Yeah. Yeah, that's mine." He said, "You're sure taking a chance walking way back there," he said. "Moose are running there, they're gonna go after you if they see you." And me and my uncle hunt 'em all over there...

above Bill Lebarge and his dogs bring freshly caught salmon (note the tails sticking out of the packs) into town near Yard Limits, south of Whitehorse, ca. 1920s. He set his nets near the present site of the SS *Klondike* and lined his dogs' packs with willow branches before filling them with fish to sell or trade.

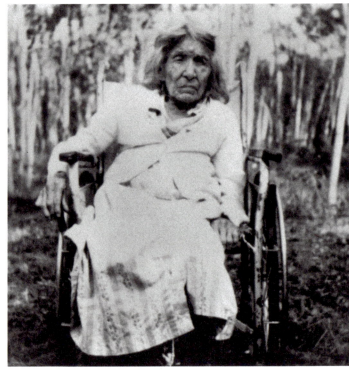

[My dad worked on the docks] just the summer... trapping [in winter]... Yeah, he went back there, straight back from Whistle Bend... This road go through there, eh?... They set up a tent there, and we would trap there... We had a dog team and things like that. And there's truck going back and forth, hauling wood. You hire one of those trucks and load on your stove and go down there. So they travelled quite a bit. But there was no four-wheeler or nothing like that.[37]

VIOLET STORER Then we moved to rapids, Whitehorse Rapids. And my dad [Billy Lebarge] built a house there, a cabin, and so was Whitehorse Billy from Marsh Lake. [From] Marsh Lake dam. And we stayed there for many years.

I guess the Indian agent told us that we couldn't stay in [town]... but at Yard Limit. I don't know what a yard limit is... I can't understand that. We stayed at... like they had a white post beside the railroad. They say, "You stay on that side. You don't build a cabin over there. You build a cabin over here." So my dad and everybody was moved over here. White Pass, I guess, didn't want people to be on their [land.]

We grew up there... The fish camp. The place people use to go and fish for salmon was at the Whitehorse Rapids. They used to gaff for them... That's why Dad moved so that we can go to Marsh Lake every July. He used to set nets. You know where the [ss] *Klondike* is? Right across from the *Klondike*. He used to have two salmon nets every August. Right there today, there's a big beaver dam, right where my dad used to set nets. I was surprised to see that. They say there's a marsh there, right where Dad set nets. Nobody touched it. White people leave it alone. Now my sister see beaver down there. She say, "How come beaver house is right where my dad used to hunt moose?" He use to live there and then take our fish back to Yard Limits by the rapids. We get all kinds of visitors.[38] ◉ ◉ ◉

left Bill Lebarge poses with large moose horns on the east side of Big Mountain near Whitehorse, 1938. At the end of each summer, Bill, his wife, Jenny, and their children went on their annual Shakaat (hunting and gathering trip to prepare for winter), which took several weeks. From their home at Yard Limits the family crossed the Yukon River by boat and walked into the mountains east of the city, where they hunted four or five moose, drying the meat along the way. They then floated down Gēs Tū'è (Tagish) or T'ahéeni (Tlingit), meaning King Salmon River (M'Clintock River) to Tàkwädàdhà (Marsh Lake), where they camped near John and Julia Joe's home and fished for salmon and lake trout. To return home, John Joe took them and their food in his boat to Wigan (McCrea), on the upper part of Kwanlin (Miles Canyon), where they had a cabin. From there, George Ryder drove them by truck back home to Yard Limits in exchange for some meat and fish.

right Jenny Lebarge at Betsy's Camp, Tàa'än Män (Lake Laberge), ca. 1976.

FAMILY FOCUS

below *Left to right:* Conshua—Rachael Baum (later Dawson) and Walter Alfred; Fred Alfred; Rachael's mother, Mary Alfred (née Campbell) and Eva Alfred; and Rachael's grandmother Ellen Campbell at Fort Selkirk, ca. 1922.

Conshua—Rachael Dawson
K'alazhaw—George Dawson

Conshua—Rachael Dawson (née Baum) of the G̲aanax̲teidí Clan was born to Mary Campbell and William Baum around 1906 at Fort Selkirk. She came from a storied family of Tlingit and Northern Tutchone descent through her mother, Mary Campbell. Her maternal uncle was Selkirk Chief Big Jonathon Campbell. Their mother, Ellen Campbell, was Tlingit, and their father was Chief Hanan, who saved the life of Hudson's Bay Company trader Robert Campbell when Tlingit warriors ransacked Fort Selkirk in 1852. The trader gave his last name to Hanan in gratitude. His father was Tlingit Thling and his mother was Tlingit as well.

Rachael grew up at Fort Selkirk speaking several languages—including Tlingit and Northern and Southern Tutchone. She travelled on the land with her family to hunt, fish, trap and gather food. She learned to tan hides, sew, cook and care for family from her mother and grandmother. As a young girl she attended Chooutla Residential School in Carcross, learning to read and write in English.

K'alazhaw—George Dawson was of the Dak̲l'awedí Clan, born at Long Lake in 1902 to Tusáxal—Jenny Boss and Dawson Jim of Lake Laberge. His maternal uncle was Kashx̲óot—Chief Jim Boss, and his grandparents were Łande and old Chief Mundessa. He grew up travelling by dog team, hunting and trapping with his family, living at Lower Laberge in his early years where his father cut wood for

the steamboats. As a young man, George worked for his Uncle Jim Boss, transporting mail and goods by horse-drawn sleigh. His first jobs were for White Pass and Yukon Railway, pounding spikes on the railroad and working as crew on the steamboats. After Jim Boss died, George was the Ta'an Kwäch'än Hereditary Chief.

Rachael and George married in 1923 at Fort Selkirk, where they lived until her mother passed away. They came to Whitehorse by dog team in 1927, where they raised their family of nine children. George built a large two-storey log house near present day 4th Avenue and Black Street,

Rachael looked after her family, cooking and preserving food, sewing moccasins and clothing, and selling beadwork to earn cash. She was an experienced midwife, helping a number of mothers with the birthing of their children. During World War II she earned enough money doing laundry and sewing for soldiers to buy a wringer washer, which speeded up her work and increased her business. Fluent in several First Nation languages and English, Rachael helped many people through the years by translating court proceedings and other government issues.

George gave up his Indian Status after the war so his children could attend public school, which meant that Rachael and all their children lost their Status too. After their log home burned, the family moved to the former RCMP house on Front Street and later to the old post office, where he worked as custodian. They moved to a large house in the Old Village in the 1960s and cared for eleven grandchildren. Rachael continued to share her stories, recording them for preservation and publication in *My Stories Are My Wealth*. Her grandchildren remember her loving care, wonderful meals, sewing doll clothes and mittens, and bedtime stories. Grandpa George drove the younger kids to school in town and bought them treats after school.

Hilda Dawson, Rachael's daughter, remembers her mother fondly:

with logs he cut at Cowley Lakes and hauled to town. He hunted and trapped around Golden Horn, taking the older children with him by dog team to his cabin there. In summers he worked for White Pass, running the donkey engine on the waterfront and as a pilot on the steamboats. In the 1940s, George guided U.S. Army surveyors to locate sections of the Alaska Highway and supervised a First Nations crew loading freight on the Whitehorse docks.

My mom was the best—she lived for her family. She took us kids with her wherever she had to go. Mom took us to Carcross to go out camping, hunt

below Ta'an Kwäch'än Hereditary Chief K'alazhaw—George Dawson wearing the ceremonial outfit of his maternal uncle Kashxóot—Chief Jim Boss at his home in McIntyre subdivision, summer 1986. The beautifully embroidered moosehide tunic, trousers and hat were made by Jim Boss's sisters for him to wear during the Governor General's visit to Whitehorse in 1952. Mr. Dawson returned the items to the MacBride Museum for safekeeping.

gopher, fish, berry picking. This was routine, going to Carcross every summer to spend time with the Patsy Hendersons. When it was berry-picking time, Mrs. Patsy (Edith) would tell Mom to come visit her. Mrs. Patsy was Mom's best friend. We went by train to Lake Bennett and we'd go to Log Cabin where the road crosses the train tracks there on the way to Skagway. We'd go there and pick berries and camp. Blueberries, any kind of berries.

In the 1970s, George organized the Chief Mundessa Club, obtaining a grant to work with Elders and youth to repair First Nations graveyards at Whitehorse, Marsh Lake and Lake Laberge. He spoke at numerous heritage conferences and shared his extensive knowledge of history with the Yukon Archives and other organizations. He was recognized for his many community contributions by Her Majesty Queen Elizabeth with a medal and Certificate of Achievement for the Chief Mundessa Club (1976), and was also recognized with the Yukon Historical & Museums Association Heritage Award (1983), the Council for Yukon Indians Heritage Award (1983), the City of Whitehorse Heritage Award (1985) and the Commissioner's Award (1988).

Rachael and George were highly respected in our community, always helping people in need with food or other assistance. Rachael passed away in 1976 and George in 1989.[39]

FAMILY FOCUS

Tàshura—Mary Smith
Tl'ukshan—Charlie Smith

Tàshura—Mary Smith of the Crow Clan was from the Big Salmon River area. Her father was Big Salmon Charlie. Tl'ukshan—Charlie Smith was of the Wolf Clan from the Lake Laberge area, related to Jim Boss on his mother's side and Klukwan people on his father's side.

Mary was born in the early 1900s. She grew up travelling, hunting and fishing with her family on the Yukon River in the area around Little Salmon.

Charlie was born at Łu Zil Män (Fish Lake) in the 1880s. His mother was from Tàa'än Män and his father was from Klukwan. They travelled widely in the southern Yukon, combining traditional hunting and gathering activities with trading. Charlie passed on many stories to his children about the first white people he and his father encountered at the confluence of the Takhini and Yukon Rivers, probably in the late 1880s and 1890s.

Mary and Charlie were married around 1920. They had seven children. The family set fishnets at Tatl'ane (Dog Salmon Slough) on the Teslin River, where they lived in a wall tent in summer, catching and drying thousands of salmon each year for their own use and to feed their dogs. They hunted moose in fall to provide meat for winter, as well as hides for clothing and sleds. They had a cabin downriver at T'äw Tà'är (Winter Crossing), where they lived for much of the winter. Their trapline in that area had small cabins to provide shelter when checking their traps. The boys went out on the trapline with their father from an early age and learned how to harvest fur-bearing animals. Mary tanned moosehides and sewed moccasins, mukluks and winter clothing for her whole family, passing on those skills to her young daughters.

In the spring time, the whole family travelled by dog team to Whitehorse, where they had a small house near the river in the vicinity of Front Street. They traded their furs at Taylor & Drury's store for groceries and some factory-made clothing. They would stay in town for several weeks, visiting with friends and family who had also come from far and wide to trade. Sometimes they travelled to Marsh Lake to visit with relatives there.

In 1937, Mary suddenly became ill with pneumonia. The family rushed to town by dog team, but she died before they could get medical help. Charlie returned to T'äw Tà'är to carry on the family's seasonal activities with his children. As the children grew up, they moved away from the Teslin River, spending more time at their home in Whitehorse as employment opportunities boomed during World War II. Trapping prices declined in the 1950s, bringing an end to their Teslin River lifestyle.

Charlie Smith lived to a very old age as a respected Elder, passing on his knowledge and stories to his many grandchildren, nieces and nephews. He passed away in 1978.[40]

Yúk'e Kwàch'e

It is winter time   1940–1973

And when the highway went through they spoil,
they just push down an old house, old cabin that ...
used to be their gathering place. They just destroyed
everything ... They dirtied up our country.

YADULTÍN—JESSIE SCARFF[1]

overleaf Setting sun in midwinter near Jackson Lake.

facing Grey wolf running in winter.

WINTER IN THE North is a time of challenges, with intense cold temperatures and long dark nights requiring preparation and skill for survival. Winter work on traplines and hunting for food is more demanding. Our people draw on inner strength and the warmth of friends, family and kin. The equinox brings lengthening days and we prepare for the return of spring.

For Kwanlin Dün, the years between 1939 and 1973 were like the darkest winter nights. It was a period of massive, overwhelming change. The U.S. Army arrived to build the Alaska Highway in the 1940s. After the war, more roads were built, ending the steamboat era and the wood camps on the Yukon River, which had employed many of our people. The Canadian and Yukon governments introduced new and intrusive laws and programs that affected us, even though we could not vote or run for election. We became a minority in our homeland, facing pressures on lands, resources and families. Many newcomers had negative views about our people, leading to segregated services, racial discrimination and forced relocations for Kwanlin Dün.

In the 1950s and '60s, increasing numbers of settlers, mining development, Whitehorse hydro dam construction and the removal of our children to residential schools created severe hardships for us. Despite these challenges we continued to practise our traditions with resilience and resistance. Our leaders began organizing to regain control of our lives and lands. With the guidance of our Elders, we survived and looked forward to a brighter future.

Shaan Tlein—Irene Smith

Shaan Tlein—Irene Smith was born at Tàa'än Män (Lake Laberge) in 1928 to the Wolf Clan. Her mother was Alice Sam (née Broeren) and her father was a white man from Austria named Andrew Emminger, who was mining for gold at Livingstone Creek. Alice later married Jim Sam, and they lived at Lower Laberge for some years. Irene was raised by her grandmother Shuwateen—Maggie Broeren at Upper Laberge. Southern Tutchone was her first language, and she spent many years teaching young people to speak her language and passing on traditional stories. She was an expert sewer and beader as well, making beautiful moccasins, vests and other garments. Irene died in 2010, leaving a rich legacy of stories and language lessons recorded for future generations.[3]

Nindal Kwädīndür
(I'm going to tell you a story)

THE OWL STORY

Told by **Shaan Tlein—Irene Smith**[2]

This story took place many, many years ago, when there were still big animals on this earth. In this one village the people were getting tired and frustrated with their situation. There was this big owl who kept coming into their village and stealing the small children and eating them. Pretty soon there were hardly any children left. The men and women carried their little ones on their backs and were afraid to let them play around outside by themselves. The people were scared and didn't know what to do. They had a meeting and decided to leave that village. They said that they would also leave this little old grandma who was no longer able to do many things for herself and was more of a burden on her people. She would be left behind to keep this big owl occupied while the people made their getaway.

So this little old grandma was left behind, and as she sat and watched her people leave, she must have felt so alone. She didn't want to be eaten by this big owl, so she started to work on a plan to help herself. So she set out to gather the things she needed. She got this big birchbark pot that the people left behind and started to fill this with pitch from the very large trees around her. Then she gathered lots of branches and wood to make a great big bonfire. She dug a hole in the ground large enough for her body to fit in comfortably. She then made a cover for this hole by weaving a lid out of tree roots, and she covered this area up with grass and dirt, making it look like there was nothing there that looked out of place. Then she sat down and waited for the big owl. While she was waiting she heated rocks and heated the birchbark pot full of pitch until it was bubbling. She then made her small fire into a big bonfire because she knew the big owl was going to come any time now.

Pretty soon she could hear his wings making loud swishing sounds. Because it was so quiet around her, she could hear him coming from a long ways off. She waited patiently. Soon he landed on this large tree beside their old village.

"Whoo, whoo, whoo," said this big owl. "Old woman, where is everyone?" he asked. She looked up at him in the tree and she said, "Hello, Grandfather Owl. Because I'm too old to travel, my people are gone and have left me here all alone."

The old woman pretended to make friends with him and called up to him. "Come, Grandfather Owl, you must be tired after your long trip. Come warm your wings by my fire so you will have strength to carry me because my bones are heavy. I'm not like those little children." So the big owl flew down across the fire from the old lady. She said, "Spread your wings and close your eyes so smoke don't get into it." So the big owl opened up his wings and closed his eyes. She could see that he still had his eyes open just a little slit, so she said again, "Grandfather Owl, why don't you turn around and warm your back too?" And so he turned around with his wings out and his eyes closed.

Then the old lady quickly pushed the pot of hot pitch over the owl and shoved him into the fire. She jumped down into her hole in the ground and covered herself because the fire was so hot. She could hear the big owl screaming. "You dirty old woman, you tricked me. Ayaaw! My feathers are burning. I could feel my eyes burning too." He kept screaming like this all night.

Early the next morning it was all quiet, so she peeked out from under the cover, and all she could see was this big black charcoal. She got out and went to look at this owl, and she got her stone knife and cut off his baby finger (claw). The people never saw big owls again after that.

She then got her things together and went behind her people. She travelled the whole day until she could see some smoke coming out far in the valley. She was walking on the sidehill when she caught up to her people. When she was close enough, she started hollering to them. Somebody saw her and told the headman. He said, "What is this old woman doing? She's going to lead that big owl back to us again." He told this young boy, "You go see her and tell her to go back." So this boy ran up to the old lady and told her she had to go back. She told him, "I killed that owl. You take his finger (claw) back to the people and show them." The people were very happy. From that day forward the little old grandma was treated with great respect.

THE OLD TOWN HAS GONE

facing top "Tent City," 18th Engineers Regiment tent camp north of Whitehorse airport, May 6, 1942.

facing bottom Canol refinery under construction, October 29, 1943. The refinery was built north of the Whitehorse townsite, next to Lot 226. It operated for only a few months before it was dismantled, but hazardous waste remained in the area, close to Kwanlin Dün homes, for decades after.

In February 1942, a route for the Alaska Highway was approved, and construction began the very next month. The coming of the highway signalled big changes for everyone in the little town of Whitehorse—including the Kwanlin Dün.

For several years the Canadian and United States governments had been making decisions about Kwanlin Dün land without including the Kwanlin Dün in discussions. In 1939 a highway commission of Canadian and U.S. members had been struck to decide on a route to take traffic from the mainland United States to Alaska, but most of its work was done in the south. Initially, there were four highway routes under consideration. Route A ran east of British Columbia's Coast Mountains, while Route B paralleled British Columbia's section of the Rocky Mountains. These two options had strong political and commercial support in western Canada as well as in Washington State, and they were approximately the same length, just over thirteen hundred miles. The U.S. Army Corps of Engineers pushed for a third choice, Route C, which sliced northwest across the Rockies, a distance of roughly fourteen hundred miles. The fourth option, Route D, rolled north from Edmonton, Alberta, into Canada's Northwest Territories and then west over the Mackenzie Mountains to Alaska—a distance of about seventeen hundred miles.

All four choices had obvious drawbacks. Route A's track would make it the most vulnerable to any coastal attack, while Route B would be susceptible to snow and floods. Both B and C also didn't go near towns—notably the railway terminus of Whitehorse—where construction supplies could be easily transported. Route D promised access to oilfields at Norman Wells in the Northwest Territories, but it was the longest option.

The commission eventually narrowed the decision down to the two shorter routes. Route A would go from Prince George to Vanderhoof, Stuart Lake, Takla Lake, along the Stikine River, then north to Atlin, B.C. There it would enter the Yukon and pass through Carcross, Whitehorse, Kluane Lake and across the White River to the Alaska border, where it would follow the Tanana River and connect with the Richardson Highway. Route B would go from Prince George to Manson Creek and onward to the Findlay River, through Sifton Pass to the headwaters of the Liard and Pelly Rivers, then along the Pelly to the Yukon, bypassing Whitehorse but going through Dawson City and then west to the Alaska border.

For the next few years the highway commission continued its work. At times reports emerged from either Canadian or U.S. members speculating about particular route choices and which one was best. Then in December 1941, everything changed—Japan bombed Pearl Harbor, and the United States was at war. Rapid decisions in Washington were quickly accepted

in Ottawa, and the Alcan Highway project was launched. In the end a combination of Routes A and C prevailed, with the road following the string of Northwest Staging Route airfields from Dawson Creek north to Whitehorse and on to Fairbanks, bypassing Dawson City, which was still the capital city of the Yukon at that time. This route had significant consequences for Kwanlin Dün, once again bringing tens of thousands of K'ŭ Ch'an into the southern Yukon just fifty years after the major upheavals of the gold rush.

On April 3, 1942, the first trainload of American soldiers disembarked at Whitehorse—a complete and total surprise to most of the residents. There had been no consultation with northern residents and little warning of what was planned for the small town.

The following Friday, the *Whitehorse Star* loudly proclaimed a warm welcome to the soldiers and support for their mission on its front page:

> On behalf of the residents of Whitehorse we extend to Brigadier General W.M. Hoge, his officers and men of the U.S. Army Engineering Corps, a cordial welcome to the Yukon Territory.
>
> To most of them it will be a new and, we trust, an interesting experience.
>
> It is the hope of us all that their stay in the north will be a most enjoyable one and that the great project they have come to undertake will be carried through to completion with outstanding success.[4]

The next month the *Star* published an editorial that declared the frontier town of Whitehorse was "gone," and in its stead would be a new sort of community:

> There are unmistakeable signs that the old town has gone and with it the atmosphere which through the years has been so familiar to most of us. Time was when, if you didn't feel inclined to do some particular work one day, you could do it the next. But

Yúk'e Kwàch'e (It is winter time)

above The 770th Railway Oper-
ating Battalion set up this camp
in a large area south of town near
where the SS *Klondike* sits today.
During the war years, the U.S.
Army took over the White Pass &
Yukon Railway. The railway went
from running one train a week to
as many as twenty-five a day to
handle thousands of passengers
and many tonnes of freight.

those days have gone forever. The town is in a state of transition.
Development work on a major scale is being carried out in various directions and transforming Whitehorse into a veritable hub
of industry. There is work for everybody and no one need be idle.
Such work as is now being carried out is by no means of a temporary nature. On the contrary the foundations for great development here in the years that lie ahead of us are being well and
truly laid. Whitehorse is to become a pivotal centre in the commercial aviation of the future. We are now on the map. Watch us
grow![5]

No one asked the Kwanlin Dün if they minded another invasion by
strangers, who would come into their lands unannounced and as unpre-
pared as the stampeders of 1897–1898 had been half a century earlier.
Within a few months more than three thousand men would descend on
Whitehorse, and over the next year more than thirty thousand in total
landed in the Yukon to build the Alaska Highway and the Canol Pipeline,
which was intended to bring crude oil from Norman Wells on the Mackenzie River to a refinery in Whitehorse and then on to Alaska. The old town
was indeed gone.

Disturbing the Peace

BY SWEENY SCURVEY

Our peaceful little camp
Situated at an ideal place
Undisturbed
By man made holocaust
The chirping of the blue jays
Chattering of the squirrels
Occasional rustles of leaves
As little animals scampered by
Dad is out hunting
Mom and the kids
Set snares for rabbits
The camp remains undisturbed
Then . . .
A noise in the distance is heard
Almost inaudible at first
Dad says it's finally happening
Life as we know it will deteriorate
And there is no way to stop it
The noise is deafening
Strange machines are tearing down our trees
Ripping up the earth that gave us sustenance
Trucks dump gravel where moments before
Rich soil remained undisturbed
The noise continues
Until it disappears in the opposite direction from whence it came
And . . .
Soon trucks cars and busses
Disturbed the once serene camp
Zooming by at ungodly hours
Life as we knew it was no more
Civilization came hard and fast
With it tin cans and the smell of gasoline and diesel exhaust
Fire raged on either side of the highway
Blackened forest still smoldering
As the car took us to an uncertain destination
Beyond our once peaceful little camp.[6]

**Sweeny Scurvey—
Kwanlin Dün Poet**

Sweeny Scurvey of the Wolf Clan
was born in May 1943 near Carmacks. His mother, Kitty Sam, was
related to Chief Albert Isaac of
Aishihik. His father was related to
Tagish Kwan people. Sweeny and
his older brother, Edwin (ca. 1940–
2020), were raised by their father,
Gus, after their mother died. Gus
combined work at wood camps
with seasonal rounds, teaching his
sons how to live well on the land.
In 1950, the boys were taken away
to the Whitehorse Indian Baptist
Mission School, where they spent
many tough years isolated from
their dad. When their father died,
they were not allowed to leave
school to attend his funeral.

Sweeny started to write poetry
in school. He and Edwin wrote a
regular news column for the *Whitehorse Star* in the 1960s and '70s,
about the lives of Kwanlin Dün and
other First Nations people during
those turbulent times. Sweeny
also worked as a labourer and as
a heavy-equipment operator. He
worked down south before returning to the Yukon in 1990 to study
at Yukon College and work on
numerous heritage projects for
KDFN. Today Sweeny continues to
contribute his knowledge for the
benefit of the whole community.[7]

OUR ELDERS SAY...

◇◇◇◇◇◇◇◇◇◇◇◇◇◇◇◇◇◇◇◇

The Alaska Highway Followed Our Trails

KLIGHEE—SAIT U—EMMA JOANNE SHORTY When I was seven, my Uncle Boson Smith and my Aunty Maggie, they came walking over from Teslin, all the way to Carcross to pick us up. And the reason I'm telling this is I want to let you know, I walked the highway, where the highway is right now. Exactly the trail the highway covers, from Johnsons Crossing, all the way into Whitehorse. They used our trail... to build the highway. And that's the reason I'm telling this. Just so First Nations will know, that they used our trails, eh?[8]

YADULTÍN—JESSIE SCARFF And the way they used to live, I heard an awful lot of stories. And I've talked about it many times... Pointing out to our people now exactly what it used to be. At Marsh Lake they used to have big gathering. Right there, Army Beach, they used to have an old-time house and I was told about it. John Joe, my uncle, told me it. There used to be people come from all over. They come by boat, they walk, those are the only two ways they get there. And they gather there maybe sometime for, for a month, two weeks, depends on how good a year they had. Some of them stay there longer... All his life, when he was a kid, he used to see that... but never, never, no white people or anything was there at that time.

They'd have a great big camp... They'd have their gathering... Everybody would, you know, give gifts away to each Elder...

And things like that. Some of the ladies, they'd bring tanned skin, give it to somebody else. Somebody else would give them tanned skin. And, and fur, things like that. Everything was just so neat...

And when the highway went through they spoil, they just push down an old house, old cabin that, that used to be their gathering place. They just destroyed everything... They dirtied up our country, that's for one thing we could say. I got a prayer at home... It says, "God help us to put our land straight. To clean up where they have dirtied"... And it's a prayer that I read practically every day. Because it's the truth.

At one time I used to be able to go from here and I'd drink water anywhere. Never worried about it polluted or anything. Now you can't do that. You have to pack your water in order to have water. Just make you sick. Everything, that what they done. Even in the air, you look at the snow. Snow is usually white. Last winter I looked at it and here the darn thing is grey. I was watching it.[9] ◉ ◉ ◉

above Four young men with pack dogs on a newly constructed road, likely the Alaska Highway, ca. 1944–1946.

facing top U.S. Army soldiers visit a First Nation family at their camp near Whitehorse, ca. mid-1940s.

facing centre U.S. soldiers and civilian workers line up at the liquor store, October 19, 1943.

facing bottom A bridge on the Alaska Highway, under construction at the Yukon River near the Marsh Lake dam, 1942. The highway ran through the front yard of one resident and close to the home of Whitehorse Billy and his family.

Tough Times during the War

GUS'DUTÉEN—FRANCES WOOLSEY

We lived in our own house... Dad rented a lot from White Pass and built a house for us... Mom worked next door in the laundry, after four... right after school, anyway, because I had to stay home and look after the kids... She went over next door and ironed shirts for them, for the American army, because a lady had a laundry business, and she did all the laundry for them, for the different soldiers. Most of them were officers and she had to have their shirts just right. But she used the old flat irons that got heated up on the stove... And then, when it got cooler, put it back on the stove and get another one. And that's how she ironed all the shirts. And they had to be done just so, because they were officers...

Mrs. Breen [was the woman]. It was in her house... closer to the river... She got water from the Shipyards... The boys went down there and brought water up. And she washed it all in the regular washing machines, the gas washing machines... she would wash all that, and hang the shirts out to dry on the line. She did that early in the morning... She would mark them all so that they wouldn't get lost. And the lady got paid for doing all the laundry. And she paid Mom. Every Friday...

It was a bad time... you know... Everybody had been drinking... because the army always had to have parties. They would bring the booze to people's houses, and they would party.

It was a bad time... during the wartime. In '43 we left here, went to Violet Creek and stayed there, for four years, five years, by ourselves. Just us. [My dad decided]... just to take us out of Whitehorse.[10]

RONALD BILL [Then my dad]...he got sick... We don't know what, what got into his lungs. He breathe in something, I guess, and they eat up his lungs, eh? Consumption... it destroyed the lung. Finally in the spring time, I was nine years old, he died, and that same summer, they hijack me for school... White Pass wanted to send him out, but he refused, yeah. He didn't want to go. He said, "Oh, it's too late, they can't do nothing"... They had some kind of hospital in Wisconsin or something... They do testing there, they send their workers there... But my dad, he didn't want to go down there... He got sick in the winter, and in the spring time he died...

American army was there [1942–1943]... because we, me and this kid there [Carl MacIntosh], we used to march around behind those army... There was thousands of them, all over the place, eh? They set up these huts, they had this pre-fab hut, they just slap 'em together in one day, yeah... [and tents]... all over the place you see down, down by the Klondike Inn... And where the mission school was, that's where they had all the huts there, too, and it's pre-fab, eh? All pre-fab. They set 'em up in one day is all, they got enormous manpower, eh? They just, they set up in no time at all... [Many changes started happening in town]... Well, mostly drinking alcohol... The social way of people deteriorated quite a bit.[11] ◉ ◉ ◉

◇◇◇◇◇◇◇◇◇◇◇◇◇◇◇

Stolen Children

SWEENY SCURVEY

THE SEASONAL ROUNDS
We went everywhere with him
In the spring out on the trap-line
We watched him chip the ice
Until he got through to the water
Near the beaver's home
The very next day
A beaver was trapped
Everywhere where we had traps
Beaver tails were our favourite

He would select a location
Where we would set up camp
He knew where to set snares

top The First Nations cemetery at the base of Two Mile Hill, seen here ca. late 1940s, is now known as Äsì Khìą Tth'än K'è (My Grandparents' Gravesite).

above The Whitehorse docks in spring were always a busy place, especially during the war. When guides, deckhands, pilots, launderers and cooks were needed for wartime projects, an experienced First Nations workforce was available.

For rabbits and squirrels
Also set traps for gophers
When we had enough
He'd leave us with an aunt

Then he went out hunting for moose
We just knew he would get one
Two day later the whole camp
Went to where he had shot the moose
We with our little packs
Men and women with theirs
Even the dogs had packs
A big fire was built
As the men and women skinned
And cut up the meat
Ribs were put on pointed sticks
To roast for our lunch
The dogs feasted on the innards
Along with bits of fat and meat
The meat was then sorted out
So that the whole moose
Would be packed to camp in one haul

Summer was time to set fishnets
He knew the exact location
Each morning and evening
He would go out
And bring in the day's catch
One day at Fox Lake
The wind was blowing furiously
The lake was much too rough
And we were all packed
Ready to head home
Dad said he had to bring in the net
So as soon as the wind slowed down
He got on the raft
On the still rough lake
We watched in fear
But he persevered
And balancing himself
He managed to bring in the net
A truck arrived shortly
To take us to Carmacks
Dad gave fresh fish to the driver

At berry-picking time
All the women and children
Would carry their packs and pails
First it would be high-bush cranberries
And then, of course, cranberries
Every now and then "Hey!" would
    be heard
That was crucial and a good way
To keep track of one another
To insure that everyone was okay

Part of our seasonal rounds
Was the wood camp
Dad worked slow but steadily
Sometimes cutting two or three
    cords a day
One day he gave me a saw and axe
And showed me a location
All alone and scared
I cut all of three cords
That took me three weeks
He was so proud of me
We then went back to mission school
I would never see my dad again.[12]

above A classroom at the Whitehorse Indian Baptist Mission School, ca. 1950.
1. Kathleen Joe (Birckel),
2. Daisy Hall, 3. Annie Broeren (Burns), 4. Bobby Joe,
5. Frank Billy, 6. Tom Dickson,
7. Eileen Chitze, 8. Unidentified,
9. Elsie Sam (Cletheroe),
10.–16. Unidentified, 17. Vera Takamatsu (Mattson) and
18. Mr. Earl Lee

CHARLIE BURNS Everything changed that time. Alaska Highway. You know? And when they started building highways... and all the Native people gathered all up, the young kids, and... take them to school. Throw them behind the truck, just like cattle.

I was—I think about seven years old... when they take us away... We were staying [in Whitehorse]. We were just coming back from gopher hunting... and we had fire outside, burning gopher... Jessie Walker, Lizzy... all those people was there and it was sometime around September. They pick us up to go to school in Carcross and put us in the train... And the police come and he said, "If any of you kids run away from this train, we're going to put your mom and dad in jail until we find you." So when the train pull out, our mom and our dad, they running beside this train all crying, and our mom be crying and running beside the train, you know, and waving at us.[13]

RONALD BILL [My stepdad] tried to get me into elementary school down here in Whitehorse, there, and they wouldn't take us... [so I went to Carcross]... Seven years. Seven years I stayed there, yeah. We only go three hours a day for school, and we had to work the rest of the hours, eh?... And when they came to see me [for residential school issues]... they asked me should students be compensated, and I told them I wanted to get paid for the work I did... I had to get wood, cut wood, and even those four feet of wood, we'd cut those four feet of wood, and then we'd bust them up, split them, and empty garbage and all these things, shovel snow... I know we cut thirty-one cords of

wood that one year there... [using Swede saws, not chainsaws]... Work in the gardens. Plant potatoes and all these beets and lettuce and turnips and things like that. Parsley and carrots. Yeah, so we become farmers...

There were three of us, me, Sammy Johnston and Douglas Johnson. Douglas is from... Dawson... Sammy from Teslin... And we made slingshots and bow and arrow and things like that. We [hunted]... grouse, gopher, rabbit and things like that. We would cook 'em up. And then we had this hooks, we make hooks, we get right in there and the most we caught there was twenty trout. We fry 'em up, we feed those kids... [The school staff,] they didn't like it. They put a boundary around the school, eh? You're not supposed to cross that boundary. And there's better hunting areas across there. So we sneak across it, and we got caught, yeah. So they told us not go anyplace like that again. But we still do things,

above Children from the communities being transported to Chooutla Residential School, ca. 1950. A former student said, "All those years they tried so hard to make us into white people, but the only time they succeeded was when we arrived at that school after 500 miles in the back of that truck... all covered in white dirt." Chris Clarke and the K'änáchá Group, *Tr'ëhuhch'in Näwtr'udäh'ǫ (Finding our Way Home)* (Dawson City: Tr'ondëk Hwëch'in, 2009), 61.

facing top Students and staff in front of Whitehorse Indian Baptist Mission School, 1950.

facing bottom Children and their teacher at the Whitehorse Indian Baptist Mission School, ca. 1950. Annie Broeren* and Charlie Burns met as children at the school and were married there when they finished school in grade eight. Annie is in the back row, seventh from the left.

because we kill a porcupine too, one time. Porcupine and things like that. We'd kill gophers... And fish, there was a lot of fish. We'd get a lot of fish... They brought me home in the summer... [not Christmas]... Frozen up, all frozen up, because they were living downriver...

I was nine years old [when I was sent to Carcross in 1945]... We learned how to read and things like that, but we never did no artwork, nothing. We just did the math and English and language... Yeah, we didn't have no art or artwork or anything. So I wanted to make a Christmas card, we did tracing and things like that... One teacher... I thought he was good, but I heard a lot of stories about him after. So he was taking advantage of those girls. They reported him, those girls. They get together and they reported him, and they all got punished. They tell [them] this guy is a man of god, and he don't do the things like that. So they punish them. They couldn't go anyplace then...

Sixteen was graduation then... Even if you were in grade two, if you were sixteen, you go. I went here. My mom and Ole Wickstrom, they move up here. They had a house. They built a house across the river... It was not hard for me to get a job in this place. I work all the time, eh? I work, and I got my mom to sign consent, and I wanted to work for the army, getting $1.05 an hour, and next thing, there was a higher-pay job, they said. At railroad tracks. I asked them how much. They said $1.17... Yeah, so I quit that job and I went to the railroad track [the White Pass and Yukon Railway]. They were giving me $1.17 an hour... I worked all summer until we finished, they

laid us off. I worked in Cowley... And next time I went to Pennington. I worked there all summer too. And I didn't want to get laid off. I got a job in the army with building a road, building a bridge in Slim River... Till freeze-up in January. It started freezing and it got too cold, so they laid us off, but I didn't go back there after that.[14]

KLIGHEE—SAIT U—EMMA JOANNE SHORTY I remember when I was four years old, that before we left to go out to the trapline, the minister, his name was Robert Ward, and he's from England, he came and took us. We had to go to residential school. My sister Mabel and myself. It wasn't a good time. Very sad. And when we got to the residential school, I remember just crying, crying. I kept telling my sister, "When is my mom gonna come and get us?"

I couldn't speak a word of English. I had to learn really fast. And there was this, ah, older lady, she is my cousin. Her name was Jane. She took us all. There wasn't just me, it was my sister Mabel, myself, Winnie, Sally and Robert. And Chris Henry, George, elder George. We were at the school, then. And Jane took us under this big tree. She told us, "Come and meet me up there, so I can teach you English. What I know of English." She said that in our language, and she was

very careful to say it, because if they heard her talking in our language, they would punish her. So we learned English.

And I was there for three years. I went there to Carcross Residential School when I was four... [Later] my sister Gladys taught me how to speak, again, in my language. And Grandma Fox. She was very upset when she spoke to us in our language and we didn't understand her. She was so upset she cried. And every day, until we had to go back, she sat us down, talked to us in our language. And we had to answer her. That's how I learned to speak my language again...

Coming home from residential school when I was seven years old... and meeting my mother for the first time in my life... that I remember her. I couldn't remember her... I didn't even know which woman was my mom... when she came up to me and she said, "I am your mother"... in our language, I couldn't understand her... And my sister had to push me and tell me that's my mom. I cried and laughed at the same time. I will never forget that.

The only time that there were hard times was when I was in residential school and the war was on and we had to bind our windows because of things flying over... planes coming close and we were short of food and we practically starved in school... We had to go out in the bush and set snares for ourselves, and the older girls used to cook whatever they found... squirrels and all.[15] ◉ ◉ ◉

◇◇◇◇◇◇◇◇◇◇◇◇◇◇◇◇◇◇◇◇◇◇◇◇◇

End of Wood Camps and Trapping

The sweeping changes that began during the war accelerated in the post-war years, leaving First Nations people struggling to find new ways to make a living. Roads replaced rivers as the transportation network, with the highway built to Mayo in the early 1950s and an extension to Dawson in 1954. The end of the steamboat era meant the loss of jobs on the boats and the shutdown of the wood camps that fueled them, displacing many families who then moved to Whitehorse seeking employment.

In the midst of these difficulties the Yukon government enacted new policies affecting the other economic mainstay of First Nations people: hunting and trapping. For decades, trapping had provided steady income for families all over the Yukon. Mining revenues mostly went out of the territory to profit southern corporations.

The Yukon government began to control how people could hunt and trap in the early 1900s. The Yukon Act of 1898 focused on protecting Canada's interests in the Klondike gold fields, with no elected representation

for residents. Political agitation among newcomers resulted in reforms to add elected members to the Yukon Council. First Nations people were completely disenfranchised from this process, with no right to vote or run for election to either the council or parliament. In 1902, soon after being sworn in, the new council passed An Ordinance for the Protection of Game in the Yukon Territory. The new law was meant to prevent waste of meat and to protect the economic value of wildlife for trophy hunting, fur farming and trapping.

In 1920 the Yukon Council passed more changes to the Game Ordinance, including provisions that applied to Yukon First Nations. No longer could they sell meat without a licence, use poison, or ship hides out of the Territory. Most notably they could no longer kill female big game animals. If the RCMP caught them, they faced heavy fines they could not pay. However, given the size of the Territory and the small number of police, the new laws were largely ignored by both First Nations and everyone else.

The situation remained stable until the 1940s and the "friendly invasion" of American soldiers. Overhunting by the highway builders caused shortages for residents who relied on wildlife for food. After the war, the Yukon government established a new Game and Publicity Department in response to negative publicity about poor wildlife management in the Territory.

Subsequent policies and legislation affected First Nations people significantly, especially the enforced registration of traplines, which disrupted traditional ways of sharing resources. When prices declined as the demand for furs dropped and more children were taken to residential schools, many families left their traplines and moved to town.

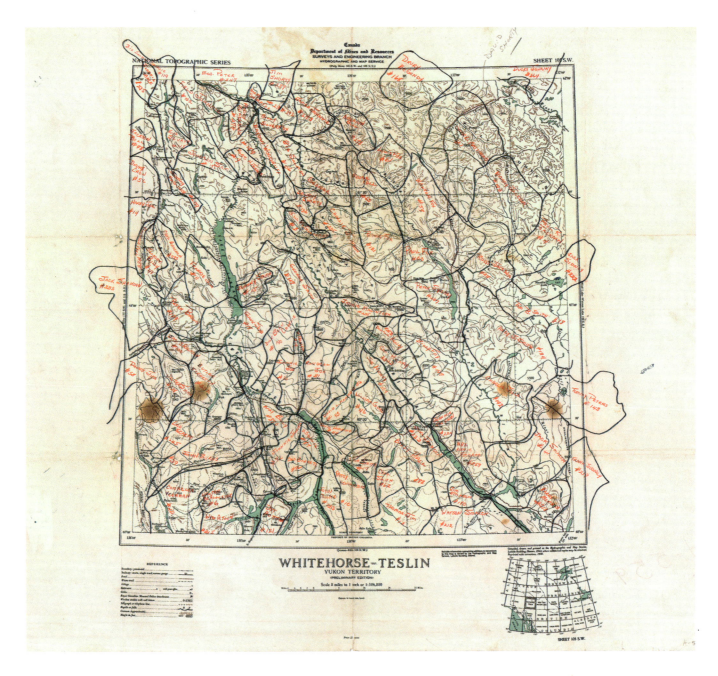

WHITEHORSE–TESLIN
YUKON TERRITORY
(PRELIMINARY EDITION)

Scale 8 miles to 1 inch or 1:506,880

YADULTÍN—JESSIE SCARFF And trapping in those days wasn't that good. The price wasn't that good. The price of the fur came up in the '50s … started coming up in 1950, around in, through there. When the Europeans wanted the fur, the fur came up high again.

And we had … the only person that used to buy fur … in the old days was … Old Bill Drury and Charlie Taylor and them. They used to buy all the fur they could get … and then we would send some of the fur back … back to Alaska. My grandparents lived there and we got a better price. Although the Canadian money was higher than the Americans … but we got better money … American money … than we did in Canada for our fur. So there is a difference in that Americans were paying higher price for their fur. Even weasel … they were paying $1.39 here, and in Alaska it was closer to ten dollars.

So, therefore … my brother-in-law, in Carcross, I got his fur. I got my uncles' fur

above This map shows trapline designations in the Southern Lakes Region. In the late 1940s, the Yukon government instituted new trapline legislation that eliminated traditional First Nations practices of deciding how to share trapping areas among family and clan members.

and another one is Jim Shorty, his fur. I would take it back to Alaska with me and I would sell the whole thing and it would cost me, say, on a big bunch, I take it through the customs, I take it through the customs in Carcross, because I knew the guy... and I say I would pay... the most I ever paid was two hundred dollars. But taking that fur across, I got about three times the money there than I would in Canada. And then when I came back, I give them their American money and they change it, they still gain, although the American money was high, the Canadian high. The money was higher. They still gained on American money.

So that is what I... we did quite some time back, in the early '50s right up until about '60, I guess. And then it seemed like the people didn't have their heart in trapping like they used to. It was just falling apart slowly. There were a few of us that kept it up but not like a long time ago. Everybody used to trap, everybody, and then when the highway went through, a lot of our people just stick up right there. They went to work for wages, and I know the Americans were paying high wages... and you go... the Canadians... like they hire you or you... you wasn't getting the money because you didn't know exactly how to do the heavy equipment on the highway and things like that. You were getting next to nothing but it was better than going out trapping.

Then it... the best years is in... in the '70s. It was good... really good price, and then it fell and after that it never came back up again. Of course, you got the Greenpeace to thank for that. They don't know what they are doing to those people. They... they say don't kill the animals.

God put that moose in that... for us to get caribou, beaver, you name it, and we use to kill them... and... when the Europeans came over, I guess, they made millions on our people... by the fur. They used to high price, I guess. I don't know how much it was... but, according to my granddad, he said that they got good money when they took it back. That is according to the history that he... he studied a long time ago... and us... our people didn't get that... They were lucky if they got one cup... Maybe you have to get them to put their cup, and they had to measure how many beaver skins fill that cup, and then you give them this skin and you get cup.

Rifle was the same thing. You can... they use to have big long rifles... And they pile it up, beaver skins, right up, and then you have the gun, and I wonder how much they got for that fur that they took back... for that... for that one rifle. They must've made quite a bit on it because you can't, those days, they said skins and things like that were pretty high and we had... they had a lot of things going on... like that.[16]

KASHGÊK'—JOHNNIE SMITH We stayed there for so many years and then we finally left there... until the war was on and after the war... I went through... went back on the trapline again. So we stayed there until the kids started going to school and left there. [At Moose Lake.] Yes.

We stayed down at Clear Lake, too. We had a big house there. We had a nice home there... but when the kids started going to school, we left... we left that trapline and we never went back hardly then. Right today, we are still here in Whitehorse... So we have been... I have been all over the place ... walked ... no truck. Walked through the bush ... fight the mosquito ... but my education is just about in the bush. I have never been to school but I know the bush good.[17]

DARLENE SCURVEY

LITTLE WHITE RABBIT MUKLUKS
I haven't been home for so long—[Mile] 932 looks so different in the winter time. Fluffy, white snow everywhere. The school bus is gone now! I take a deep breath of pure fresh cold air and sigh! I am home.

I see familiar surroundings; ámą (Mom) is waving at us and smiling from the winter cabin. I see átà (Dad) walking on the packed snow trail towards me and my younger brothers, Eddy and George. I see the brown cabin covered in white snow with woodsmoke billowing out of the stovepipe. Papa kneels down and hugs and kisses our cold brown faces. We follow átà back toward the cabin, and ámą quickly rushes towards us with warm hugs and kisses. We are finally home with ámą and átà. They have moose stew simmering on the stove and golden brown bannock frying in the pan.

Ámą quickly takes me aside to give me my birthday present. She goes to the corner of her bed and pulls out a worn canvas sack and gives it to me. Dad says, "It's for your birthday." I could not be any happier in those special moments with my parents. I reach inside the canvas bag, feeling silky soft fluffy fur. I pull out a pair of little white rabbit mukluks. I start smelling the foot of the mukluks. I remember the familiar smoked tanned moosehide my mother and father worked so hard to make. I gently caress the

smooth red beaded flowers on my moosehide mukluk tops. I could feel my mother's anticipation for me to try on my new mukluks. I jump on the bed and quickly as possible try on my little white rabbit mukluks.

I am going to go snare rabbits. Ámą is excited to have us home with them again for Christmas holidays. She is getting the rabbit snares out of her secret compartments and giving them to me. Ámą always makes sure we are dressed warm for the winter season. She puts on my scarf and mittens and sends me out the door.

I am feeling free as the snow falls on my face. I look down at my white rabbit skin mukluks with such pride as I walk on the snow trail across the highway. I walk into the white covered forest with the happiest feeling. I am very familiar with this rabbit trail route. I have walked through this trail so many times before, setting rabbit snares with ámą. In my happy thoughts I am looking down at my feet, admiring my beautiful beaded warm mukluks. Without any thought of looking at where I am going, I slam into a tree and fly backwards into the snow bank. I get up and dust the snow off my beaded mukluks and continue my hunt for rabbits.[18]

◉ ◉ ◉

above Kashgêk'—Johnnie Smith and his wife, Annie Smith, cut up a moose, ca. late 1940s.

FAMILY FOCUS

Kuk'eitłeł—Kwajalein—Elsie Suits Family

Kuk'eitłeł—Kwajalein—Elsie Suits was the oldest daughter of Dak'alaa Maa—Sadie Jackie of Marsh Lake and an American named James Morgan Baker. She was born in 1913 on Kluane Lake and raised on the Baker family homestead, at the confluence of the Boswell and Teslin Rivers, with her older brother, John, and younger siblings, Dorothy and Jack. Sadie died suddenly when her children were very young. Their father sent the two oldest children to St. Paul's Hostel to attend the Dawson Public School.

When Elsie was twenty-two her father chose fellow American John Suits as her husband. Married in Whitehorse in 1935, they had five children: Marion, John (Sandy) and Robert were born in the old Whitehorse Hospital, while Joe and May were born at their Marsh Lake home with Elsie's aunty, Mary Billy, as midwife.

The family's first home was close to the confluence of the Mary and Teslin Rivers. John was a trapper and hunter, working a long trapline west as far as Michie Lake. On trips to Whitehorse for supplies, they walked or travelled by dog team, crossing the M'Clintock River using rafts located on each side. Around 1938 they moved to Marsh Lake, at the mouth of the M'Clintock River, where the Joe family gave a warm welcome. Elsie and Julia were first cousins and shared similar childhood experiences of residential school. John continued trapping and hunting while the family tended a large garden. Food was plentiful, with nearby meadows and marshy areas providing ideal habitat for moose and bear along with waterfowl, and the big lake teeming with salmon and other fish.

Elsie's high energy and physical fitness were essential for the endless hard work of homesteading. Often left alone with the kids, she made the long hike to M'Clintock River to fetch water for cooking, washing and gardening, as well as keeping the fire going at home. Still, she always found time to take the kids on long walks. They hunted for grouse, rabbits and gophers. The boys had a snare trapline, fished for pike in the slough and went berry picking with the Joes—strawberries, raspberries, saskatoons, cranberries, moss (crow) berries and rosehips. The Suits and Joe kids were cousins and best friends, with the bush as their playground, along with the old traditional Longhouse close to the graveyard by Rocky Point.

In the spring of 1942, U.S. Army bulldozers suddenly appeared at M'Clintock River. It was a shocking event for the kids—Marion was eight, Sandy six, Robert three and Joe three months. Their two-room cabin was close to the new road. Soon the soldiers built a Bailey bridge across the river and a camp on the south side. Friendships flourished with soldiers who were generous with gifts, including axes, saws, eiderdown bedrolls, insulated clothes and winter boots—and even silver dollars! Food items

included five-gallon drums of preserved peaches, cases of dried fruit, cans of Klim (powdered milk), hams, bacon and many bags of candy. The Suits had to fix up an old cabin to hold all the goods.

After the highway was built, Elsie's sister Dorothy Webber and her children could drive out from town, spending many happy summer days with all the cousins together at Army Beach. With so many new people travelling into the area and no public health services or vaccinations, the full range of childhood illnesses circulated through the families.

The Suits kids had no access to formal schooling at Marsh Lake. The highway brought closer scrutiny from government officials, who insisted the children should be attending school, forcing the family to relocate to Whitehorse. John secured an old army building and they moved to Black Street. The house had no insulation, so they pitched a tent inside while fixing up the house. The kitchen had a well with a trap door for access. Like most homes in town, there was no sewer connection and the "honey wagon" came to pick up the slop buckets.

With all the children in school, Elsie went to work washing dishes at the Whitehorse Inn and cleaning at the mining recorder's office and the post office. John was a security guard for the Canadian Air Force at the airport and walked up the clay cliff for his night shifts.

top Elsie Suits with Gus Viksten and their daughter, Joan, at their home in Horsefly, B.C., ca. 1957.

bottom Suits and Webber cousins on a family fishing trip, ca. 1950s. *Left to right:* two unidentified boys, Robert Suits, May Suits, Marion Suits and Albert Webber, Donnie Webber.

Whitehorse was a wonderful place to be a kid. Everyone knew each other, so parents didn't worry about their children playing outside. The paddlewheelers were still running, and those that were dry-docked made exciting playgrounds.

About this time, Elsie fell in love with a Swedish immigrant named Gus Viksten. He had a truck and took her and the kids fishing every summer weekend to Aishihik, Little Atlin, Kusawa, Teslin, Braeburn, Laberge and Quiet Lake. Family and friends were always welcome and well documented with Gus's camera. Elsie, Gus and their six-month-old daughter, Joan, moved to Horsefly, B.C., in 1956.

The Suits children stayed in Whitehorse with their father, but the older brothers frequently visited their mother in her new home. John Suits passed away in 1962. Elsie and Joan returned to Whitehorse in 1968 after Gus died, reuniting all of her children. Elsie continued her active interest in the outdoors, enjoying excursions with her grandchildren in later years. She passed away in 2002, leaving a legacy of happy memories among her large extended family.[19]

OUR ELDERS SAY...

Whitehorse Hydro Dam Flooded Everything

CHARLIE BURNS Well. All that salmon used to... stay here for a little while, eh? Have a rest. And then they go up toward Marsh Lake, you know? Then... they go up M'Clintock River... to Big Salmon Lake. Up M'Clintock. So that's where they spawned... All the Native people from Carcross... Grandpa Joe, Johnny Joe, all of his family, all go up to get salmon, and they dry salmon there... And lots of Native people used to camp along where the road is there now...

At that time, when they built the dam, that's when they break the trails for the salmon, you know? The salmon used to go up there and spawn, and all the little, the little [fry], used to come back down, and they know the trail, eh? So when they come back up... the dam was here, eh? And they can't find their way up, they know the way up... But... they go up to the dam... they come floating back down again, because the river is too swift, and they can't jump the high place there, you know where that water rolling there. They can't get by that... And they're all wounded when they come back down here, you know? And they're all cut up and everything like that.

But the salmon... they were all in here, you know, that island there, all over. They were all there... because they can't go anywhere... [thousands and thousands]. But they all die once they [go] down the river. There's eagles, all the way right down to Lake Laberge, you know? So there was a lot of eagles, lot of eagles. In here [islands across from Robert Service campground].

Well, what could [the people] do? You can't talk to the governments, and they got no ears, you know? They don't... talk to you, tell you, go up there set off the dam. You can't do it, eh? Because you got no authority, no nothing, see?... They don't listen. It's like this dam... we didn't want it, but they build it. Because we got no authority to say anything.[20]

HAROLD DAWSON And before the dam here, my dad used to trap up that way for mink. Catch a lot of mink... After the dam, no more mink, no more things there. Blueberries [gone too]... It flooded all down the bushes and everything.[21] ◉ ◉ ◉

Forced from Our Homes

ASHIĀ—ANN SMITH Well, again, I keep going back to, you know, the residential school, because that's all I knew when I was... quite young. I must have been about five years old when I started going, and I was very small. It was, the school part was probably one of the difficult

things in our life, because basically we didn't live with our parents for ten months of the year. So two months, in the summer time, and the holidays, like during Easter break, Christmas time, those were the special times... So I was lucky to have my mom and dad come for us during the school and, you know, take us home.

But every time we came home, it seems like it was different every time. And every time we came home, we came home to a different home, and a different location. I can remember being down at the Shipyards, or over by, you know, where the bridge is now, the Yukon River Bridge, and that was the area that we first stayed, and where they have the big boat now is where we had a small little house that we rented. And so, sitting right under there is where the house used to be, where we stayed.

But the thing I can remember, back then, was, I don't remember living there, but I can remember being in an old car. My dad had an old car, and it was one of those old-fashioned black cars, so I can remember that. And that was the only time I can remember staying there, is,

you know, these old cars. And then we went to residential school, and then we came back from a break from the school, and where we came to, we were down by where Klondike Inn is, so, you know, we were down there. It was pretty swampy around there, and we had a little cabin, a black cabin, it was just a one-room.[22]

KLIGHEE—SAIT U—EMMA JOANNE SHORTY They just, somebody just came. Would go from door to door and say we have to move. Like, brought a letter to us. I'm really sorry I didn't keep that letter. We had to move. And they gave us a time, about a couple months, to, you know, move us.

And how my mother-in-law, she moved her house, up... by the Yukon River Bridge, south of here, close to Marsh Lake. She did it in a sneaky way, you know. She told me, "I have to move, and could you come with me, to meet with an Indian agent." So I said okay, I went...

So we walked and walked. We didn't have a car then. Her and I walked from Whiskey Flats, all the way where the government building is now, went upstairs,

facing Whitehorse dam, 1959. When the hydroelectric dam was completed in 1958, it blocked upriver migration of two salmon runs to Marsh Lake. A 366-metre fish ladder, visible at left, was built soon after to allow some salmon to return, but the damage was done: tens of thousands of fish died, despite efforts by our people to transport them above the dam in gunnysacks and trucks, and many families went hungry. The runs have still not returned to their pre-dam levels.

above Indian Affairs constructed small houses in the Old Village (Lot 226) from the 1950s through 1960s.

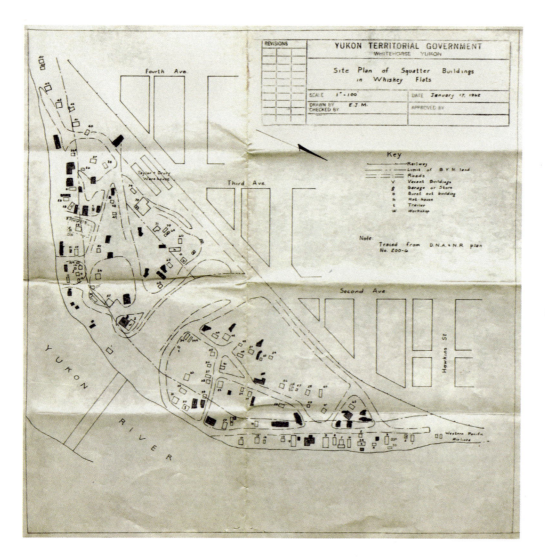

left Annotated site plan of Whiskey Flats showing the bridge to Riverdale, 1962. Kwanlin Dün and people from many Yukon communities along with newcomers crowded together in makeshift homes on haphazard lanes with no services in this riverfront neighbourhood.

facing top Homes burn in Whiskey Flats, ca. 1960. Government officials destroyed the homes of Kwanlin Dün and other residents of waterfront "squatter" neighbourhoods in the 1950s and '60s.

facing centre Lot 226, ca. 1960s. Lack of services and substandard housing contributed to poor living conditions for Kwanlin Dün in the Old Village.

facing bottom View of the Old Village (nearest to viewer, to right of centre) and Whitehorse from the north, ca. 1960s. Remnants of the Canol refinery and other industrial development can be seen behind and to the left of the Village, adjacent to Kwanlin Dün homes.

and we told them, "We want to meet with you." And they said, okay. And right away she said, "I was told that I have to move." And they said, "Yes, you have to." And they told her, "You have to move your house. And give up your house. And we're going to build you a house, down in the village, you know, the one down the hill, under the bluff there."

So . . . she said, "Okay, how big a house are you going to build for me?" "Oh, enough for you." And then there was some other questions they had for her, and they said, "Well, what are you going to do with your house? Oh, we're going to pay you a thousand dollars," they tell her, "if you knock your house down." And we spent quite a long time there. They asked

her quite a lot of questions. Told her that they were going to build a place for her down in the old, in the village. They didn't say how big a house. So she said, "Okay, it's time to go now.". . . So we went home.

And I told her, "What are you going to do?" "You just watch me," she said. And the next day I was going to go and visit her. I went home. We had a little tiny cabin, two-room shack . . . It was me . . . my husband, [my daughter] Norma and . . . I went down to her house. Oh, I got all ready, I fed my children, gave them breakfast, and I tell them, "Let's go visit Grandma." So we put on our coats, we get ready, close the door, lock it and walk down the hill . . .

And we walked, and we walked there, and we looked. "Holy smokes. What happened to Grandma's house?" they said. And this Maggie... she came out and she said, "Oh, she got Andy Hooper to haul her out, up by the dam, twenty miles from here," she said. "They did it last night." So that was the trick she played on them... I kind of wanted to laugh, and I couldn't feel sad, because she did something for herself, eh? Her and Andy Hooper hauled it out...

It was very sad. Very sad. We were good neighbours, helping each other... It was a really good community.[23] ◉ ◉ ◉

Taking Charge of Our Housing

RONALD BILL [When I left the army] I took a course in Vancouver... eighteen months course, they give you the whole bit, everything about doors, windows, how to fix doors and windows, and cabinet and things like that... [at] Vancouver Vocational... I never got no benefits from the army at all. Now they do, but the only thing I got was eighteen dollars a month... I worked weekends, picking strawberries and things like that. And we do some raking, stuff like that, cutting grass... For spending money... Indian Affairs paid for [school]... I had to do that for two years. I wanted to quit one time... They talked me back into it... I graduated as a carpenter, coming from a carpenter course, and then they needed a draftsman down in Vancouver, and I worked for this consortium there... So I worked for two years there. I quit that job after that, and I wanted to work as a carpenter, and of course I came back here [in

1964] and I worked as a carpenter here all the time...

When I came back they come see me... Roy Sam and they had all these houses down at Marwell area there... [the Old Village]... [Roy and Carl McIntosh said], "We want to take you on a tour for tomorrow and look at the village, see what you think of it"... So I told my dad... "They're gonna show me the village down there, the houses." So he tell me, "... Just take a look at these house. They're too small for these families." He said, "They should've build them bigger houses instead of this little house." So I went the next morning... and I see... they were all overcrowded, these houses. There's a house there fourteen by sixteen feet, same as a big tent frame... Here there were eight people sleeping in it... Well, we found out later that they weren't built to CMHC [Canada Mortgage and Housing Corporation] standards... They were using two by eights for the floor joists and that, and they're splitting along there when you walk...

So Roy and some of those people... they talked together that they had to change things. So Indian Affairs had control of all... everything there. Every time you wanna do something, you've got to set a meeting with Indian Affairs... They were reading... newspapers from other First Nations down in Alberta, mostly... [They were] orchestrating to take over the business from Indian Affairs... And they used sawdust for insulation. Sawdust going down about two feet, and you could see frost all around, on a cold day...

And Roy and a whole bunch of us, we talked about taking it over, the control from Indian Affairs, so... we made a plan to run in an election, and we got in. We

CASCADING FROM TAKHINI TRAILER COURT is this continuous waterfall of raw sewage. It flows into the swamp behind the Whitehorse Indian village where children from the village play. --Star photo

got in, Roy [as chief]. And I was about five votes ahead of the last place on council. They didn't know me, I guess. I was mostly in army, you know. Finally we got in and we set our meeting with Indian Affairs and we told them we'd like to take over control from you guys, because we best know what's needed down there than you guys, because we hardly see you around there. So they said, "We'll have to go and caucus to talk about it. See if... they could give you guys control"... But every time they went into caucus, there was always somebody pulling for

above Sewage outfall above the Old Village, 1973. Untreated sewage from Takhini Trailer Court flowed into a swamp on Lot 226, beside the rodeo ground and village playground. According to Chief Roy Sam, the smell in the summer was "sickening."

us, and they let us know what's going on. And here, they get in contact with us, and they tell us that they agree to let us have control. But to leave it open so if we start having any trouble, that they come back in and take over again. So they tell us, "You gotta build a Band Office." I was a carpenter then, eh? You gotta build a Band Office, and here they state some budget, it has to be within this budget. So they gave me a job to figure out everything...

We had to do it in a certain budget. We did it right on budget. We finish it in good time, and... then we start getting these funds... to run the Band. And they let us have it. And then... we tried getting water in those houses down there, but they wouldn't let us because there were all these houses... were not built to standards. So we had to move or build these houses, tear them down or something. And then they did a survey... they want to find out the water table. Water table under town... So, and then... they put in a pump down there. They sink a pump down, and a whole bunch of kids got sick from it, because the water was contaminated [from the sewage coming down from Takhini].[24] ◉ ◉ ◉

◇◇◇◇◇◇◇◇◇◇◇◇◇◇◇◇◇◇

First Native Family in Riverdale

CHARLIE BURNS When I was in Camp Takhini... we used to talk lots together, and [Annie] ask me why we're paying rent... She says... we had lots of money, because none of us drank. And I drove [truck] right to Dawson, hauled fuel to Dawson... [worked for White Pass and Yukon Railway].

Eleven years. [In] 1960... we moved to [Teslin Road]... There was only fifty people... in Riverdale at that time... There was no Native people...

So when we come here, we didn't have—no voting rights, no nothing, and there was no Native peoples supposed to be here... So we went around about four or five houses here, and we come to this house and we looked at this house and we... I know the people who live in here. Leslie Grant her name was, that's the daughter [of the principal]... from Carcross School... So when they come to this

above Edith Dawson protests living conditions in the Old Village, ca. 1980.

house, and she [Annie] said, "I want this house," the salesman . . . said, "I don't know." He says, "There's not supposed to be no Native people here, you know." My wife says that she wants to know why . . . and that fellow went and talked to somebody else . . .

So he [another real estate agent] come over here . . . All four of us in the kitchen, and we were talking there, and they said, "How much money you willing to put down?" Well, my wife says, "Me and my husband, we've been working together," and she says, "I can put fourteen thousand dollars down or ten thousand cash because we have that money in the bank." "Well, okay," he says. "Well, let's go and do up the papers." So . . . I said, "I just heard you say that no Native people . . ." "Well, now," he says, "everything's changed."

Changed, yeah, so we went down and we had our own lawyer . . . [He] took all the papers to his place. I think it was about two weeks . . . He says, "Well, I guess you guys have a house!" . . . So there was lots of white people all around here, and we had a big motorhome too, you know. So I drive my motorhome back up in there [behind the house], and I had a pickup truck, brand-new pickup truck, and all those people—all outside looking at us moving our furniture in the house here, Indian people . . . So that's that, yeah. And I'm still here.[25] ◉ ◉ ◉

top left Charlie Burns at his home in Riverdale, 2020. Annie and Charlie Burns bought their home in the 1960s.

top right Annie Burns and her husband, Charlie, at Marsh Lake, ca. 1970.

left Charlie's mother, Bessie Burns, outside his Riverdale home with her grandson, Joe, ca. 1970.

TREATED AS SQUATTERS
IN OUR OWN COUNTRY

In the early 1900s, the White Pass & Yukon Railway had surveyed and then purchased from the Canadian government large tracts of land on the west side of the Yukon River below the Whitehorse Rapids for its rail and river transportation businesses. The company sold lots to individuals to establish the Whitehorse townsite, while other lots were reserved for government services like the post office and police. The company retained large tracts for its operations and also the right-of-way running along the river, meaning that people who located homes in those areas were considered squatters on White Pass land. Over the years the company allowed many of its employees to live there, including numerous First Nations families and others who crowded into the town during World War II when employment opportunities boomed.

The Alaska Highway turned Whitehorse into a transportation hub for the whole territory after World War II, and a key stopping point on the corridor linking southern Canada and the United States to the North, including Alaska. Wage employment drew many Tagish Kwan families, who traditionally occupied areas from Marsh Lake to Lake Laberge, into the fast-growing town. Families from Big Salmon, Teslin and elsewhere also relocated to Whitehorse.

There was no organized approach to settling families as both federal and territorial government services were minimal, and the new City of Whitehorse was only established in 1951. People of many origins and backgrounds crowded into haphazard neighbourhoods scatterd along the waterfront, from Yard Limits at the south end of town north to the Shipyards and surrounding areas. There were no sanitation services, and few homes had electricity in these neighbourhoods. Other serious social problems resulted from overcrowding, poverty, fire hazards and the illegal sale of alcohol by local bootleggers. Labelled as "squatters" by townspeople in more fortunate economic circumstances, they lived in difficult conditions and faced constant pressures to leave—but had nowhere to go.

The White Pass company and government mostly tolerated the neighbourhoods as the residents constituted a significant part of the local workforce. But there was grumbling from some officials and non-Indigenous residents about the "squatter neighbourhoods," with numerous campaigns aimed at cleaning up the town to be more attractive to visitors. Then in May 1953, a major polio outbreak resulted in dozens of people being hospitalized and several deaths. Public health officials ordered schools closed and banned public gatherings. The town was gripped by fear, and officials ordered the destruction of condemned homes and eviction of people from the "squatter neighbourhoods." The *Whitehorse Star* carried sad details of the horrendous chaos for the families involved: "Many a tear fell . . . as citizens, Indian and white, watched

their rickety homes being crushed under the might of a bulldozer... wheel barrows and wagons were piled high with dishes, bedding and clothing. Those... [with] cars and trucks were busy loading, most with a glum resentful frown on their faces, and above the roar of the menacing bulldozer sounded the ripping of boards."[26]

The Kwanlin Dün faced difficulties in getting work, including racist attitudes and government policies, along with restricted access to education and skills development. Housing for them in the 1950s and 1960s was scarce and substandard, even as the federal government built new housing subdivisions for army, air force and government workers.

Families of all backgrounds faced similar hard realities—there was no plan for their resettlement and few options for rebuilding their lives. Evictions and cleanups along the waterfront continued for decades, justified in the name of beautifying the town and creating public park spaces, dislocating residents who loved their life by the river and who had a hard time finding another place to live. If their homes were not condemned and could be moved, Status Indian people could relocate to Lot 226, at the north end of town, which had been established as Whitehorse Indian Reserve No. 8 in 1921. Non-Status people had to find places around the edges of the reserve or move in with relatives elsewhere in town.

Many Kwanlin Dün families have fond memories of living in Whiskey Flats, Moccasin Flats, Sleepy Hollow and the Shipyards. First Nations people lived alongside white squatters in these locations. Both groups were treated like outsiders by some townspeople, but this helped to create a strong sense of community, where neighbours looked out for one another.

Outside these neighbourhoods, Yukon First Nations people experienced a very different world. They were barred from "Whites Only" restaurants, restricted to the "Indians Only" section at the movie theatre and segregated to the "Indian ward" at the hospital. They did not have the right to vote, attend public schools, purchase alcohol or secure bank loans and were often subjected to demeaning treatment. The inequality of these times was obvious and unbearable.[27]

above Aerial view from east of Whitehorse, ca. late 1950s. Whitehorse General Hospital is under construction on the east side of the river (*at bottom left*), squatter communities are visible across the river near docked floatplanes, and the airport is visible west of town (*at top*).

facing Kwanlin Dün were forced from their homes and their traditional fishing, hunting and gathering areas on many occasions from the time of the 1897–1898 gold rush through to the 1980s.

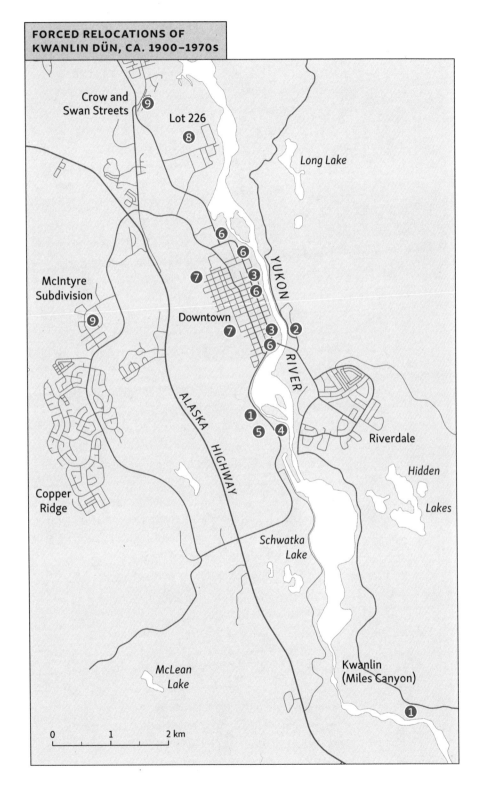

FORCED RELOCATIONS OF KWANLIN DÜN, CA. 1900–1970s

Crow and Swan Streets

Lot 226

Long Lake

McIntyre Subdivision

Downtown

Riverdale

Copper Ridge

Hidden

Lakes

ALASKA HIGHWAY

YUKON RIVER

Schwatka Lake

McLean Lake

Kwanlin (Miles Canyon)

0   1   2 km

1. **Canyon City and White Horse Rapids: Gold Rush, 1897–1900**
   Stampeders displaced Tagish Kwan and other First Nations people.

2. **Seasonal camp at White Horse Landing, east side Yukon River: 1897–early 1900s**
   Settlers displaced Tagish Kwan and other First Nations people.

3. **White Pass & Yukon Railway (WP&YR) Waterfront Lands: 1912–1920s**
   WP&YR officials, town residents and government officials forced First Nations people to relocate north of town. Canada designated Whitehorse Indian Reserve No. 8 (Lot 226) in 1921.

4. **Robert Service Campground: 1920s**
   Townspeople developed tourism facilities, displacing Tagish Kwan and other First Nations people who had fished and lived there seasonally for countless generations.

5. **Yard Limits: 1950s**
   Town officials bulldozed First Nations homes in "squatter clearances."

6. **Whitehorse Waterfront Neighbourhoods: 1950s–1970s**
   Town officials launched annual cleanups of waterfront neighbourhoods, with no consultation and minimal compensation for homes destroyed to establish Rotary Park and the SS Klondike site.

7. **Clay Cliffs Neighbourhood: 1940s–1980s**
   First Nations and other peoples' homes near the Clay Cliffs were dismantled after mudslides.

8. **Lot 226 (The Old Village), Whitehorse Indian Reserve No. 8: 1920s–2000s**
   At first, Tagish Kwan and other First Nations people lived at Lot 226, but after WWII only Status people were permitted. Non-Status people lived on the edges or elsewhere. Overcrowding, lack of services and open raw sewage led to the 1969 Whitehorse Indian Band Council resolution for relocation.

9. **McIntyre Subdivision: 1980s–present**
   KDFN relocated people from Lot 226 to new homes on Crow and Swan Streets in the early 1980s, and to McIntyre from 1986.

FAMILY FOCUS

Dak'alaa Maa—Dorothy Webber
....
Fred Webber

sent to Dawson City to join their older siblings, John and Elsie, at St. Paul's Hostel, attending Dawson Public School for ten years. They begged their father to let them return to the Boswell homestead and finish their schooling by correspondence.

As young women, Elsie and Dorothy worked hard raising vegetables in their large market garden, running fishnets, looking after the family dog teams, keeping house and trapping small game. The family traded goods with the Taylor & Drury riverboat and other river travellers. They had many adventures together—including raising two bear cubs that stayed several years with the family as pets. After the boys left home, the sisters stayed on a few more years with their father.

After Elsie married and moved away, Dorothy decided she wanted to move to Whitehorse. She walked to town with her dad and their dogs when she was twenty-one, packing all their gear. He helped her get a job with the postmaster's family, the Porters, where she lived as a nanny, helping to care for their younger children.

Dorothy met Fred Webber, and they married in late 1939. Fred was born in 1912 and raised in Carmacks as a boy but later moved with his parents to B.C. He returned to Carmacks during the Depression years to work with his relatives, and then came to Whitehorse where there were more opportunities. During World War II, Fred worked as a tradesman for the U.S. Army. He became a master tinsmith

Dak'alaa Maa—Dorothy Webber was the youngest daughter of Dak'alaa Maa—Sadie Jackie of Marsh Lake and American James Morgan Baker. She was born at Livingstone Creek in 1918 and raised on the family homestead at Boswell River on the Teslin River with her siblings John, Elsie and Jack. After their mother died, Dorothy and Jack were given to Celia and Frankie Jim at Tàa'än Män (Lake Laberge) to raise, as they had no children. When they reached school age, their father and the RCMP came to Celia and Frankie's home and seized the two youngsters. They were

top Fred and Dorothy Webber with their children Helen, Donnie and Bill (*in dad's arms*), ca. 1940s.

bottom Dorothy (Dot) Baker holds a coyote in her lap, ca. mid-1930s.

and plumber, working for Matt Nelson after the war and eventually buying his tin shop business in the 1960s.

Dorothy and Fred had five children: Helen, Donald, William (Bill), Albert and Bruce. Fred bought two lots for twenty-five dollars each in the early 1940s and built a log home for his family at Third Avenue and Jarvis Street. Dorothy was very busy as a homemaker, taking care of the children. She taught them to be independent, giving them a lot of freedom to roam the town on their bicycles, trusting them to look after themselves and each other. The family fished and hunted, and went berry picking to add to vegetables raised in their garden. They spent fun times with Dorothy's siblings and their children, enjoying their large extended family with many cousins.

Uncle Jack Baker, Dorothy's brother, was an avid trapper, hunter and prospector. He would be gone for days in the wilderness with just a small pack, a bit of fishing gear and a .22 rifle. A friend once found a note from Jack on a tree. It said: "I have been walking for 29 days and never seen a soul" and was signed "Lonesome Jack Baker." He never married but spent a lot of time with all his nieces and nephews. He played fiddle and violin with his brother, John, while his sisters played harmonica. Jack and John worked on the White Pass & Yukon Railway and often sent huge boxes of blueberries picked near Log Cabin to Dorothy's family.

Fred's business prospered during the 1960s as Whitehorse boomed, with many new houses being built. His sons joined his business for a few years and then moved on to other work. Dorothy enjoyed many years as a mother, aunty and grandmother and passed away in 1974. Fred worked hard all his life and passed away in 1994.[28]

left *Left to right*: Solomon Charlie, K'alazhaw—George Dawson and Fred Boss perform with traditional dancers at a celebration in Whitehorse, ca. mid-1970s.

right Tut.Latseen—Susie Fred performs at Sourdough Rendezvous, ca. 1958.

LOOKING TO THE FUTURE

Building Our New Reality

Despite segregation and racial discrimination, our people worked hard to be part of the city growing up in our midst. Our Elders wore their regalia and brought our culture into public settings at many events, such as the Whitehorse Winter Carnival—later renamed Sourdough Rendezvous. Yukon First Nations people excelled at the annual dog-mushing events, bringing us all great pride as our relatives from many communities took home big prizes.

Our people worked in many different professions, contributing to the economy and literally helping to build the city. Young men worked at the cinder-block factory in Marwell, which produced the materials for the Qwanlin Mall and many other buildings constructed from the 1950s onward. Although spelled a different way than the Southern Tutchone term for our namesake canyon, the mall owners adopted our name for their building! With people working and earning money, families started moving out of the Old Village into rental accommodations around the city, and some purchased homes in neighbourhoods that previously were all white.

top left Dancers including Fred Boss (*second from left*), Kashxóot— Chief Jim Boss (*third from left*) and Annie Ned (*fifth from left*) plus drummer Tììnah Ts'atìi—Chief Johnny Fraser perform on stage, at the winter carnival in Whitehorse, in 1948. Tììnah Ts'atìi means "Copper Holder."

top right Kashxóot—Chief Jim Boss drives a horse and wagon during a winter carnival celebration, ca. 1948. Even his horse is wearing regalia—an octopus bag!

left Ch'e'a Mą—May Hume (*centre left*); her mother, Kàdùhikh— K'ałgwach—K'odetéena—Kitty Smith (*behind and to right*) and father, Whitehorse Indian Band Chief Kanéł—Billy Smith (*behind and to left*); and Carcross/Tagish Elders Patsy Henderson (*in beaded jacket*) and wife Edith (*in beaded dress*) welcome Queen Elizabeth II (*centre right*) at MacBride Museum, 1959.

top Skookum Jim dancers perform at Sourdough Rendezvous, ca. mid-1970s. **1.** Charlotte Darbyshire, **2.** Kathy Darbyshire, **3.** Donna Nolan, **4.** Tammy Yardley, **5.** Marilyn Yadułtin McLean, **6.** Elaine Chambers, **7.** Denise Beattie, **8.** Shirley McLean, **9.** Carmella Jones, **10.** Unidentified, **11.** Kathy Rear and **12.** Donna Chambers.

above Kanéł—Billy Smith, the first chief of the newly formed Whitehorse Indian Band, with his wife Kàdùhikh—K'ałgwach—K'odetéena—Kitty.

Skookies: Centre for Socializing and Action

Skookum Jim Memorial Hall was built in 1961–1962 in downtown White-horse with funds from the estate of Skookum Jim. It still houses the Skookum Jim Friendship Centre, one of the first Yukon Indigenous organizations. The hall was the birthplace for many more groups that were instrumental in the political development of Yukon First Nations, including the Yukon Native Brotherhood (YNB, see p. 181), the Yukon Association of Non-Status Indians (YANSI, see p. 183) and the Yukon Indian Women's Association (YIWA, see p. 198).

"Skookies" was also an important centre for social programs, community events and youth activities—Cubs, Boy Scouts, Girl Guides, Brownies, Indian Dance Club, weekly teen dances, bingo, movies, hootenannies, well-baby clinics and after-school homework sessions. Whitehorse Indian Band members were strong supporters and fundraisers for these programs. For years, "Skookies" served as the only community centre for the Whitehorse Indian Band and other Indigenous people in Whitehorse.

An Administrative Convenience: Whitehorse Indian Band

In 1956, the Department of Indian Affairs amalgamated the diverse groups of Tagish Kwan and other Status Indian people from many different communities who were living in Whitehorse into the Whitehorse Indian Band (WIB), known today as the Kwanlin Dün First Nation. The WIB was created as an administrative convenience for the Indian agent and ignored traditional territories and leadership practices.

Billy Smith served as the first Chief of the Whitehorse Indian Band, along with two councillors, Scurvey Shorty and John McGundy, all of them

unpaid advisors in the new administrative structure established by the Department of Indian Affairs. Problems of overcrowding, substandard housing, polluted water and lack of sanitation services increased as more and more Yukon First Nations families were forced to relocate from waterfront neighbourhoods. WIB leaders worked hard to bring those concerns to the attention of the department and the public. In 1965, the department instituted the first WIB elections for Chief and Band Council. Scurvey Shorty was elected as Chief and continued to fight for better conditions for Band members.

By the late 1960s, Whitehorse and the rest of the Yukon were booming with new economic opportunities, but little of that prosperity was flowing to First Nations people. WIB members needed a strong leader to bridge

left Kishwoot Hall in the Old Village, ca. 1980s.

right K'alazhaw—George Dawson calls bingo at Kishwoot Hall, ca. 1970s, under a poster of Ann Smith (incorrectly identified as "Anne") for Sourdough Rendezvous Queen.

differences among the various peoples and to foster unity. They found one in Tämbey—Elijah Smith, elected Chief in 1967. Elijah was well placed to become a leader: he was an independent heavy-equipment operator, work that gave him connections throughout the Yukon. He was the eldest in a very large family headed by his mother, Annie Ned, a strong matriarch and leadership mentor in her own right.[29] He had spent six years as a Canadian soldier in Europe, where he saw action and was seriously injured. Like other Indigenous soldiers, in order to enlist Elijah had to enfranchise, giving up his Indian Status. To be "equals on the battlefield, but not at home" gave him much to think about when he returned to the Yukon.

As Chief, Elijah spearheaded the development of Kishwoot Hall on Lot 226 to give Whitehorse Indian Band members a centre close to home. The hall was an old World War II barracks that he relocated in 1967 and named in honour of Kashxóot—Chief Jim Boss. The WIB offices were located there, as were community services, social events and fundraisers to support programs. Kishwoot Hall housed a very successful kindergarten program sponsored by Skookies in the days when kindergarten was not offered in Yukon public schools. The Kishwoot kindergarten was so popular that three full-time teachers were employed, including Emma Joanne Shorty, who had lobbied for the program and took training offered in Whitehorse for kindergarten teachers.

Kishwoot Hall was the site for Yukon Indian Days, held from September 18 to 20, 1970. The event featured a rodeo, dances, bingo, traditional foods and a homegrown midway. It drew Yukoners from all over the territory, including many white residents, and was a huge success.

Organizing for Change: Founding the Yukon Native Brotherhood

In 1902, in the wake of the Klondike gold rush stampede, Kashxóot—Chief Jim Boss made several attempts to safeguard the lands and hunting rights of the Tagish Kwan people at Tàa'än Män (Lake Laberge). Little came of his efforts other than government protection of a small parcel of land at Tàa'än Män, but his actions are recognized today as an early statement of claims for his people.

Decades later, events both inside and outside the Yukon influenced the development of modern land claims. Yukon First Nations soldiers serving oversees in World War II risked their lives to defend human rights and unlawful invasions in Europe, yet returned home to a country where they had fewer rights than other Canadians. Their families lived in marginal conditions without opportunities to participate fully in Canadian society. Yukon First Nations veterans, along with other Indigenous veterans, experienced further racial injustices when Canada deprived them of many benefits and compensation extended to other veterans.

Promising land claims developments were underway in nearby Alaska. The Tlingit and Haida Tribes of southeast Alaska sued the U.S. government over the loss of their lands and resources, and were awarded compensation in a 1968 settlement. That successful claim caught the attention of Yukon First Nations that had direct family ties to the Tlingit of southeast Alaska and possible beneficiary status in Alaska. Settling land claims was an urgent priority for the American government as a result of oil and gas discoveries in Alaska and the imminent need to build pipelines across unceded tribal lands. The Tlingit–Haida claim led the way to the 1971 Alaska Native Claims Settlement Act (ANCSA), at the time the largest land claims settlement in U.S. history.[30] It appeared that pipelines and land claims had a connection. Settlements in Alaska gave hope for Yukon land claims, but the need for better organization was becoming very clear.

above Children enjoy creative play at the Kishwoot Hall kindergarten in the Old Village, 1969. *From left to right:* Barbara Dawson, unidentified, Darlene Jim, Hilda Dawson, and John Tom Tom.

top Yukon chiefs, including Teslin Tlingit leader Frank Sydney (*fourth from left*) and Tämbey—Elijah Smith (*obscured, second from right*) speak to federal government officials including Jean Chrétien (*third from left*) at hearings on proposed changes to the Indian Act, Whitehorse, 1968.

above Carcross/Tagish Elder Ch'óonehte' Má—Stóow—Angela Sidney addresses the minister and officials at the hearings, 1968.

The Yukon Chiefs founded the Yukon Native Brotherhood (YNB) in 1968, during consultations in Whitehorse with the federal government over changes to the Indian Act. Elijah Smith was no longer Whitehorse Indian Band Chief at that time, but he attended the consultations on behalf of the Chief, who was ill. Elijah presented a blunt report on the circumstances facing WIB members and all Yukon Indian people at the time: "We didn't know if you people from Ottawa were going to listen to us talk about something that wasn't in your book. That's the book called 'Choosing a Path' [an information booklet prepared by the government]. Because we felt that our biggest problems weren't in that book. Also many of the questions you have in that book don't apply to the Yukon."[31] Among the issues Elijah presented were the lack of paid positions for Band Chiefs and councillors; problems with Indian Act definitions of Status and non-Status people; the terrible conditions at Lot 226 in Whitehorse, with open sewers and contaminated drinking water; the desire for self-government among Yukon Indians; and the lack of revenue or grants for Bands to develop services for their own people.

Finally Elijah concluded: "The last problem is of course the biggest one. We want the land and treaty question settled as soon as possible. Many of us

feel we are just wasting our time until this is settled . . . We need a treaty to tell us what our rights are—where our land is—we want to plan for the future of our people. We have no future until we clean up this unfinished business. We have several ideas of what we think the terms of the treaty should be. We intend to put a high price on our right to the land of the Yukon. Every year that goes by, and a new mine opens up, our asking price will go up."[32]

Representatives of other Yukon Indian Bands presented their reports; then the Chiefs announced that they had decided to hold a closed session that afternoon and would reconvene with department officials on the morning of October 22. The next day the record of the meeting states: "Mr. Elijah Smith reported that at the meeting held among the Indians themselves yesterday, Monday, October 21 at 3:00 PM. they had founded the Yukon Native Brotherhood. President—Elijah Smith, Vice-President—George McLeod, Secretary—Edna Rose."[33] This was a turning point in Yukon history. It was recorded with little fanfare in the federal report on the Whitehorse meetings, but the outcomes would be far reaching for decades to come.

The primary objective for creating the YNB was to achieve a negotiated land claims settlement for Yukon First Nations and to build a strong political organization to support that goal. This was not easy. The organization was small, poorly funded and operated out of temporary offices at Skookum Jim Hall.

Elijah believed in grassroots political development and face-to-face communication, spending much of his political career travelling from community to community and house to house. All the while, he was seeking support for land claims and encouraging all the Bands to establish offices, install phones and hire staff. He believed that economic opportunity, community development, training and self-government were the best means

top left Yukon chiefs enjoy a break during a land claims research trip to First Nations in southern Canada, 1971. *Left to right*: unidentified, Harry Joe (Champagne & Aishihik First Nations), Tämbey—Elijah Smith, Ánálaháash—Sam Johnston (Teslin), two unidentified men.

top right Tämbey—Elijah Smith attends a function, ca. 1980s.

for overcoming racism and poverty. He earned respect by paying particular attention to Elders in each community.[34] Elijah was also very skillful at gaining access to government leaders through his political connections. He was respected by many in the white community in the Yukon, within national Indigenous organizations and among Ottawa officials. He was a powerful, charismatic leader, able to give eloquent voice to the rights and needs of Yukon First Nations people—a critically important skill in the difficult times ahead.

Hearing All Voices: The Yukon Association of Non-Status Indians

Status Indians were recognized by Ottawa and entitled to benefits under the Indian Act, but many Yukon First Nations people had lost their Status and were left out of federal housing and health programs, as well as the newly formed Yukon Native Brotherhood. Some had enfranchised (that is, given up their Status) in order to obtain work, and others had done so because they wanted their children to attend public schools. Women who married non-Status or white men automatically lost their Status, as did all their children. Status men who married non-Status or white women did not lose their Status. Many families were split between those with and those without Status, causing deep concerns about who would benefit from any future land claims settlement.

The Yukon Association of Non-Status Indians (YANSI) was created in 1971 to represent all those Yukon people who were of First Nations ancestry but were denied Status under the Indian Act. George Asp was elected as interim president. Joe Jacquot became president when the organization incorporated in March 1972. Their first tasks focused on setting up YANSI locals throughout the Yukon and pursuing a role in the land claims negotiations. YANSI was soon active in every possible way, addressing housing needs and raising concerns about Yukon River pollution and many more issues.[35]

Klighee—Sait u—Emma Joanne Shorty: I remember that, when they had YANSI... Yukon Association of Non-Status Indians... I was one of them, because my husband, Norman Shorty, and myself, we belonged to YANSI at the time. And it was not our own choice, but we had to, because we were First Nations.

And the reason is because... Norma, my daughter, oldest daughter, she was ready to go to school. And a year before she was ready, she was only five, I went to Indian Affairs, and I told them, "I want my daughter to go to public school," and they said, "No. First Nations are not allowed to go to public school. They have to go to residential school." I fought with them all summer. Just about every day, I used to go up. "Did you make up your mind yet?" Finally they got mad, and this lady came with a paper, threw it at me, and she said, "Sign it." So I took it home... I showed it to [Norman] when he came home. We lived in that little shack up there, and he took a pen, and he said, "Sign it." So I signed it, and he signed it, that's giving up our Status. I still got that little blue card. Yeah. And then in 1985, or '84, we got our Status back. During that time we had a hard time with doctor's bills and all that. It's okay. It's over. All is forgiven.[36]

Together Today for Our Children Tomorrow

In 1973, seventy-one years after Chief Jim Boss first tried to secure the land rights of the Tagish Kwan people, a delegation of Yukon Chiefs, led by Elijah Smith, presented their position paper on land claims to Prime Minister Pierre Trudeau in Ottawa. The 1973 meeting in Ottawa was a pivotal moment for Yukon First Nations people, both Status and non-Status—and ultimately for all Yukon people—but it would prove to be just the first step on a very long journey. The paper they presented was titled "Together Today for Our Children Tomorrow: A Statement of Grievances and an Approach to Settlement by the Yukon Indian People." It became the foundation for the modern negotiated land claims treaties in the Yukon and a standard for others that followed across Canada. The paper was emphatic that "This is a Settlement for tomorrow not for today... This settlement is for our children, and our children's children, for many generations to come. All our programs and the guarantees we seek in our Settlement are to protect them from a repeat of today's problems in the future."[38]

top Emma, Elaine, and Norma Shorty. Norma cut the ribbon for the new Bay Store, ca. 1960.

bottom Ugut—Norman Shorty Sr. with his children, Christmas ca. 1969. *Back, left to right:* Norma, Eileen, Jacqueline. *Front:* Norman Jr., Jason, Norman Sr.

FAMILY FOCUS

Klighee—Sait u—Emma Joanne Shorty
Ugut—Norman Shorty Sr.

Klighee—Sait u—Emma Joanne Shorty had two Tlingit names given to her by her maternal grandma and aunties. She was born in Teslin in the 1930s to the Gaanax.ádi Clan, Pit Cache house, with ancestral roots in Taku, Juneau and Angoon. Her husband, Ugut—Norman Shorty Sr., was Tagish Kwan through his father Jim Shorty's mother, one of the twin sisters of Tagish John, who moved to Big Salmon upon her marriage to Long Shorty.

In their early years together, Emma and Norman Sr. lived in Teslin and along the Alaska Highway in several places, following Norman's employment with highway crews. In the 1950s, Norman's work brought them to Whitehorse, where they lived at Whiskey Flats. When the city expropriated their waterfront home to create parkland for the sternwheeler SS *Klondike* around 1964, they moved to a home on Black Street with their family of five children. In the mid-1970s, the city again expropriated houses along the clay cliffs owing to the danger of mudslides. With compensation from the city and their savings, the Shortys bought land and started building a new home at the Marsh Lake dam.

In addition to raising her children and following her traditional food-harvesting practices, Emma undertook many activities to teach children and preserve her culture throughout her life. She taught in the first kindergarten for Kwanlin Dün children at Kishwoot Hall, developed curriculum

top Jason and Norman Jr. with roasted gophers, ca. 1970.

bottom Norman Jr. and Jason Shorty in a boat made by Ugut— Norman Shorty Sr., at Big Salmon, ca. 1970.

projects with staff at the Council for Yukon Indians, and recorded stories for oral history projects with Kwanlin Dün First Nation, the Yukon Native Language Centre and many others.

Norman Sr. worked as a truck driver with the Yukon Highways Department for many years. He was a pioneer broadcaster for CBC Yukon together with his sister Gertie Tom, bringing news and the music of Yukon First Nations to the airways in the 1960s. He had a professional reel-to-reel recorder that he used to record people speaking and singing in their languages, creating one of the first sound archives of Yukon First Nations people.

Emma and Norman decided to give up their Indian Status and all their benefits under the Indian Act in the 1950s so that their children could attend public schools rather than be taken to residential school. It gained them the right to vote and access to employment in government, but it meant that their children also lost their Indian Status. Through Bill C-31, Emma, Norman and all their children regained their status in the 1980s.

Norman passed away in 1990 and Emma in 2017. Their children and grandchildren continue their traditions of harvesting from the land, preserving and teaching First Nations languages and culture, and contributing to the well-being of their communities.[37]

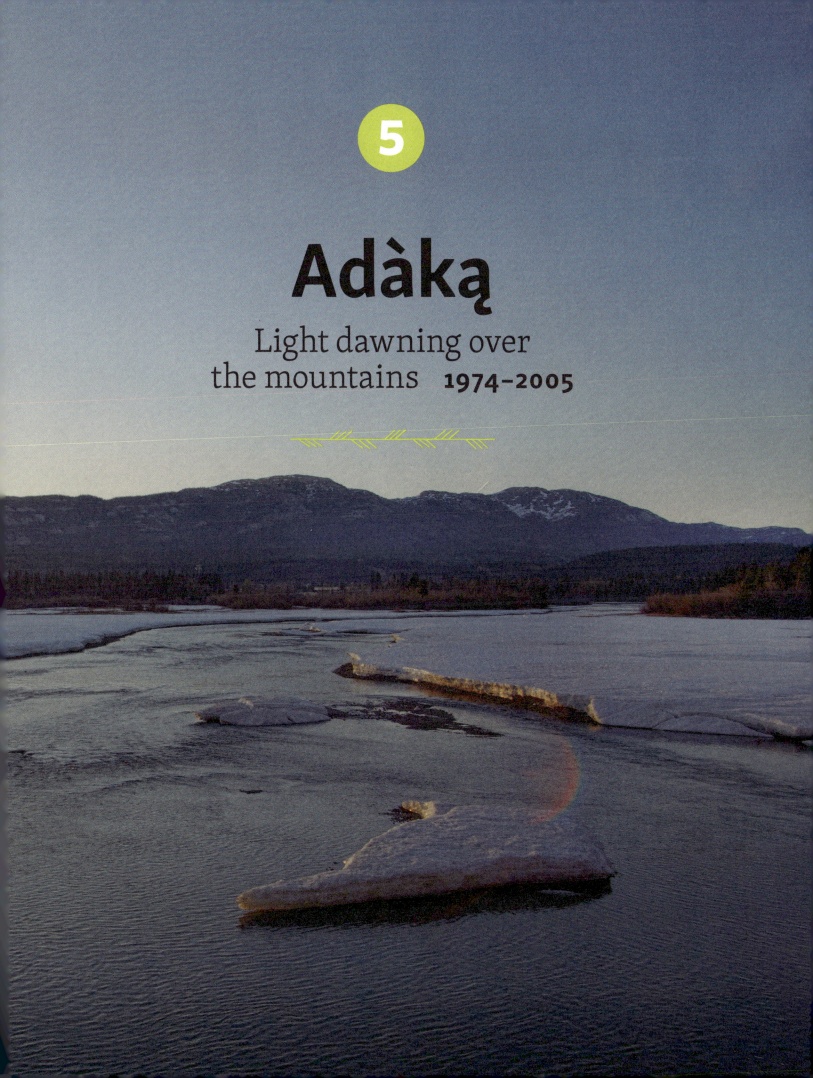

5

Adàką

Light dawning over the mountains 1974–2005

We are not here looking for a handout,
we are here with a plan, that will cost the
Canadian tax payer much less than if the present
government policies and programs continue.

ELIJAH SMITH, President, Yukon Native Brotherhood[1]

ADÀKĄ SPEAKS TO the new light of dawn radiating from mountain peaks and spreading across the land. In spring, every day brings more and stronger light, continuing the full circle of life and the cycle of seasons for our people. This is a time of renewal, regeneration and revitalization. Northern days are sweetly scented with crocus and lupine, fresh green leaves appear on trees, skies are filled with the calls of swans returning to the North. People shed the heavy clothes of winter, taking up new opportunities in our beautiful land.

In 1973, First Nations people throughout the Yukon came together to develop a manifesto for our future called "Together Today for Our Children Tomorrow." Our leaders went to Ottawa to present our claims to the Canadian prime minister. For twenty years we worked in our communities to develop a new vision for ourselves, and in the process we helped to transform all aspects of Yukon society and governance. This was an era of great hope, when we staked our claims and regained our self-determination as Yukon First Nations. Many Kwanlin Dün were leaders in achieving the 1993 Umbrella Final Agreement. Then in 2005 we negotiated our Final and Self-Government Agreements. We worked hard and peacefully to reconstruct our own destiny and to create new relationships for the benefit of all Yukon people.

Kàdùhikh—K'ałgwach—K'odetéena—Kitty Smith

Kitty Smith of the Crow Clan was born around 1890 near Juneau on the Alaska coast. Her mother was Tatl'èrma from Marsh Lake and her father, Tàkàt'à, was from the Alsek and Tatshenshini region. After her mother died when Kitty was very young, she was raised by her father's mother, travelling extensively in the southwest Yukon, following her people's traditional seasonal rounds for hunting, gathering and trading. Her father's family gave her three Tlingit names at a potlatch: Kàdùhikh, K'ałgwach and K'odetéena. As a young woman she married Kanéł—Billy Smith from the Tagish area, and they raised their children in the southern Yukon. She refused to send her children to residential school. In the pre-war years she lived far enough from white settlements to resist the reach of the RCMP and the Chooutla school, keeping her kids on the land with her and her husband to provide them with skills and knowledge drawn from their traditional ways and languages. Kitty was an energetic entrepreneur, combining hunting and trapping with sewing, carving and mining to earn a living. She was a respected storyteller who loved to entertain her audiences, and a frequent contributor to heritage gatherings to the end of her long life. She passed away in 1989 at the age of one hundred.[3]

Nindal Kwädīndür
(I'm going to tell you a story)

HOW INDIANS GOT FIRE

Told by **Kàdùhikh—K'ałgwach—K'odetéena—Kitty Smith**[2]

Crow was the one who first got fire.

You know that Chicken Hawk? He got long nose, first time, they say.

Crow got King Salmon. He can't eat it without fire, you know. Some-place he see fire come out salt water. He don't know how to get it. He don't know which way he's going to get it. How he know fire, Crow? He don't know which way he going to get it. Somebody's got to get it, he think. That time he tell birds, "You think we get it, that fire?"

"No."

Chicken Hawk, he got long nose. "I'll try," he say.

Crow get pitch from wood, tie up his beak for him. "Try now," he say.

He wait for that fire going to come out. Soon it come up. He poke it with his beak. He start to burn now, that beak. Chicken Hawk beat it home. "My nose start to burn," he scream.

"You're doing good," call Crow.

Just on shore he fall down. But he got it already, that Crow. That Chicken Hawk pretty sick though.

"Come on," Crow tell him. "I'm going to medicine you." He fix him up little beak. "Just nice-looking boy, you now," he say. "Women going to like you now."

They cook now that fish. Put away tail so it won't make foolish people. Everybody eat that fish now.

They build fire and from there Crow take rock, flint. He throw it all around. That's why you sometimes find that rock all around.

STATING OUR CLAIMS

Elijah Smith, president of the Yukon Native Brotherhood (YNB), secured funding and support from the federal Indian Claims Commissioner, Lloyd Barber, in 1972 to develop a statement of Yukon Indian claims for presentation to the federal government. YNB leadership decided the statement should be based on text generated from extensive community consultations. Dave Joe chaired a steering committee for the process with a deadline of November 30, 1972.

Preparing the statement was complex work involving all Yukon Indian Bands and many individuals. Field workers met with each community to gather input. YNB officials attended meetings in all communities and organized land claims conferences, hired interpreters, designed questionnaires, trained staff, recorded sessions and reviewed huge volumes of information.[4]

Three representatives of each Band and all the Chiefs came to Whitehorse to review and approve the final draft of the statement. The title of the document—"Together Today for Our Children Tomorrow"—was selected from a list of ideas gathered by the research team. It may have been inspired by a quote from the Hunkpapa Lakota leader Sitting Bull: "Let us put our minds together and see what kind of life we can make for our children."[5] The distinctive gold and black document cover featured a photo collage of Yukon First Nations individuals representing four generations: Elders, adults, youth and children, superimposed on drawings of stretched beaver skins.

On February 14, 1973, the delegation of Yukon First Nations Chiefs presented "Together Today for Our Children Tomorrow" to Prime Minister Pierre Elliott Trudeau in a packed committee room on Parliament Hill. Elijah opened the meeting with a direct and succinct message: "We are here with a plan." When Prime Minister Trudeau asked the delegation of Yukon Chiefs how long it would take to complete a land claims settlement, the reply was "Six months."[6]

Jean Chrétien, the minister of Indian Affairs and Northern Development, was also present that day. In 1969, Chrétien had put forward the White Paper (officially titled "Statement of the Government of Canada on Indian Policy"), which would have abolished the Indian Act, eliminated Indian

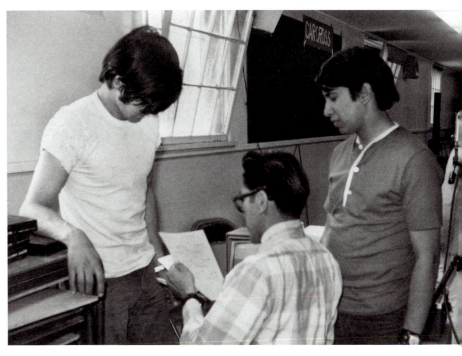

above Ray Jackson (*centre*) of the Yukon Native Brotherhood works with two student trainees, including Shaakóoni—Mike Smith (*right*), to prepare for the YNB land claims community video project, at Kishwoot Hall, 1971.

status, and forced the assimilation of Indigenous people into Canadian society.[7] Elijah handed a copy of the "Together Today" document to him, reportedly saying: "Here, Mr. Chrétien, is a copy of your New paper!"[8]

We Had More Rights Than They Thought

Timing was vital to the presentation of "Together Today for Our Children Tomorrow." Prime Minister Trudeau had not been a supporter of land claims and Indigenous rights, maintaining it was impossible to right the historic wrongs of the past. His position changed in 1973, when the Supreme Court of Canada ruling in *Calder v British Columbia* (named for Nisga'a Chief Frank Calder) confirmed that the Royal Proclamation of 1763 was still applicable in regions where the majority of land was unceded territory. The decision affirmed that the Nisga'a had legal claims to their traditional lands in British Columbia. It also implied that Indigenous land rights were legally enforceable in many other areas, including the Yukon. As a result, the federal government changed its view of obligations to Indigenous people in areas of Canada where land had not been ceded to the Crown through past treaties. Prime Minister Trudeau stated: "Perhaps you had more legal rights than we thought you had."[9]

Other issues also affected federal government views on northern land claims. Major oil companies were planning to construct the Mackenzie Valley pipeline in the Northwest Territories. This included a possible pipeline extension across the North Slope of the Yukon to Prudhoe Bay, Alaska. These developments would require clarification of land ownership and the land rights of northern Indigenous people. Everyone was well aware that pipelines and land claims were converging with urgent deadlines.

On April 2, 1973, the Yukon Native Brotherhood assumed ownership of Coudert Residence, a vacant building in Riverdale (a neighbourhood in Whitehorse) that had formerly been used as a residence for Roman Catholic First Nations students. The Yukon Indian Centre Corporation was established to manage the building, with space leased to the Yukon Association of Non-Status Indians (YANSI), the Yukon Indian Women's Association (YIWA) and other groups with plans to offer cultural education and economic development programs. The Yukon Indian Centre became a gathering place to imagine a new future, honour a proud past and foster a vital political movement. The old gymnasium was packed for important meetings during the week and for community dances on Friday nights.[10]

Working Together: The Council for Yukon Indians

In November 1973, YNB established the Council for Yukon Indians (CYI) as the Yukon land claims negotiating organization. The executive included the chair, vice-chair and secretary-treasurer, who worked with a Board of

Directors with one delegate from each community, plus one representative each for YNB and YANSI. Elijah Smith served as the appointed interim chair.[11]

Formal negotiations with the federal government began in 1974 in Vancouver, led by lawyers hired by CYI. Community people turned their attention to site selections for each Band. The negotiations began as two-party discussions between the federal government and Yukon First Nations, with the territorial government excluded from the table. To appease Yukon politicians and organizations critical of the land claims process, the federal government appointed a Yukon citizen representative as a non-government observer.[12] The projected end date for negotiations was December 1977, but it was several years after that before an Agreement-in-Principle was reached.[13] CYI continued as the joint negotiation body for YNB and YANSI, while the two organizations remained separate entities for another seven years.

Bill Webber, President, Yukon Association for Non-Status Indians: YANSI reps began a public protest picketing outside of the Coudert Residence . . . We wanted to be able to fully participate in the talks, which were leading up to the development of a statement of claim. Finally we had a response from Elijah [Smith] and he indicated: "Don't worry we will take care of you." We responded that we wanted to fully participate. It was not good enough that someone was going to look after our interests.

facing top Yukon Chiefs stand on the steps of Parliament Hill on February 14, 1973. The delegation, including Yukon Native Brotherhood Secretary Judy Gingell (*front row, second from left*), her father Chief Kashgêk'—Johnnie Smith (*front row, fourth from left*), Shaan Tlein—Irene Smith (wife of Elijah Smith) and Tämbey—Elijah Smith (*front row, far right*) presented their land claims paper, "Together Today for Our Children Tomorrow," to Prime Minister Pierre Trudeau that day.

facing bottom The cover of "Together Today for Our Children Tomorrow" featured images of nine Yukon First Nations people representing Elders, adults and youth.

above Yukon First Nations Chiefs and the Yukon Native Brotherhood executive meet in Whitehorse, 1977. *Front row, left to right*: Gerald Isaac, YNB Vice President; Willie Joe, YNB President. *Back row, left to right*: Chief John Joe Kay; Chief Joe Johnson; George McLeod, YNB Secretary-Treasurer; Chief Robert Hager; Chief Danny Joe; Chief Max Skookum (*in front of Joe*); Chief Dixon Lutz; Chief Harry Joe (*in front of Lutz*); Chief Roy Sam; Chief Percy Henry; Chief Stanley James; Eric Morris.

In Berger Submission

CYI Calls For Settlement Before Pipeline

By ANDREW HUME
Staff Reporter

The Council for Yukon Indians recommended to the Berger Inquiry this week that no pipeline be built until Yukon Indian land claims are settled and implemented.

The recommendation is one of nine points in a presentation to summation hearings before the inquiry in Yellowknife by Whitehorse lawyer Ron Veale, pipeline cousel for the CYI.

The Berger inquiry into a proposed natural gas pipeline from Alaska across the Yukon and down the Mackenzie Valley is scheduled to conclude this week in Yellowknife after 18 months of hearings.

provide the baseline data for all Indian communities affected by these routes as was done in the case of Old Crow," Veale told the inquiry.

There are 12 Indian communities in the Yukon and before the Alaska Highway route is considered, the CYI wants government funding to undertake a pipeline information program to inform these communities of the ramifications of a pipeline and to obtain their reaction.

A major section of the CYI final argument was taken up with the principles of the Old Crow land settlement, which covers all the area north of the 65th parallel in the Yukon between Alaska on the west and the Northwest Territories on the east.

the Old Crow River for the people of Old Crow and asks that they be withdrawn from any plans for development by any level of government or industry.

The final principle would grant the people of Old Crow the power to control their way of life and the environment within which they exist.

The brief contends that the pipeline routes, the energy corridor concept and the subsidiary developments of the Dempster Highway and the Beaufort Sea exploration all violate these principles.

The CYI sums up the position of the Yukon Indians. It was heard along with final summations from the two pipeline applicants during the final day of hearings in Yellowknife.

The two applicants are Canadian Arctic Gas, who propose a 48-inch natural gas pipeline from Purdhoe Bay, Alaska across the Yukon and down the Mackenzie Valley, and Foothills Pipe Lines, which has proposed to build a 42-inch, all-Canadian line from the Mackenzie Delta down the valley to Canadian markets. Foothills also has an interest in the alternate Alaska Highway route.

When final summations from the applicants and all interveners have been heard, Mr. Justice Berger will write a report and make recommendations to the federal government on conditions under which a pipeline could be built. It does not lie within his

terms of reference, established by the cabinet, to decide whether or not a pipeline should be constructed.

The lengthy submission by the Yukon Indians examines in detail the impacts of both northern routes across the Yukon and their social-cultural impacts, manland relationships, economic impacts and draws conclusions that in neither case should a pipeline ever be considered.

The brief concludes with the view that "the construction of a gas pipeline and subsequent corridor developments will have disastrous impact upon the people and the environment of the North and may trigger a violent reaction if native rights and title are not fully recognized.

above The Council for Yukon Indians opposed any pipelines being built in the Yukon before land claims were settled and implemented.

We were still excluded in the development of the statement. It was not until negotiations were going to begin that it was agreed to form another entity rather than let Yukon Native Brotherhood represent our interests. The Council for Yukon Indians was then founded and included equal involvement for the non-Status Indians in Yukon Indian land claims negotiations.[14]

Pipelines and Politics

In the wake of the 1970s oil embargo by Middle East oil-producing countries, and in the midst of rising gas prices and discussions between the United States and Canada for pipeline rights-of-way in northern Canada, there was a lot of pressure from Ottawa to begin pipeline projects. As had happened in Alaska, pipelines, politics and land claims converged. The CYI knew that pipeline developments could significantly undermine land claims, so their position was definitive: "No pipeline until land claims are settled and implemented."[15] In 1975, YNB and YANSI negotiated with Ottawa to issue a twelve thousand–square-mile land "freeze" to stop further land alienations during negotiations. It was in the best interests of all parties to settle land claims, but there was conflict on what to do in the meantime. The freeze was often ignored, as when Ottawa established the Alaska Highway Gas Pipeline right-of-way and made exceptions for other developments considered too important to delay.

Justice Thomas Berger began the Mackenzie Valley Pipeline Inquiry, or Berger Inquiry, in 1974. He was commissioned by the Canadian government to assess the impact of a pipeline to carry gas from Prudhoe Bay, Alaska, across the Yukon North Slope to join with a pipeline that would carry Beaufort Sea gas down the Mackenzie Valley to southern markets. His final report in 1977 recommended a ten-year moratorium on building a pipeline through the Mackenzie Valley route in order to settle land claims in the Northwest Territories, and recommended against any pipeline across the Yukon North Slope.[16] The federal government accepted the recommendations but quickly turned its attention to the Alaska Highway as an already developed transportation corridor that could provide an alternative route for American gas to reach southern markets. Ottawa appointed Ken Lysyk chairman of the Alaska Highway Pipeline Inquiry in mid-April 1977 and gave him a deadline of August 1, 1977—just three months—to gather input and make recommendations on the highway route. Despite fierce opposition from many Yukon groups, including CYI, the inquiry concluded the project could proceed if appropriate regulatory oversight was in place.[17]

Falling oil and gas prices halted momentum within a few months, causing oil company proponents to delay their northern development plans. The "pipeline rush" evaporated, but it had served a very useful purpose in the Yukon—spurring on land claims organization and political development at all levels. New federal monies were flowing to support CYI and numerous social and economic initiatives throughout the North.

The federal government appointed Elijah Smith as Yukon Regional Director of Indian Affairs in 1977, the first time that a Yukon First Nation person held that position. Many First Nations people had mixed feelings about the appointment, given past racist and colonial treatment from Indian Affairs. Elijah viewed the appointment as an opportunity to represent Yukon First Nations at the source of political power. He soon found his position as a civil servant challenging and frustrating, as his department was entrenched in colonial and bureaucratic processes. Elijah stayed in government for only a short time, then returned to work at CYI on the land claims.[18]

Historic Political Changes

Since the beginning of negotiations, Yukon territorial government (YTG) politicians had lobbied to be an equal party at the table, but their efforts were unsuccessful. That changed in 1979, when the minority Conservative government led by Prime Minister Joe Clark was elected. The new minister of the Department of Indian Affairs and Northern Development (DIAND), Jake Epp, wrote a hasty letter to the commissioner of the Yukon, establishing in the territory a system of "responsible government" composed of elected officials. Erik Nielsen, Yukon's long-standing member of Parliament, had substantial sway as a minister in Clark's cabinet—he pushed hard for the YTG to be included in the land claims negotiations, and finally succeeded. Now the YTG had full political support in Ottawa, and land claims negotiations became a three-party process.[19]

History was made in February 1980 when YNB and YANSI amalgamated with CYI to form one organization representing all Yukon First Nations. It was a bold move ending the separation of Status and non-Status people created by the Indian Act. Amalgamation wasn't a simple matter of joining two organizations to negotiate a land claim. It represented breaking the influence of a powerful institution—the federal bureaucracy at DIAND administering the Indian Act—and required tremendous sustained efforts by CYI leaders. For Yukon First Nations people, the amalgamation was a homecoming, reconnecting families and communities separated for generations by government policies and restrictions. For Elders, it meant the return of their grandchildren.[20]

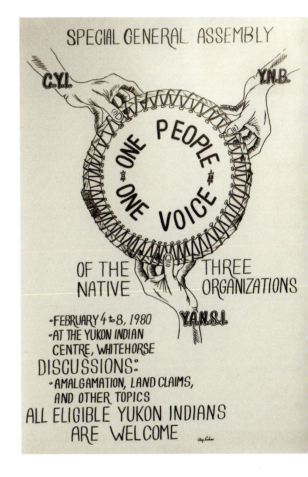

above Kaska artist Ray Ladue created this poster for the 1980 Special General Assembly, which approved the historic agreement to amalgamate the Council for Yukon Indians, the Yukon Native Brotherhood and the Yukon Association of Non-Status Indians.

The 1984 Agreement-in-Principle

From the mid-1970s, intensive land claims negotiations continued between CYI, Canada and the Yukon government. Many Kwanlin Dün First Nation (KDFN) leaders and members, including Elijah Smith, Mike Smith, Judy Gingell and Bill Webber, devoted years to this process. The negotiations were often difficult, hampered by the federal insistence on "extinguishment" of Aboriginal rights—meaning that any agreement would require the First Nations to relinquish any and all rights that weren't covered by the agreement. At the same time, some important CYI positions were opposed by the YTG. Despite the challenges, in January 1984 the parties reached a tentative Agreement-in-Principle (AIP).

The next step was for the CYI to ratify the AIP at a General Assembly. The federal government wanted a decision by the end of the year. The timing was a concern for CYI, with another federal election due that year or the next. Except for a nine-month Conservative government in 1979–1980, the Liberal Party had been in power for the duration of negotiations. The CYI negotiating team was very apprehensive that a change in governing party in Ottawa could not just undo the gains made in the AIP, but also threaten the entire land claims process, perhaps requiring another new start for the negotiations. An election was called for September 1984, and the Progressive Conservatives won in a landslide victory over the Liberals—but that was not what stopped the AIP ratification.

First Nations delegates met in Whitehorse in October 1984 for the CYI General Assembly. The Kwanlin Dün First Nation, formerly the Whitehorse Indian Band, voted to accept the AIP on condition that two clauses were added: that only certain Indigenous rights would be extinguished, and that financial compensation would be directed to individual First Nations and not to a central organization. Chief Johnnie Smith wanted assurance that recognition of self-government in the Canadian Constitution would be extended to Yukon First Nations, especially given that a one-government structure for the Yukon, with the YTG in the lead, had been accepted in the AIP.

Other delegates, however, adamantly opposed key provisions of the AIP. The primary concern was the extinguishment of Indigenous rights. Federal policy at the time did not support the entrenchment of Indigenous rights. In the end, after much passionate debate, the AIP was rejected in a close vote by the General Assembly delegates. It was a major and shocking setback for those who had devoted so many years to negotiating the AIP. Some people worried that land claims were doomed forever. It was difficult to see a way forward from this point.

BUILDING INDEPENDENCE

Before 1973, economic development initiatives within the Whitehorse Indian Band (WIB) community were almost impossible. The discriminatory policies of banks and government granting programs prevented First Nations people from obtaining start-up funds, federal grants or bank loans. Since WIB members had no access to capital, white contractors were supplying all the basic community services such as water and wood delivery to homes in Lot 226.[21]

above Whitehorse Indian Band Community police constable trainees Lesley Smith (*left*) and Sally Jim, ca. 1979.

This changed in the mid-1970s, when the Yukon Native Brotherhood accessed federal funding for economic development projects, allowing for the purchase of a delivery truck for each First Nation community. This was the first economic development venture for many Yukon First Nations and a significant one, since everyone benefited directly as recipients and some as providers of essential community services. It was also a concrete example of economic development benefits supporting the economic independence goals of the land claims process. A few years later the YNB established the Yukon Indian Development Corporation to support more initiatives, which continues to this day.

The availability of federal grants helped WIB undertake many small economic ventures in the late 1970s. A parka-sewing centre opened in Kishwoot Hall, supplying parkas to the Yukon Indian Arts and Crafts Society retail outlet on Main Street and later to Yukon Native Products. It operated until 1982, when Yukon Native Products secured a larger production and retail centre on Fourth Avenue.[22]

The WIB was anxious to begin exercising its self-governing rights in service to the community. Safety was of great concern, as was the often ineffective response of the RCMP at the time. In 1979, WIB began its own policing program, which involved training its own constables and creating its own bylaws. Looking back, this might seem like a minor expression of

above Yukon Indian Women's Association members, including Bobby Smith (*far left*), protest at the cemetery on Two Mile Hill, now known as Àsì Khìą Tth'än K'è (*My Grandparents' Gravesite*), Whitehorse, ca. 1975. Other protesters include Kaushee Harris (*behind the group of women*), Albert Webber (*front centre*) and Jenny Jack (*far right*). The YIWA led community opposition to the Yukon government's promotion of First Nations burial grounds as tourist attractions.

fresh possibilities in comparison to later First Nation self-government initiatives, but at the time, WIB bylaws required approval from the Minister of Indian Affairs. Nevertheless, Yukon people took notice, and while some were excited by the opportunities for self-government, others were uncertain. The WIB Community Policing Program was a bold step and a concrete example of possibilities for a new future.[23]

Women Claim Their Place: Yukon Indian Women's Association

Community concerns and political interests led a group of Indigenous women from all over the territory to form the Yukon Indian Women's Association (YIWA) in 1974. The organization was active on numerous fronts. At the founding meeting, YIWA protested cheap imported copies of First Nations crafts, which undermined incomes for Indigenous women. They tackled the disrespectful designation of First Nations gravesites as tourist attractions, persuading the City of Whitehorse and Yukon government officials to remove the tourism sign at the Two Mile Hill cemetery in Whitehorse and similar signs at other First Nations gravesites around the Yukon.[24]

YIWA also took an active role in land claims. In 1975, President Adeline Webber and Vice-President Judy Gingell lobbied CYI to include YIWA in the negotiations. While they were unsuccessful, YIWA was involved in various land claims committees.

In 1980, YIWA joined the national fight against gender discrimination entrenched in the Indian Act. At the time, if First Nations women married non-Status or white men, they and their children automatically lost their Status and all the rights and privileges associated with it. First Nations men were not subject to this provision of the Indian Act. If they married non-Status or white women, those women gained Status and so did their children. YIWA representatives flew to Ottawa to demonstrate against this unfair policy and the violation of their Indigenous rights. It required major lobbying, but Parliament finally passed Bill C-31 in 1985, abolishing this section of the Indian Act. It took many more years for the First Nations women and children who had lost their Status to regain their benefits and rights.[25]

Many YIWA leaders were Whitehorse Indian Band members, including Judy Gingell and Ann Smith. YIWA involvement was formative training for their later political and leadership roles. In 1988, Ann Smith was elected as the first female chief of Kwanlin Dün First Nation. Judy Gingell served as the first female chair of the Council for Yukon Indians and later was the first Yukon First Nation person appointed as commissioner of the Yukon. YIWA continues today as the Yukon Aboriginal Women's Council.

Time for Celebrations and Hockey

After years devoted to building Yukon First Nations organizations and attending meetings, it was time for some fun. In September 1977, YNB and YANSI sponsored Yukon Indian Days at Airport Lake, a traditional gathering site where Northern and Southern Tutchone people from Hutchi, Lake Laberge, Marsh Lake, Carcross, Carmacks and Pelly came to trade. The three-day event drew First Nations people from the Yukon, British Columbia, Northwest Territories and Alaska. Events included stick gambling, tug-of-war, tea and bannock-making competitions. The highlight was a greased pole contest. Yukon Indian Days continued as an annual event until 1982.

The YNB and YANSI recreation departments organized the first Northern Native Hockey Tournament at Whitehorse in 1977. The first event drew only a few teams from First Nations communities, but the tournament rapidly grew each year and continues today under management of the Yukon First Nations Hockey Association as an annual celebratory highlight.[26]

Leaving the River: Relocation to McIntyre

During the 1970s, WIB leaders had focused much of their energy and efforts on CYI, the central organization fighting for land claims. Meanwhile, in the community, the lack of services and unhealthy living conditions that resulted from living on the swampy lowlands of Lot 226 had reached a crisis point. The debate about where Band members would relocate had been going on since 1970, and all proposed relocation sites had encountered numerous roadblocks. Many years were devoted to studying the move and site selection, with much effort lost to failed negotiations, political interference and logistical delays—all while the community endured unhealthy living conditions. It was time for the immediate concerns of the KDFN community to take precedence over land claims.

Finally, in 1984, the question of where to move was decided when several events converged. WIB had a budget to build six new houses, but no new location had been identified. Department of Indian Affairs funding

above Fans cheer on the Council for Yukon Indians Warriors at a hockey game in Whitehorse, ca. mid-1970s.

above A little relocation humour! A "cabin" for rent in the Old Village, ca. 1989.

policies required housing to be built on "trust" lands, but it was too early in the land claims process to allocate land ownership for WIB. A deadline attached to the funding further complicated the issue—time was running out on the unused housing budget.

At this time there was a vacant four hundred–site subdivision in McIntyre, with service infrastructure already in place. The site had been developed in the 1970s, in anticipation of a housing boom from the proposed Alaska Highway Pipeline project—but it was no longer needed after the project was dropped. The newly elected Yukon territorial government under NDP premier Tony Penikett and the new Yukon Regional Director of DIAND, Phil Fontaine, offered financial support for WIB relocation to the McIntyre subdivision.

The new location was not entirely supported by all Band members. In 1981, most had voted to relocate to Long Lake on the east side of the Yukon River. However, this site required the building of a costly new bridge across the Yukon River, which would delay the move for many years.

In the end, the move to McIntyre became a reality because it received support from all the key players—Chief and Band Council, City of Whitehorse, federal government, and particularly the YTG. In order to save the federal housing money from lapsing, the YTG immediately purchased the needed lots in McIntyre, allowing construction to begin. This was a departure from the stance of previous territorial governments, which maintained the federal government should assume all responsibility for First Nations programs. This kind of coordinated effort occurred because new political relationships and a cooperative spirit were forming at all levels to pave the way for the settlement of land claims.

WIB signed the final relocation agreement with the federal and territorial governments in 1986. By then WIB had established a new name and identity as Kwanlin Dün First Nation (KDFN). The original community plan identified eighty-three homes to be built—about twenty homes per year. Kwanlin Dün established the Tagish Kwan Corporation as its construction and business agency. The new corporation played a significant role in the development of McIntyre, providing carpentry training to Kwanlin Dün members along with management for housing projects.

All told, the relocation took twenty years, from 1969 to 1989. The move to McIntyre was not a simple process of relocating—KDFN had to build a new community away from the traditional lands occupied for many generations. Beyond the new buildings there were much-needed programs to foster wellness and deal with alcohol and drug issues, plus cultural events to nurture "community" in a new place. Once the community foundations were taking shape, KDFN could concentrate more on land claims negotiations again.

left Construction begins on homes for Kwanlin Dün in the new McIntyre subdivision, 1986.

right Kwanlin Dün Relocation Office at Kishwoot Hall in the Old Village, ca. 1987.

Four Years Old at the Old Village

BY JESS RYDER

Once upon a hot summer day, I was playing in a field of tall grass, taller than me at the time. The smell of fireweed and dried meat all around. At that age, I was worried about the bears but no one else was: there was a lot of dogs.

I was playing in a bare patch in the grass and got my hand caught in a clamping gopher trap, and I cried a while. No one heard, so I sat there watching the gophers play right in front of me for half the day until someone stumbled upon me that was wondering where I went. Turned out a lot of people were looking for me.[27]

Gopher Gopher

BY SWEENY SCURVEY

Gopher, gopher everywhere
You see them here and there
Every which way you go
There's one thing you should know
They are tasty, mmmm
When cooked in the right way
But first catch 'em
And eat 'em every day.[28]

above Mayor Don Branigan turns on the water at the first new home in McIntyre subdivision, with Kashgêk'—Chief Johnnie Smith (*far left*) and other leaders, ca. 1986.

right Elder Kàdùhikh—K'aƚgwach—K'odetéena—Kitty Smith at the opening of her new home in McIntyre subdivision, with her son Kashgêk'—Chief Johnnie Smith (*far right*) and Yukon Commissioner Doug Bell (*far left*), ca. 1986.

above KDFN members dance at a street party with Bob Charlie and his band to celebrate the opening of McIntyre subdivision, ca. 1987.

left The new KDFN administration building opened in 1989 in McIntyre subdivision. It was named Kashgêk' in honour of former Chief Johnnie Smith. In 2020 that building was demolished to make room for a larger one, to accommodate the requirements of the KDFN as a self-governing First Nation.

Tagayme—Renee Peters

George Peters

Kwakúghwät—Field Johnny

BY TINA WILLIAMS

"Shortyville," on the Yukon riverbank at Marsh Lake dam, was "Grandma's Place" when I was a child—a place I called home, where I felt loved and safe. My sanctuary. It was a small one-bedroom cabin.

Growing up with my grandparents was very special and made a huge impact on my life. From them I learned to support myself and my children. Grandma used to say, "It is good to have something to fall back on in case there is no work." My grandparents— Renee Peters, Field Johnny and George Peters—were always busy and worked a lot. My grandmother had two husbands who were both alive at the same time, and they all worked together to support each other and their whole family. My grandmother was originally given to my grandfather George Peters from Carmacks in a traditional marriage. They had one child, Tsäl Yénjáél—Jessie. My grandmother married my grandfather, Field Johnny, some years later. The story was that when the "white" people came, they [First Nations people] were told it was a "sin" to live together, so she had to choose one. She chose Grandpa Field. He lived at Grandma's house, while Grandpa George had a home in Carmacks.

From witnessing my grandparents' marriage, I learned that age does not matter when there is love and commitment. Grandma was eight years older than Grandpa Field and younger than Grandpa George. I learned that what matters is

working hard together, helping each other and loving each other. Their busyness was about survival and doing what they needed to thrive from one day to the next.

Both grandfathers supported our little family. My mom was an only child for all of her childhood. Both her dads doted on her. When Mom was an adult, Grandma and Grandpa Field adopted Dale and Donald. Mom was single after she separated from Tammy's dad, Harold. Dwayne, Ronnie, Tammy and I lived with her in a little two-bedroom house across from Jamieson's store in downtown Whitehorse. Grandpa George used to bring us meat, moose, rabbit and other game when he came to town.

When I was very young, Grandma Renee and Grandpa Field and my uncles lived in a canvas tent frame at the Marsh Lake dam. Inside the tent to the left there was a wood stove that was used for cooking in the winter and to heat the tent. To the right of the door was a small table for storage. At the back of the tent were bunk beds. My grandparents slept on the bottom and my uncles slept on the top. Under the bed there were boxes for storage, and behind the tent there was a little shack that stored belongings that did not fit in the tent. Outside of the tent frame there was also a firepit for cooking.

My grandparents did not own a television for most of my childhood. Most of our time as kids there was spent outside

facing top Swans return in spring to the upper Yukon River below Marsh Lake dam.

facing bottom Fall colours signal the arrival of hunting season.

exploring. Our boundary was from the river to the highway and not past Great-Grandmother Jessie's cabin. Grandma Renee and Grandpa Field could not read. I do not know if Grandpa George knew how to read. Grandma eventually learned to sign her name. Grandpa Field would wave away books. As a child I took this to say hands are for providing. Grandpa Field spoke more than Grandma, and he treated me with kindness all the time. Grandma talked to people in Northern Tutchone but did not speak much English. I asked her why she did not teach me her language. She said there was "no room for it anymore."

During the summer my grandparents were busy all the time. Grandma usually sat down outside because she was tanning hides or sewing. I would watch her, even though the smell was not great! She would not let me help until Grandpa told her to let me because I wanted to learn. She said, "What is she going to do with it?" So I did not completely learn to tan hides. She had one of those older wringer washing machines with the rollers. I was amazed that she would do her laundry and then wash a moosehide in it.

I followed Grandpa Field around while he worked at home or at camp. He had a garden behind the cabin. He would repair his snowshoes, clean his guns, pack water and chop wood. He spent time with his dogs and cooked meals for them every day. When he was not home he was out hunting with Uncle Dale and my brother Ronnie. I always wanted to go but was not allowed because I was a girl—with one exception: I could go across the river and up the mountain to help carry a moose home! I packed a heavy load and made sure not to slow anyone down. Grandma would usually bead

and sometimes check her gopher traps while waiting. We would have a meal prepared for them when they arrived home.

Grandpa Field did the hunting and gathering when I was smaller. Then later Uncle Dale helped him. It was so exciting when Grandpa was getting ready for a hunt! There was such a flurry of energy. Grandpa would be checking his dogs, his dog sled and their backpacks. Grandma would be repairing his pack and moccasins.

As a child, I did not hear my grandparents disagree about anything. They spoke to each other gently, supported each other and always helped each other. Grandma sewed Grandpa's clothing, and Grandpa brought home the hide for her to tan. They worked as a team. I knew my grandparents loved each other. I saw their glances, the slight touches, the smiles and the kind words. My world was safe and quiet when I was with them.

What did I learn from my grandparents about life, parenting, culture, identity and love? I saw how they treated other people with kindness and respect. I could tell when they did not like someone or something— by their silence. They were non-violent in their teachings—it would be a look of disapproval or a tone of voice, and because they spoke so gently with me, when their tone changed I paid attention!

In later years the Band built them a one-bedroom cabin and they moved there. They had no electricity and no running water. In the evenings, we used candles and oil lanterns for light in the winter. My grandparents took the bedroom and my uncles had beds in the main room. There was a wood stove in this cabin for cooking. Later on, electricity was installed and an electric stove was brought in. We used an outhouse and carried water. Back then my grandparents and family still drank alcohol. When I was a teen, the Band built my grandparents a two-bedroom rancher-style house. The new rancher-style house was right across the road from the cabin. Grandma lived in it almost until the time she passed.

In July, we would go camp with Grandma or with our Aunty Kitty Jonathan, to her fish camp at Carmacks. We learned to prepare salmon for drying in the smoke house. Later in the summer my grandparents would live at Fish Lake in a tent frame that had a wood stove for heating. At this camp, there was a lot of wild meat to eat. It was a feast, and Grandma cooked everything on the campfire.

My mother was born at Sheldon Lake near Ross River, Yukon, where both of my grandfathers and grandmother lived in their early years together. They lived by travelling between Ross River and Carmacks. Grandpa George used to travel the river to Whitehorse for food supplies in the spring. Mom told the story of when she was taken to residential school. She was seven years old and an RCMP officer showed up at the camp and she had to go with him. She was there until she ran away at the age of fifteen. She and a friend walked from Chooutla Residential School in Carcross to Whitehorse on the railway tracks. It was because of this legacy that going to Grandma's was such a relief, because Mom raised us the way she was raised at residential school—which was very strict.

I hold Grandma's place as a place of serenity in my mind and go there in meditation when this world becomes too challenging. The land at Grandma's house has changed beyond recognition. Gone are the trees and the clean landscape. Grandma passed in 2004 and Grandpa Field passed in 1999.[29]

Finding Our Way as Kwanlin Dün First Nation

The years following the move to McIntyre were a time of uncertainty for KDFN, a time to question and reconsider community goals. Long-time Chief Johnnie Smith had retired in 1988, and there were frequent changes in leadership over the next eleven years. KDFN leaders were often criticized and challenged by members during these years, sometimes requiring outside intervention to resolve divisive issues. KDFN land claims negotiations were underway but moving very slowly and centred around land site selection. Celebrating a KDFN land claims agreement was still a decade away.

Despite the uncertainty, KDFN continued building a strong community, offering social programs, cultural activities, educational opportunities and training. Many programs targeted youth development. The community policing program initiated with community bylaws in 1979 evolved into a Justice Department guided by a Justice Council, with crime prevention strategies, circle sentencing support and family court circles for those facing child protection proceedings. KDFN social programs and community supports were slowly replacing the services of outside government agencies.

top Demonstrators protest governance issues, ca. late 1980s.

above Children playing hand games while a counsellor drums at youth culture camp, ca. 1985. At far left are Elaine Shorty and Derrick Dennis Smarch.

Adàką (Light dawning over the mountains)

BUILDING A NEW YUKON:
GOODBYE TO THE INDIAN ACT

In 1985, negotiations resumed on a new land claims framework agreement. Sitting at the table with the federal government now were CYI chair Mike Smith and representatives of the newly elected Yukon NDP government. The NDP had run on a platform to settle claims as a first priority. Mike Smith, a lawyer and KDFN member, had been elected chair of CYI in 1984, on a platform to decentralize CYI and increase the flow of benefits from program funding to communities. In particular, he wanted to see more employment opportunities for communities and improved communication on land claims.

The new negotiation teams created a very different process, dropping the former adversarial style focused on winners and losers typical of court proceedings, and adopting a more cooperative approach based on openness and trust. All three negotiating parties took training in this style of negotiations. The process significantly improved by moving away from meetings of lawyers in Vancouver to enhanced community involvement, including municipal and other local groups who were sometimes invited as observers. As a result of better communication and transparency, greater trust began to develop between Yukon First Nations and other Yukon residents.

The 1989 Agreement-in-Principle

Looking back, the rejection of the 1984 Agreement-in-Principle, though very discouraging at the time, allowed an opportunity for all parties to regroup and rethink their positions. The goals established for the next phase of negotiations encompassed protection of Aboriginal rights and provisions for self-government, increased financial compensation and more land. The process was further helped along by a new federal land claims policy in 1987, which finally abandoned the demand for extinguishment of Aboriginal rights as a condition of any agreement.

Once again a pending federal election added urgency to the negotiations. All parties reached consensus on a new agreement the following year, though it was not officially signed until 1989, shortly after the November 1988 federal election. Signatories were CYI chair Mike Smith, Yukon premier Tony Penikett and federal DIAND minister Pierre Cadieux. The agreement required ratification by all fourteen Yukon First Nations. Ratifying the agreement fell to a new CYI chair when Mike Smith resigned in 1989. KDFN member Judy Gingell was elected as CYI chair and took up this responsibility. It was a challenge, but each Yukon First Nation ratified the Agreement-in-Principle.

facing Youth at a KDFN summer camp, Baha'i Jackson Lake property, 1985. **1.** Mary Ann Scurvey, **2.** Stacey Quock, **3.** Marie Dick, **4.** Bruce Wilson, **5.** Melissa O'Brien, **6.** Shawn Sam, **7.** Wynett Dawson, **8.** Billy Gill Scarff, **9.** Crystal Edzerza, **10.** Floyd Charlie, **11.** Tanya Andre, **12.** Rachel McLeod, **13.** Kenny Quock, **14.** Ray Shorty, **15.** Norma Shorty, **16.** Byron Kudowat, **17.** Hailey Bowe, **18.** Sandi Porter, **19.** Teresa Dawson, **20.** Kathleen Dawson, **21.** James Dawson, **22.** Trevor Dawson, **23.** T.J. Linville, **24.** Marie Charlie, **25.** Cheryl Dawson, **26.** Mark Porter, **27.** Derrick Dennis Smarch, **28.** Rae Mombourquette, **29.** Cheyanne Tizya, **30.** Pricilla Dawson, **31.** Terrance MacIntosh, **32.** Jacqui Shorty.

Akhwäda—Judy Gingell, Chair, Council for Yukon Indians, 1989–1995: We involved all the people of the Yukon. We had to make our case, we had to really let the government know that we are the full, first people in this territory. We gathered everyone from all the communities. Brought them in to Whitehorse, sat down, and we worked on the agreement document. We worked on every chapter of what's in those documents. There were lots of Elders who worked along with us. They were right with us, and many times they brought us back on track. Some of us younger ones, we did see things different and we were moving fast. It is one of the most beautiful resources we have as Aboriginal people, to have our Elders there, because they really know. You give them the time, they will tell you and it just helps you, guides you.

It's a total difference, like night and day, as to how things were back then and where we're at today. Our people are so empowered. We have authority, jurisdiction, we have responsibility. There is a lot of work in implementing those agreements, doesn't come easy. And the partnerships that you have to develop with the people that you live with, there's a lot.[30]

Tony Penikett, Yukon Premier, 1985–1992: This is the most important time in our history. We are building a new Yukon together—a marriage of the best traditions of both cultures.[31]

The 1993 Umbrella Final Agreement: A New Era for Yukon First Nations

From the Agreement-in-Principle of 1989 came the Umbrella Final Agreement (UFA) in 1993. The UFA provided the framework of provisions common to all Yukon First Nations for their individual land claims agreements and provided the option to address areas of unique interest to each Yukon First Nation. In addition, the Final Agreement for each First Nation would include a self-government agreement. In 1993, four Yukon First Nations signed their Final and Self-Government Agreements—Champagne and Aishihik First Nations, Teslin Tlingit Council, Vuntut Gwitchin First Nation and Na-Cho Nyak Dun First Nation.

Nearly 120 years of subjection to the Indian Act came to an end with the passage of the Yukon First Nations Land Claims Settlement Act:

> When a final agreement is given effect, the Indian Act ceases to apply in respect of any reserve, within the meaning of that Act, that is identified in the agreement as settlement land.[32]

With the signing of individual Yukon First Nation Final and Self-Government Agreements, it was clear that each First Nation would operate predominantly as an independent government. The authority that the Council for Yukon Indians once had as a central organization was greatly reduced. After the completion of the UFA, the CYI undertook community consultations on the future role of the organization, which resulted in significant restructuring and downsizing. CYI passed a new constitution to reflect the provisions of the Umbrella Final Agreement, choosing a new name to

above Council for Yukon Indians Chair Akhwäda—Judy Gingell celebrates the signing of the Umbrella Final Agreement while Na-Cho Nyak Dun Chief Robert Hager (*seated*) looks on, May 29, 1993. She is flanked by Yukon Government Leader John Ostashek (*left*) and Indian and Northern Affairs Canada Minister Tom Siddon.

above Elders and leaders from Kwanlin Dün First Nation and Ta'an Kwäch'än Council (TKC) signed an agreement to finalize the separation of the two First Nations in 1997. **1.** Sophie Smarch (KDFN), **2.** Alicia Vance (KDFN), **3.** Violet Storer (KDFN), **4.** Henry Broeren (TKC), **5.** Chief Joe Jack (KDFN), **6.** Hereditary Chief Glenn Grady (TKC), **7.** Irene Adamson (TKC), **8.** Irene Smith (KDFN), **9.** Kathleen Jones (TKC), **10.** Sharon Martin (Canada), **11.** Shari Borgford (Canada), **12.** Gail Anderson (TKC), **13.** Ruth Massie (TKC), **14.** Hazel Campen (TKC), **15.** Bruce Campbell (KDFN), **16.** Annie Burns (KDFN), **17.** Colleen Williams (KDFN), **18.** Frances Woolsey (TKC), **19.** Evalena Beisser (KDFN), **20.** Edythe Maloney (TKC), **21.** David Jennings, **22.** Glenn Sigurdson, **23.** Unidentified, **24.** Louie Smith (KDFN), **25.** Unidentified, **26.** John Suits (KDFN), **27.** Johnnie Smith (KDFN), **28.** Carl Rumsheidt, **29.** Liz Hanson, **30.** Gord Harvey, **31.** Unidentified, **32.** Donnie Burns, **33.** Daryn Leas, **34.** Anne King, **35.** Tom Uylett

facing Traditional territories were negotiated as part of the 1993 Umbrella Final Agreement, with some subsequent modifications. Historically, however, there was much overlap, sharing and collaborative use and occupancy among First Nations in what is now the Yukon.

reflect the identity of First Nations no longer governed by the Indian Act—the Council of Yukon First Nations (CYFN). Kwanlin Dün First Nation leaders were still critical of the centralizing nature of the organization and refused to sign the constitution, opting out of CYFN.

Ta'an Kwäch'än Council

In 1956, the Department of Indian Affairs arbitrarily amalgamated all the Status Indian people living in the Marsh Lake, Whitehorse and Lake Laberge region into the Whitehorse Indian Band. This upset Tàa'än Män (Lake Laberge) people for many years, as they valued their original identity. The Ta'an Kwäch'än Council (TKC) re-established itself as a distinct First Nation on February 14, 1987, to represent Lake Laberge families.

This decision led to complex negotiations over many years about which families would join each nation; overlapping land use; and the division of programs, funding and services. These discussions were still underway when TKC and KDFN each signed the UFA, as separate First Nations, in 1993. Some families have members belonging to TKC and other members belonging to KDFN. In the end, 11 percent of the people joined the Ta'an Kwäch'än Council, resulting in reductions of federal funding for KDFN by that amount. The families of the two nations met together for a formal signing ceremony at the conclusion of their negotiations on January 22, 1998, to ensure goodwill as they followed their individual pathways to the future.

The term "Kwäch'än," meaning "the people of," was chosen to identify the new First Nation as "the people of Tàa'än Män." The word "Dün" or "Dän" in the Kwanlin Dün First Nation name refers to any First Nation person regardless of origin, reflecting the group's very diverse makeup.

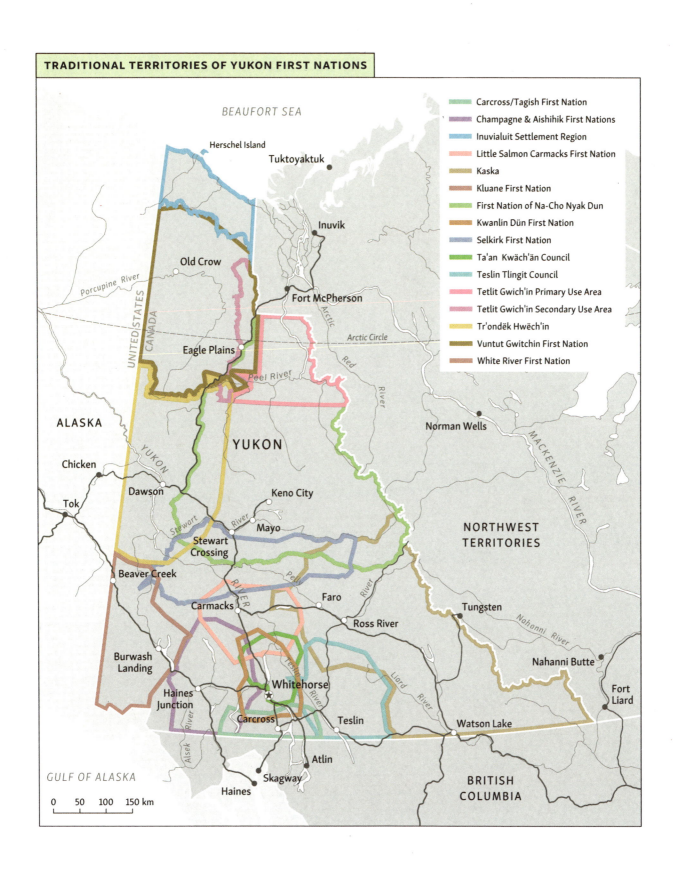

TRADITIONAL TERRITORIES OF YUKON FIRST NATIONS

Carcross/Tagish First Nation
Champagne & Aishihik First Nations
Inuvialuit Settlement Region
Little Salmon Carmacks First Nation
Kaska
Kluane First Nation
First Nation of Na-Cho Nyak Dun
Kwanlin Dün First Nation
Selkirk First Nation
Ta'an Kwäch'än Council
Teslin Tlingit Council
Tetlit Gwich'in Primary Use Area
Tetlit Gwich'in Secondary Use Area
Tr'ondëk Hwëch'in
Vuntut Gwitchin First Nation
White River First Nation

BEAUFORT SEA

Herschel Island

Tuktoyaktuk

Old Crow

Inuvik

Porcupine River

UNITED STATES
CANADA

Fort McPherson

Eagle Plains

Arctic Circle

Peel River

ALASKA

YUKON

Norman Wells

Chicken

Dawson

Keno City

Tok

Mayo

Stewart Crossing

Beaver Creek

Carmacks

Faro

Ross River

NORTHWEST TERRITORIES

Tungsten

Burwash Landing

Whitehorse

Nahanni Butte

Haines Junction

Carcross

Teslin

Watson Lake

Fort Liard

Atlin

GULF OF ALASKA

Skagway

BRITISH COLUMBIA

Haines

0   50   100   150 km

Getting Back on Track with Land Claims

The years between 1996 and 1998 were especially challenging for KDFN, as members began land claims enrollment and determining who would be beneficiaries of the land claims agreements. Some community members enrolled as KDFN beneficiaries, but some were beneficiaries of other First Nations. Some KDFN members questioned the relationship between citizenship and beneficiary status and who should hold political office. A group called the Coalition for Democracy challenged the authority of an elected Chief who was enrolled as a beneficiary in another First Nation. The dispute, including an impending lawsuit, caused serious disruption in all aspects of KDFN affairs, requiring the Department of Indian Affairs and Northern Development to intervene and mediate. Federal and territorial negotiators decided to suspend negotiations until these controversies were resolved.

The KDFN election on March 22, 1999, was an important turning point. Newly elected Chief Rick O'Brien made land claims his first priority and focused all possible resources on negotiations. This was an urgent necessity—the federal mandate for negotiating Yukon agreements ended on March 31, 2002. Chief O'Brien established a new negotiating team with Mike Smith as chief negotiator. Several KDFN citizen advisory groups formed to review specific aspects of the negotiations. The Land Claims Caucus, consisting of KDFN beneficiaries, provided overall guidance to the land claims department.

Relationships with the City of Whitehorse improved in 2000 when Ernie Bourassa was elected mayor with a more responsive council. The City was interested in an exchange of the Motorways riverfront property for development that promoted tourism and First Nations cultural events. Getting back to the river and renewing cultural traditions were also priorities for KDFN.

The negotiators decided to restart the KDFN land claims discussions by addressing three key issues: securing riverfront property (including the old Motorways property) for KDFN; waiving taxation on undeveloped KDFN lands within the city until the development of the properties; and providing economic opportunities in exchange for a reduced landmass for KDFN. These issues were fundamental to a successful KDFN land claim. Once negotiators agreed on these issues, KDFN secured a Memorandum of Understanding from the federal government to extend negotiations beyond the 2002 deadline.

As negotiations were moving forward, KDFN was also in a constant race to keep up with new development projects in the city. Staff were hired specifically to stay abreast of new projects, to remind the Whitehorse and Yukon governments of KDFN interests and to participate in project planning. At times this required the city to redesign plans that had been undertaken without consideration for KDFN interests. As the Kwanlin Dün newsletter noted in 2001, "KDFN is the first urban land claim to be negotiated in Canada, and there is no precedent to follow."[33]

Between 2002 and 2003, negotiators finalized various segments of the KDFN agreements. On March 12, 2004, Kwanlin Dün First Nation, the Government of the Yukon and the Government of Canada agreed to a comprehensive land claims settlement with many unique features. Like all Yukon First Nations land claims agreements, the KDFN Final Agreement included the UFA provisions, along with sections specific to aspects of KDFN history and current circumstances.

From March to November 2004, Bill Webber chaired a community review and ratification process. Voting on November 5 and 6, 2004, consisted of two ballots. Ballot One was specifically for members who were KDFN beneficiaries to vote on the Final Agreement and related financial agreements. Ballot Two was for all KDFN members to vote on the Self-Government Agreement, including the terms of the KDFN constitution and ownership of Lot 226. The turnout for Ballot One was 88.7 percent of eligible voters with a 61.2 percent yes vote. For Ballot Two, the turnout was 88.5 percent with a 59.7 percent yes vote.[34]

KDFN Final Agreements: We Are Building a New Government

There was a great deal to celebrate on February 19, 2005, as the community gathered at Yukon College to witness the signing of the KDFN Final and Self-Government Agreements. The KDFN agreements broke new ground, bridging multiple interests and competing land uses, all within the largest urban centre in the Yukon. In the years between 1973 and 2005, Whitehorse Indian Band/KDFN members contributed to the development of the community and helped to establish YNB, YANSI, CYI and YIWA, all of which brought Yukon First Nations together on land claims and to address issues of common concern to all Yukon First Nations people.

> **Shaakóoni— Mike Smith, Chief of KDFN, 2003–2011:** We were finally accepted as real, real owners of this land. You think back on that, that was like a turning of the page for us, and really critical, and really important, and, we hope, future generations would come back and think about that, because it was really important, and especially for the young people. They have to know, get some pride and realize that they can't come and take you away anymore.[35]

> **KDFN Constitution:** We acknowledge the many aboriginal people from other first nations who have enriched our lives.[36]

"We've been working the land claim for quite a while, many years now, and I think this land claim agreement, it's a pretty good agreement... I hope everybody vote for this land claim so it settles, we can have things going, have business going...they read it to me and I said that's the best agreement I've ever heard, so I hope everybody... come vote to get land claims settled." – *Johnnie Smith, former KDFN Chief*

Ługûn—Lugóon—Sophie Smarch, Elder: It would be nice if we could just turn the page back and go back to them days when things were so nice. We never recognize one another as just from Dawson, or she's from Haines, or she's from Juneau, or Carcross or Teslin or Atlin, or any place. We were all people. We were, we have so much respect for one another that we just live in harmony. We share stories. We give people in marriage. We share births. Babies. And if there should be a death, it was honoured and it was looked after, taken care of. Mainly, in our old, old, olden days, we cremate one another. Because we travel so much, to all different places, in the Yukon and in B.C., that we don't leave our deaths wherever they die, we take them back to where they belong. We take their ashes. Put them away, where they're from. That's why we used to believe in cremation. And I guess it stopped. I don't know when it stopped, but it stopped, because there's transportation and everything now that things are so different. The world has changed so much since our ancestors.[37]

Chief Mike Smith: We don't have such a thing as non-Status, or Metis. You're a Yukon First Nation, period. You know, we've delved into that, we don't have those issues anymore. So, really, really, really important, bringing back people.[38]

Land provisions consist of three classifications: Category A lands (with surface and sub-surface ownership) amount to 62 percent of the total KDFN land quantum; Category B lands (with surface ownership) are 37 percent of the total; and Fee Simple lands (lands previously owned privately) are 1 percent. Lands were selected as rural blocks, community lands and site-specific lands. The overall KDFN land quantum is 1,043 square kilometres.

Since Lot 226 had been set aside as Whitehorse Indian Reserve No. 8 in 1921, it required special consideration during the land claims negotiations. Parts of the reserve had been expropriated for other purposes by government through the years. KDFN won a lawsuit in the Federal Court of Canada in 2001, confirming rights to all of the original Lot 226 and paving the way for negotiations to determine compensation for lands affected, including the Takhini Trailer Court, Range Road and hydro rights-of-way.[39] Under the Final Agreement, Lot 226 was designated in 2005 as KDFN Category A Settlement Land.

Land claims gave KDFN opportunities to reclaim traditionally used and culturally significant sites along the Yukon River. Securing the old Motorways property on the waterfront provided a site large enough for a long-desired cultural centre. This project was already in the planning stages in 2000, with the Cultural Centre Working Group created to assist in the design, location and development of the centre. In 2002, KDFN received $200,000 as the first installment of $1.25 million from the Yukon government for construction. Canada provided $6 million for the project. These contributions were part of the KDFN land claims compensation.

Special management areas were established for a proposed Kusawa Park, bordering Kwanlin Dün First Nation, Champagne and Aishihik First Nations and Carcross/Tagish First Nation (CTFN) lands. A steering committee includes representatives from each First Nation to assist in park development. The Lewes-Marsh Habitat Protection area, between the Yukon River Bridge and M'Clintock River, was established with a steering committee of KDFN, CTFN and TKC representatives. The agreement formalized KDFN and YTG partnership in the Canyon City Historic Site to oversee archaeology and interpretation so that traditional Indigenous uses are not overwhelmed by Klondike gold rush stories.

The KDFN Self-Government Agreement includes provisions to support KDFN's self-governing powers in relation to jurisdictional overlap with the City of Whitehorse and the Marsh Lake Local Advisory Area. Along with the KDFN Self-Government Agreement, KDFN members ratified a new KDFN Constitution, with new governing principles and structure.

These were all remarkable achievements. The KDFN Final and Self-Government Agreements are a testament to KDFN perseverance in meeting multiple challenges and sustaining a united focus over decades of hard work. The agreements made it possible to reconnect to homelands on the river, renew traditional practices, build a strong government and create a new future.

Rick O'Brien, Chief of KDFN, 2000–2003; 2011–2014: It has been a long road, but the journey has been worth it.[40]

Andy Scott, Minister of Indian Affairs and Northern Development, 2004–2006: The proof is in the agreements . . . The relationship between Ottawa and the Kwanlin Dün First Nation was entirely new. It is now a government-to-government partnership.[41]

Chief Mike Smith: Kwanlin Dün's journey to settle our land claims has been longer than most. We are the Yukon's largest First Nation. We are a people of diverse cultures and backgrounds. We live in the most populated part of the Yukon, in an environment that is far removed from the one known to many of our ancestors. We have witnessed the best and worst aspects

above Chief Shaakóoni—Mike Smith (*centre*), Minister of Indian Affairs and Northern Development Andy Scott (*left*) and Yukon Premier Dennis Fentie hold aloft the signed KDFN Final and Self-Government Agreements, February 19, 2005.

of the history of Yukon settlement. We have experienced social upheaval, the loss of our homes and forced resettlement from our traditional lands and from the Yukon waterfront. We have witnessed extensive alienation of our lands without ever having surrendered our title to them. And we have struggled to govern our traditional lands from an urban centre where three other governments—federal, territorial and municipal—also occupy the seat of power.

I thank the people, the Elders who have waited long for today, and I thank the Kwanlin Dün children and youth who share with us their hopes and dreams. Kwanlin Dün First Nation people have made the choice to take responsibility for our future. We look forward at this time to pass on our legacy to future generations. We are marking a new beginning for our people in economic prosperity, cultural strength and our rights under the law, which will be accepted and respected by other governments.[42]

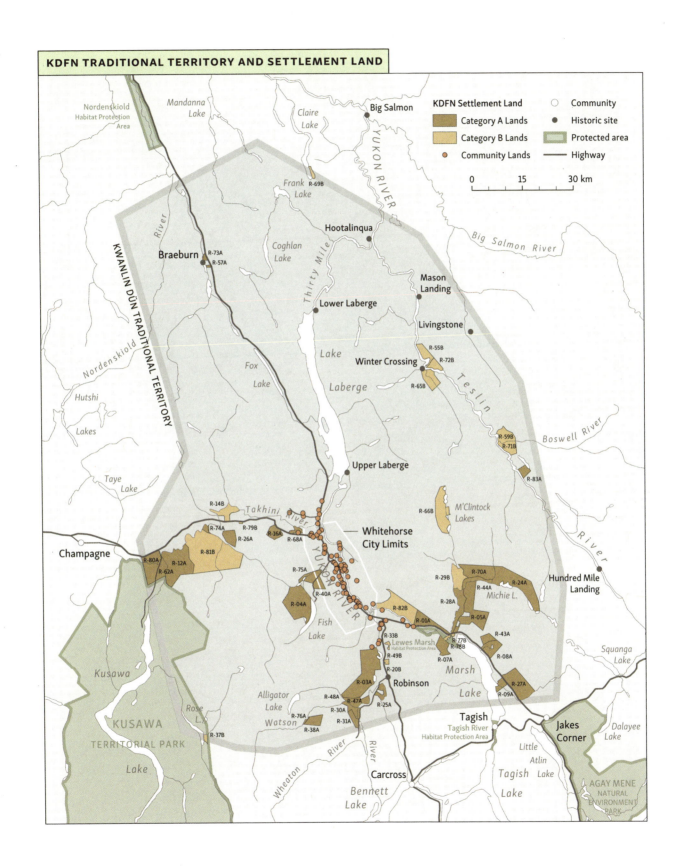

KDFN TRADITIONAL TERRITORY AND SETTLEMENT LAND

KDFN Settlement Land

- Category A Lands
- Category B Lands
- Community Lands ●

○ Community
● Historic site
Protected area
— Highway

0   15   30 km

Nordenskiold Habitat Protection Area

Mandanna Lake

Claire Lake

Big Salmon

YUKON RIVER

Frank Lake
R-69B

Big Salmon River

Hootalinqua

Coghlan Lake

Thirty Mile River

Braeburn
R-73A
R-57A

KWANLIN DÜN TRADITIONAL TERRITORY

Mason Landing

Lower Laberge

Livingstone

Nordenskiold River

Fox Lake

Lake

Laberge

Winter Crossing
R-55B
R-72B
R-65B

Teslin

Hutshi Lakes

Boswell River

R-59B
R-71B

Taye Lake

Upper Laberge

R-83A

R-14B *Takhini River*

R-66B

M'Clintock Lakes

River

R-74A R-79B
R-26A
R-16A R-68A

Whitehorse
City Limits

R-80A
R-81B
Champagne
R-12A
R-62A

R-75A

R-40A

R-29B R-70A
R-44A R-24A
R-28A
Michie L.

Hundred Mile Landing

R-04A

YUKON RIVER

R-82B
R-01A
R-05A
R-43A

Fish Lake

R-33B
R-49B
R-20B

Lewes Marsh Habitat Protection Area

R-77B
R-78B
R-07A

R-08A

Squanga Lake

Kusawa Lake

Rose L.

Alligator Lake

R-03A
R-48A R-47A
R-30A
R-76A R-25A
R-38A R-31A
Watson

Robinson

Marsh Lake

R-09A
R-27A

KUSAWA
TERRITORIAL PARK

R-37B

Wheaton River

River

Tagish
Tagish River Habitat Protection Area

Jakes Corner

Dalayee Lake

Little Atlin Lake

Tagish Lake

Carcross

Bennett Lake

AGAY MENE
NATURAL
ENVIRONMENT
PARK

KWANLIN DÜN FIRST NATION SIGNATORIES:

6. Edith Baker

7. Jessie Dawson

8. Leonard Gordon Sr.

9. Lesley Smith

10. Jason Shorty

11. Allan Taylor

12. Helen Holway

13. Victoria Fred

14. Charlie Burns

15. Elizabeth (Betty) Miller

16. Darwin O'Brien

17. Dianne Smith

18. Joey Lebarge

21. Chief Mike Smith

KWANLIN DÜN FIRST NATION ELDERS AND BENEFICIARIES:

25. Ann Smith

26. Annie Burns

27. Pat Joe

28. John Suits

ST NATION

Cermony

2005

N TERRITORY

FEDERAL AND TERRITORIAL REPRESENTATIVES:

5. Larry Bagnell, Yukon Member of Parliament

20. Andy Scott, Minister of Department of Indian Affairs and Northern Development

22. Dennis Fentie, Premier of Yukon

OTHER PARTICIPANTS AT THE CEREMONY:

1. Carl Rumsheidt (Yukon Government); **2.** Dermot Flynn (YG); **3.** Amos Westropp (Canada); **4.** Brian McGuigan (Canada); **19.** Elsie Wain (Canada); **23.** Lynn Black (YG); **24.** Greg Kent (YG).

above The signing ceremony for the KDFN Final Agreement and Self-Governing Agreement took place at Yukon College in Whitehorse on February 19, 2005.

FAMILY FOCUS

Sùkusen—Barbara Fred

Sùkusen—Barbara Fred of the Crow Clan was born at the old Whitehorse Hospital in 1946. Her mother was Tut.Latseen—Susie Fred of the Marsh Lake Tagish Kwan people. Barbara's maternal aunt was Lily Kane, and her maternal uncle was Frank Slim. Susie was first married to Casey Fred from Angoon, Alaska, and they had nine children, including Barbara's sister Annie Smith.

Barbara's father was Ralph LaVallée, a French Canadian from Rimouski, Quebec, who had trapped around Hudson's Bay before coming to the Yukon with the Canadian army after World War II. Susie and Ralph met at the Shipyards, where she was working in a cafe. They had three children together and lived in a small two-room home at the Shipyards during the summers when he worked in town. In winter the

family moved to a wall tent in the bush, where Ralph cut wood to sell as heating fuel for homes in Whitehorse. Their winter wood camps were at Tagish, Annie Lake and the Carcross area.

Barbara remembers their wall tent home as cozy, warm and fragrant with spruce boughs on the floor. They had a kitchen table and chairs, with mosquito netting as room dividers. Susie and the kids set snares for rabbits, squirrels and other small game. Susie prepared the skins and sewed moccasins and other clothing to sell in town. When the Whitehorse dam was under construction in the mid-1950s, Ralph worked as an explosives expert and at other jobs in town.

At five years old, Barbara was taken in the back of a big stake truck to the Whitehorse Indian Baptist Mission School. It was a difficult life away from her parents, living with hundreds of other kids in crowded dorms. Her mother came to visit when she could on weekends, but often her parents were out in the bush, trapping and woodcutting.

In summer the family would be reunited at Robinson, where they had a cabin. Barbara has fond memories of going hunting with her parents, her sister Annie, Annie's husband, Johnnie Smith, their children, and the Burns, Craft and Shackoon families, who were all relatives. By day the children walked the trails with the adults as they hunted for moose. They learned to set up camp and to identify berries and other

foods safe to eat. They also learned respect for the land and that they had the responsibility to look after one another. In the evenings, Johnnie and his sister, May Hume, would sing songs and tell the old stories while the women sewed by the crackling fire in the wood stove.

When she was fifteen, Barbara left home and went to Edmonton, where she worked as a nanny for a few years, married and had three children—Victoria, Joseph and Clifton. In 1971, she returned to Whitehorse as a single mom and quickly set to work finding employment. She enrolled in a business management course at the Yukon Vocational School and did her practicum at the Department of Indian Affairs. That was the beginning of her thirty-two-year career with the federal government. She moved up progressively through senior positions, working on housing programs and in finance. After training as a social worker, she became Director of Education, managing post-secondary education funding for First Nations students. She was seconded to CYFN for a few years, then came back to the federal land claims office. During these years, Barbara had four more children—Kerry, Jason and twins Mike and Michelle.

Barbara has always taken an active interest in her community, contributing to many projects, boards and committees. In the early 1970s she participated in Whitehorse Indian Band committees that were organizing for land claims. Later, at DIAND, she worked on the Relocation Project when people moved from the Old Village to McIntyre. As a federal employee she attended land claims negotiating sessions leading up to the 1993 Umbrella Final Agreement. She sat on the Lotteries Commission as a volunteer, then on the Yukon College Board of Governors for several years and as chair from 2002 to 2003. With her education background she worked with other KDFN members to establish the House of Learning, where citizens could pursue training and education close to home.

In retirement, Barbara enjoys spending time with her children and grandchildren, camping and being out on the land. The stories and experiences of her early years still inspire her. She is concerned about the rapid pace of change in our world today and cautions people to remember to take care of our environment for the sake of all future generations.[43]

6

Shakaat

A hunting and gathering trip in late summer   *2006–2020*

Our community is strong and resilient, and with the increasing health and well-being of our citizens, Kwanlin Dün First Nation is a growing force for good in our Traditional Territory.

DORIS BILL, CHIEF OF KDFN, 2014–PRESENT[1]

SHAKAAT IS THE TIME in late summer when we travel together on the land—hunting, gathering and preserving the resources that will sustain us through the coming year. We celebrate the bounty of our land and give thanks for all that it offers, taking only what we need so that future generations will have a good life here as well. The signing of our Kwanlin Dün Final and Self-Government Agreements in 2005 launched a new era of hope for our people, when we began to harvest the benefits of long years and hard work in land claims negotiations.

We regained control of our cultural heritage, along with significant lands and resources in our Traditional Territory and important economic benefits. We now determine policies for language revitalization, health, justice and the education of our children, enabling us to plan for our future generations. In the *Kwanlin Dän Ch'a* newsletter after the signing ceremony, Chief Mike Smith wrote about the collective vision of the Kwanlin Dün First Nation that is embodied in the agreements: "We will maintain and strengthen our identity through our relationship with the land, culture and language, all of which will make life better for ourselves and our children."[2] As the past fifteen years have shown, that vision is being realized in many ways within our community and our government. We are reclaiming our hope, sense of pride,

community and connection to the land. KDFN has prospered.

We continue to work hard in many ways to develop our First Nation based on our fundamental values of family, land and culture. Our *Kwanlin Dän Ch'a* newsletter reflects our lively and busy community: carrots sprouting in the community garden, children playing at a new neighbourhood playground, youth pushing kick sleds along our trails. Citizens are invited to community cleanups and to help build a community safety plan. Our pride in our First Nation is visible in the artwork on display in bus shelters and on banners, and in the Southern Tutchone language on street signs. We have returned to the river with our magnificent Kwanlin Dün Cultural Centre, bringing our culture to the forefront of life in our city, welcoming neighbours and visitors from around the world. This has been a time of reaffirming and renewing the values and strengths we have held throughout our long history: the importance of children, family and community, of protecting the land and making a living.

Although much work remains to be done, with our strength and resilience the future of KDFN is bright. We are a strong, vibrant community evolving as the largest urban self-governing First Nation in Canada. Together we uphold our identity, languages, traditions, lands, waters and resources for the benefit of all children, today and tomorrow.

Kashgêk'—Johnnie Smith

Kashgêk'—Johnnie Smith was born near the Marsh Lake dam in 1922. His parents were Kàdùhikh—K'ałgwach—K'odetéena—Kitty Smith and Kanéł—Billy Smith. His father was a nephew of Keish—Skookum Jim. As a child, Johnnie travelled with his family throughout the southern Yukon, hunting, trapping and gold mining. He learned the traditional languages, drumming and stories of his parents and continued to share those with audiences to the end of his life. He served as Chief of the Kwanlin Dün First Nation for three terms between 1969 and 1988. He died in 2010.[2]

SALMON BOY

Told by **Kashgêk'—Johnnie Smith**[3]

This is another story about the fish . . . The salmon they come up, okay? And them people, they hook fish just like Klukshu [a salmon fish camp in southwest Yukon], I guess . . . So this boy . . ., what I said, you have to respect the game, eh? You have to respect fish, too. So [this boy,] he tell him mom, "I'm hungry."

His mom take out dry fish, but the fish was kinda mouldy like, eh? And he cooked that by campfire, he say, "Here son." He give it to him.

Then his son get mad. He call down that fish or something, "Mouldy fish!" Or something. "You want to feed me the mouldy thing!" He mad, that kid, just a little kid.

But he tried to snare that seagull. [Of] course, nice-looking bird, ah, you know eat eggs all the time. He finally snare 'em. He got small toggle, I guess . . . That kid get excited, he run. He want to catch a seagull before he get too deep a place. But still he go a little farther and he got a deep place and that kid gone, drowned.

But he wasn't drowned. When he went in the deep water, he fell in the boat 'cause he call down the fish, eh? So when the fish went back to ocean, went back to ocean, I think. And he went down to ocean too, that boy. He fell in a boat that took him down to ocean.

Then he stay round there. He hungry. He can't eat nothing—nothing to eat. But a lotta eggs all over . . . all kinds of eggs. And this one, he try to eat that to find out, don't know he eat that. They told 'em, the one kid, he got friend there. He starvin', and he said, "You want to eat?" He said, "I'll tell you what to do."

"Go ahead," he said.

"Back there they play around. Kids are play around. They play, play place, eh? And that kid runnin' ahead of you, you push him," he said. "Then he gonna turn to fish," he said. "Then you cook it. But make sure the bone," he said, "don't let it fall in that . . . where ya stick to poke 'em in the ground? Don't let it fall in there. Make sure you put the bone together after you finish eat it."

And that fish he eat, the same kid when he come home, the same kid, the one he eat, he run around down there? . . .

So he, that boy been there I don't know how many years. He must have been down there . . . well, fish come back about four years, ah. After they been to ocean, four years they come back, I guess, ah.

Well when that kid gone, he's got copper around his neck, copper? They got copper something to put just to, you know, they fix for him fancy, I guess.

So he finally came back. He could see his mom and dad. His mom work by cut fish on the beach, ah? Was it. Same place, he's looking at 'em. And eh, another fish warn him. He said, "You want to go back? If you want to go back," he said, "you got to get hooked." And him, he try come there as soon as that hook, big hook come out on top of him, he duck away. He's scared, you know, he's gonna be hurt. You know, he could see that hook.

"No. I don't want to go back."

People [the fish] goin' back now. That boat's all goin' back now.[4] "Okay," he said, "you don't go back now, you're goin' back no more." He said, "When that hook go on top of you," he said, "you jump back into the boat."

So when that hook go on top of him, he make up his mind. That hook come on top of him. Just the time that hook, he jump back. And he got hooked out. Oh, worst then, I guess. He could see his mom, could see his dad. He got hooked out. And the worst thing was, I guess, was they take a knife, he could see the knife, of course, he was person. But the cutter, he cut right here.—Keech, keech, keech—in the throat, you know, they cut the head off?

And that copper, I don't know how wide it is, but it was there. And that's where that knife hit. I guess that's the will of the fish, I guess. Otherwise, he could cut different place, ah. And here, that fish was last fish. He come out lottsa time. Yeah. Last fish he come there, his momma sees. He gets this fish, is nice-lookin' fish to eat. That's his son. But the rest of the fish go back, they all die off, you know. And that's where he got hooked.

So he, when he start cut his throat, he cut that copper—keech, keech— so he . . . What's the matter thing, he can't cut off. So he open up, he look at it. "It's copper! What the copper doing in fish, around the neck?"

So "Okay," he tell his husband. "Come here. Look at this," he said. He opened this. "You see copper here?" And his husband say, "Yeah, copper there, how come?" "Well, do you remember our son got copper around his neck?" He hear 'em talk about him, but he can't talk, eh? "Oh, that's right!" he said.

So in old Indian way, they know that's what happen, I think. So what they do, they take 'em . . . they take that fish way back to bush. They bring feathers and everything. They put him inside feathers. And his dad lay down there—fast. Stay there, stay there. I don't know how long he stay there with no eat, nothing, his dad. He stay there, finally he move around. He look—that's his son, big man. Copper here, it turned to people. Come back to be people again.

And he's the one tell story about fish story. Fish been war too, they been war, that's why you can see it in the jawbone, and a few little things around the head. They got knife. They got axe, you know, all kinds of spear in their head. That the story about the fish, they been fightin' war long time ago. And that's the boy tell story about that when he come back. And that's how he designed, coast Indian designed all that boat, designed from that boy—he come back to alive again, to be man again, to be a fish . . . how a fish they got boat. Look, that's how he made it.

They got certain place to go to. When they're gonna go from ocean. "We're gonna go there," they said. They got certain town, eh, certain place what creek to go. They got name for it. They got name for slough and stuff like that where the fish spawn. That's why they can't go up past any farther.

Like Klukshu, you go down a slough there, you see them swim around there. When they finish spawn, they go there far as they go, they can't go up to the lake, from there on to the lake they swim up the river, go to the lake. As far as they go there, that's where they die and that's where they turn back from, eh—back to ocean.

And that's how they find out by that boy how the fish live and how they got boats and stuff—how they build it, everything. That's how the fancy boat the Indians got along B.C. coast, they make big boat. And that's what it is.

That's far as the end of that story.

above Kwanlin Dün Cultural Centre opened on June 21, 2012.

KWANLIN DAŃ GHÀÌCH'E (KNOWING WHO WE ARE): BACK TO THE RIVER

Dawn Waugh, Citizen: It's the family connection that's important, and it's important to keep that going. That's what this place means to me. It's lots of family connection . . . and that's what I want to carry on for the kids, right? To keep that family connection. It's good—it's a good feeling, it's a good place. It brings good energy.[5]

Teagyn Vallevand, Youth: We have such a strong connection with the river, just as Kwanlin Dün people. I mean, if you look at our name, it's "people of the water, flowing through canyon," like, right there, it just tells you that we have such a strong connection to that river.[6]

Through its long history, Kwanlin Dün First Nation developed a unique identity as an urban First Nation with a diverse mix of people from different places and backgrounds. In the years since our agreements were signed, through building a government; healing from the impacts of colonization; following pathways to education, employment and empowerment; securing financial resources; and holding up both old and new generations, KDFN has shown its identity to be a strong, resilient and vibrant First Nation rooted in our values, beliefs and traditions passed down through

top Kwanlin Dün and other First Nations people drum and dance in a procession, along with many community well-wishers, beside Chu Nįį Kwan (Yukon River) on their way to the grand opening of the Kwanlin Dün Cultural Centre, June 21, 2012.

above Áyenjiátà—Louie Smith accepts a Council of the Federation Literacy Award while his tutor and friend Ted Ackerman (*centre*) looks on, September 2019.

generations. It is who we have always been and who we continue to be—we walk in two worlds, a modern First Nation proud of our history and culture. With the tools and opportunities provided by our agreements, we are reaffirming and revitalizing our nation and our place in the Yukon.

The land of our Traditional Territory has been our home for millennia. We have always been stewards of this land. Back in 1973, when the delegation of Yukon First Nations first presented the principles for negotiating a land claim to the federal government in Ottawa, our leaders realized that an agreement was essential to protect our identity, rooted in the land. The Final Agreement has accomplished this reaffirmation of our rights and our connection with the land, which continues to sustain our values and provide the foundation of identity for our young people.

Central to the final agreement was Kwanlin Dün coming back to the river from which we had been displaced, with land and resources to build a cultural centre. When first envisioned, the centre was not only a place to re-establish our cultural connection to the river, but also to tell our stories and to teach others about our history and our ways. The Kwanlin Dün Cultural Centre highlights our identity and our resilience through time.

We celebrated the completion of the centre with a wonderful gala and cultural night, full of laughter and pride. The public grand opening was held on National Aboriginal Day, June 21, 2012. Drummers led a procession from the site of the old Kwanlin Dün community, on the flats of what is now Rotary Park, along the river to the Cultural Centre. Hundreds of people celebrated with song, dance, storytelling, food and fun. The Chief and Council

described the occasion as "a wonderful opportunity to exercise our traditional role of hosting people from different cultures and communities on the riverbanks. It was also a spectacular celebration of years of hard work by our negotiators, Elders, staff and leaders to give life to the vision we had of regaining our place by the river and in the City of Whitehorse."[7]

Our Wolf and Crow moiety crests welcome people to the centre. The main meeting room follows the Longhouse design of the Tagish Kwan people, recognized in our Constitution as the original people within our Traditional Territory. Outside, the sacred fire circle provides a place for the community to share celebrations and pay respect in times of loss. The Yukon River flows swiftly past along the clay cliffs—as it has always done. The canoe house holds our large painted dugout canoe, ready to take us back on the river. The sacred healing space is open to all. An Elders' room hosts gatherings and teaching sessions. Small meeting rooms provide space for arts, business events and special projects. The exhibit spaces showcase our history and culture. Following our traditions, we welcome all to gather at the centre—it represents who we are as a strong and resilient people.

The first summer it was open, over five thousand visitors from all over the world came to our centre. In the years since, it has become an important gathering place. Thirteen thousand visitors attended the Adäka Cultural Festival in 2012, and each year thousands of people enjoy the art, song, dance and food of our Yukon Indigenous peoples. KDFN members and Whitehorse residents came together there to listen to the final report of the Truth and Reconciliation Commission in 2015. Two thousand people walked alongside the moccasin vamps during the Walking with Our Sisters commemoration of missing and murdered Indigenous women. We host many nations in cultural and government gatherings in our centre. Anyone who spends time there feels the power of our culture back in its place on the Yukon River.

left Members of the Kwanlin Daghalhaan K'e group dance at the opening of the Kwanlin Dün Cultural Centre, June 21, 2012.

right Dakhká Khwáan Dancers perform at Kwanlin Dün Cultural Centre grand opening, 2012.

above In 2017, Nàkwät'à Kù (Potlatch House), located in the McIntyre subdivision, was expanded and upgraded to accommodate increasing use and improve the safety and functionality of the community space.

Our identity comes to life at community events such as our Culture Night in the Cultural Centre in 2012, and at the 2015 Celebrating Who We Are gala honouring ten years of self-government. Such events deepen our sense of community and our values of caring and sharing. We also individually honour and respect our citizens as their efforts strengthen all of us. We have held ceremonies on the renaming of the Dusk'a Head Start Family Learning Centre to honour Dusk'a—Emma Burns. We celebrated the election of our new Council in 2011 at a swearing-in ceremony in front of the community. We honour with pride all our graduates. Many of our citizens have achieved awards and recognition for their work, including Gary Bailie, Judy Gingell, Jessie Dawson, Rachael Dawson, Louie Smith and Darlene Scurvey, to name just a few.

We also honour our losses, when we draw on the strength of our spirituality, our traditional ceremonies and our support for each other. Many sacred fires have been held at the Kwanlin Dün Cultural Centre and at Nàkwät'à Kù (Potlatch House) for the passing of our Elders and leaders, to mourn tragic deaths in our community and to support those who have shared their stories.

We draw strength from knowing who we are, and continue to welcome others and share the traditions of our homelands. In the summer of 2013, we hosted the Assembly of First Nations General Assembly. It was fitting that the Assembly started with a procession of past and current leaders in recognition of the fortieth anniversary of "Together Today for Our Children Tomorrow," the twentieth anniversary of the signing of the Umbrella Final Agreement, and the unique accomplishment in Canada of the Yukon having eleven self-governing First Nations. We have welcomed many people from our local city and around the world to gatherings at the Cultural Centre, where Indigenous and non-Indigenous have come together in the spirit of reconciliation, sharing and learning.

Beyond our own community, KDFN is becoming a force for good as we take a leadership role with others who are looking to us to share our experience. We have contributed to the lives of people in the city with our work on homelessness and mental wellness. The Cultural Centre has become our new home on the river and a beautiful place for sharing our stories with visitors from around the world.

Klighee—Sait u—Emma Joanne Shorty, Elder: For First Nations people, living by the water is very spiritual because it gives us a lot. If I'm feeling down, I go to the water and I sit down for a while

and collect all my thoughts. I pray near the water. This is what really draws us to the water. We are part of the water. We get our food from the water. We quench our thirst from the water. We are born into the world from the water. We receive our life by water.[8]

Cassis Lindsay, Youth: The river is life, right? The river is everything you need to survive, so I understand that that's what Kwanlin Dün did, right? They stuck by the river, and as the settlers came they got moved away, but now they're coming back to reclaim their heritage.[9]

Emily McDougall, Youth: When I travel the river, I look at some of the same scenery that my grandfather [Frank Slim] would have looked at when he was navigating the river. And I only do it in a canoe. He had to do it in a huge boat, so I feel just amazed at how he did it. It's very humbling, it's just amazing to think that our family has that kind of history and heritage along the river.[10]

Katelyn Dawson, Youth: That's my family, and it's amazing to have those roots, honestly. Like, just the tradition and the culture—you know, they're survivors and . . . it's inspiring, you know, it's inspired me . . . A lot has changed, but, you know, they still live on, in me, in my family . . . My people were right down there [at the river], you know, they were all brought up down there, and I've heard a lot of stories from my mom and dad and, you know, it's a really important part of their upbringing . . . It's traditional land . . . That's where our roots are, so it's really important . . . It's like we reunite with that land and come back . . . It feels really good, it's powerful. You feel it.[11]

top People gather around the sacred fire during the Adäka Cultural Festival, 2019.

above People gather behind the Kwanlin Dün Cultural Centre to celebrate the arrival of the Healing Canoe, 2012.

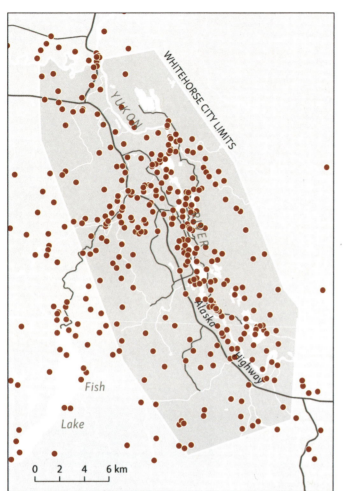

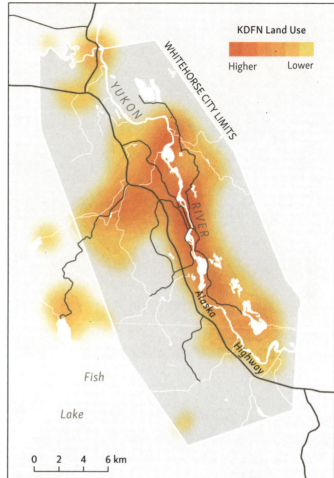

above, right These maps show locations for KDFN traditional and contemporary land uses in and around Whitehorse, including fish camps, berry picking, gravesites, old village sites, medicinal plants, tool making, trails and wood camps. The map on the left indicates points for particular activities and the map on the right is a "heat map" indicating the range of concentration of these activities. Both are based on information provided by KDFN beneficiaries and citizens during the development of the KDFN Community Lands Plan (2018 community meeting seen at right).

above The Kwanlin Dün Cultural Centre (*centre*) is an important part of Kwanlin Dün's return to the waterfront of Chu Nį̨į Kwan (Yukon River).

Sweeny Scurvey:

THE WATERFRONT

It was an ancient meeting place
Where the nations gathered
To celebrate and to trade
To gather fish and meat
Drums were heard on the waterfront
Where teams of men
Squatted on mats playing games
That held no language barriers
Further up the banks
The womenfolk congregated
While the children played games
Of their own devices
As the women cooked meals galore
The locations alternated
Above Miles Canyon
Or below the Whitehorse Rapids
On the east side of the river
Where Riverdale now sits
And where the hospital stands
And where Wickstrom Road ends

On the west side
Which was once Whiskey Flats
Now the site of the *Klondike*
And Rotary Peace Park
Where the YTG building
And the library sits peacefully
Where the White Pass Depot squats
And where the ships were docked
And flood lands of Sleepy Hollow
Yes the whole waterfront
Was the ideal meeting place
For many nations
May it continue as it did before
White Pass moved in and took over
The waterfront belongs to First Nations
Who willingly share it with other nations.[12]

Artistic expression has long been important for our people, as seen in carvings, weaving, clothing, regalia and other forms. Our artists' works, like those shown here, are included in Kwanlin Dün Cultural Centre displays, the MacBride Museum of Yukon History and the Yukon Permanent Art Collection.

Shakaat (A hunting and gathering trip in late summer)

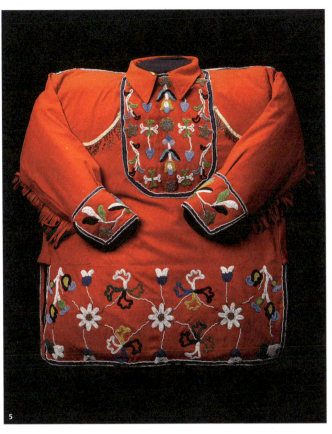

1. Edith Baker, beaded mukluks with pink flowers.

2. Evalena Beisser, embroidered stroud weskit, 1984.

3. Karen Bien, beaded Wolf headdress.

4. Nathan Dawson, painted paddles, ca. 2014.

5. John Joe's beaded dance shirt, ca. 1900.

6. Annie Smith (sewing) and Dianne Smith, Lesley Smith MacDiarmid and Irene Smith (beadwork), Judy Gingell's hide commissioner's dress, 1995.

7. Ann Smith, *Grandmother's Time*, merino wool robe with beaver fur trim, 1994.

8. Annie Smith, traditional doll (girl) with beads, beaver fur and cotton on home-tanned hide, 2004.

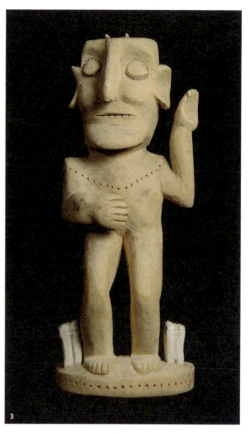

1. Justin Smith, *Between Two Worlds*, carved yellow cedar paddle, 2008.

2. *Between Two Worlds* (detail).

3. Kitty Smith, untitled sculpture (#1), poplar and ink, 1940.

4. Old Tlingit-style vest (back).

5. Wanda Webb, Old Tlingit-style beaded hide vest.

top left Elder Et'äts'inkhälme—Gertie Tom with her beaded mitts, ca. 2018.

top right Elder Ashiä—Ann Smith weaving a Raven's Tail robe on her loom, ca. 2005.

left Elders Violet George (*left*), Margaret Blake (*top*) and Dianne Smith (*right*) work on sewing projects with young Natalie Moen at Degay Zhra (Swan Month) Elders Day Camp, Jackson Lake, 2017.

FAMILY FOCUS

Joanne Luger

Joanne Luger never imagined she would become a dentist or a respected artist. Growing up in Whitehorse, her family was poor and she was always getting into trouble—she was even kicked out of high school. Now she's the director of a busy public dental clinic in Bismarck, North Dakota. Local galleries feature her drawings, paintings and pottery. "I'm not one of those people who grew up with professional people in my family to pave the way," she reflects. "The journey was not a nice clean one. But I look at my journey and I think, if you have the drive, anybody can do just about anything."

Joanne says she was lucky because she stumbled upon a rare opportunity. In 1979, when she was only eighteen, she signed up for the Dental Therapy Program—a fully subsidized three-year course in the Northwest Territories to learn basic dental services to serve remote communities. She worked two years, travelling across the North as a dental therapist. Then another life-changing opportunity presented itself. The University of Manitoba offered her a spot in its School of Dentistry. "I only got to where I am now because I happened to be in the right place at the right time, there was funding available and I was willing to work," says Joanne.

Joanne says the cultural values and skills she learned from her family also paved the way. She remembers when she was a child how her Aunty Gertie Tom, and her mother, Elizabeth Wilson, taught her to sew moccasins. "If there was even one thing wrong, they would cut it all off and tell you to sew it again and again and again and again," she says. "That's just instilled in my head. I'm not going to quit. I'm going to just keep going no matter what. Those are old traditional values. You gotta hunt, doesn't matter what the weather is, you have to eat. You get up and do it or you die. That's my aunty and my momma."

Growing up doing traditional arts with her family—like sewing, beading and hide tanning—also taught Joanne incredible hand-eye coordination that enabled her to excel in dentistry and fine arts. "It has definitely helped me with my fine motor control," she says. "I give my granny and my aunty and my mother credit for that because I am very, very detail-oriented."

While at dentistry school, she met someone from the Sioux Nation of North Dakota. She moved to Bismarck, and together they had two daughters while she completed her dentistry program at the local state college. In 2004, she opened Bridging the Gap, a public health dentistry clinic that offers full services to anyone who walks through the door—mostly Medicaid or low-income clients who pay on a sliding scale. "Dentistry is so unbelievably expensive," says Joanne. "I feel I am doing this because of how I grew up and the people that I grew up with. Those values are deeply integrated in me. Services should be available to everybody, not just the wealthy. I can't be in a private office because I can't ask people for money. It's just not who I am, it's not part of my system. I'll do it for free if I have to. And that's because I'm from the Kwanlin Dün First Nation."

The hardest thing for Joanne is being away from her family in the Yukon. "It was always my intention to come back but there was no work for me." She built a life for herself away from home, always yearning to return to the Yukon while her roots grew deeper every day in North Dakota. "I grew up in a really tight community with tight family relationships, and it was very difficult for me to leave that, but I had no choice." She has travelled home for visits every summer since she moved away in 1979, usually with her two daughters—now young adults. "Those visits are important for my own personal development, my own spiritual development. I'm still a Yukoner no matter how long I've been gone."

Those annual visits have also given her a lens through which she could observe the steady growth and development of her First Nation. "It is phenomenal the changes I've seen. There's a huge push towards reviving cultural activities: dancing, storytelling, language. I remember going to potlatches when I was a little girl and there were only a handful of people who even knew how to dance. Most of them were Elders." She remembers hearing Northern Tutchone spoken by family members and wishing she knew what they were saying, what they were laughing about. "Recently, I was at the airport in Whitehorse and there were two teenage girls speaking Inuktitut, and they were chattering away having a conversation. It just brought tears to my eyes that these young people were so proud of their language. It's happening now in the Yukon and I just love, love, love it."

As Joanne nears retirement, she's making plans to spend more time in the Yukon so

she can participate in and give back to the community. "I'd like to see Kwanlin Dün First Nation achieve independence, being a sovereign nation with control over their health care. I would love to be involved with that, to help set something up for people in the community. Dentistry is very, very expensive. Crown work is not accessible to many people."

For this level of independence in health care, Joanne believes we need more highly trained KDFN citizens with absolutely no financial barriers to pursuing higher education, plus real opportunities to return and work in the community. "If there was a system whereby people wanted to pursue higher education—doctors, lawyers, dentists, physiotherapists—there should be absolutely nothing to block them. There should be a system in place to ensure that."

She reflects on her own life and how a lucky chance set her on her path. "If it were not for those opportunities that presented themselves along my journey, I would never be where I am now." Joanne wants to share her story with youth and hopefully inspire them. "How wonderful to be able to tell our children there are opportunities in the world that are available to you. You don't have to be really smart. You don't. Because I'm not really smart. You just have to want something bad enough and work hard enough for it. I just work hard."[13]

top Youth clean lake trout during one of several wellness events held at the Jackson Lake Healing Camp, 2011.

above Màn Kų, a dwelling used in pre-contact times, built by youth at Jackson Lake Healing Camp, 2017.

HEALING OURSELVES TOGETHER WITH DADZE NASAT—OUR STRONG HEART

Chief Mike Smith: We are all survivors. We have endured for many years. As First Nations people throughout the world, we have endured pain for over five hundred years of European colonization ... We want to put this hurt behind us ... As we heal our spirit, we will again be strong. Thankfully, we have come a long way.[14]

Judy Gingell, Elder: Residential school played a huge role in our people's lives ... [We] need to somehow gain back that independence and sense of community we had prior to residential schools. We need to instill pride in our culture once again. The good news is that I believe that it is starting to come back.[15]

U'yenets'echia—Sean Smith, Councillor, 2014–2020: Our steps, as people and as a community, as families grow and learn ... we do carry that pain, that anger and, you know, some of us are farther along our healing journey, but it's built [on] resilience within the people of Kwanlin Dün, to be strong and to push beyond where they're at in their lives, and to seek out things like education, wellness, healing, cultural knowledge, cultural awareness. These are all tools for empowering our people, and that's something that we want to hold close and pull together.[16]

Unidentified counsellor, Jackson Lake Healing Camp: The land heals. Everything is moving, alive and healing. It knows what we need.[17]

People of KDFN have endured much suffering over many generations, but citizens draw strength from their families, from deep cultural roots and from special places. With strength and courage we are finding paths to healing. KDFN has organized key events where people can share their stories, gain knowledge and tools, and support each other on personal healing journeys.

In 2009, KDFN held a cleansing ceremony after the demolition of the old Yukon Hall residential school building in Riverdale. To commemorate the demolition, KDFN hosted several hundred residential school survivors and family members from across the Yukon and northern British Columbia for a three-day healing gathering and celebration potlatch. People paid

tribute to survivors, who courageously told their stories. They spoke of the intergenerational effects of residential schools. They also spoke of survival and resilience. By telling their stories and healing their spirit, they hoped to help others find their own path to healing. Elders Annie Smith and Irene Smith named the event Uyid Ynji Tl'aku—I let it go now.

In 2008, Councillor Ann Smith described Jackson Lake, a natural setting not far from town, as a healing location connecting Kwanlin Dün directly with the land. She recalled Elders telling her: "If our people have a hard time in this modern world, they must go back to the land."[18] Through a program called Caring for the Circle Within, Kwanlin Dün set up land-based healing camps in 2010 at Jackson Lake. At these camps, men, women and youth participate in programs based on contemporary and traditional healing approaches. Participants address the spiritual, mental, emotional and physical needs stemming from the effects of residential schools and related issues. The two pilot camps have grown into programs with long-term funding that serve as models for other First Nations. Coming back to the land at Jackson Lake is part of our healing journey as Kwanlin Dün, for our families and for our Nation.

In 2011, KDFN jointly hosted the national Truth and Reconciliation Commission hearings in Whitehorse with Ta'an Kwäch'än Council and the Council of Yukon First Nations. It was an opportunity for residential school survivors to tell their stories and for those in the broader Whitehorse

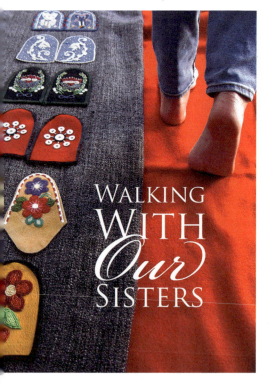

WALKING WITH Our SISTERS

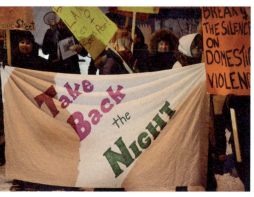

top left and right Poster and display of moccasin vamps created for Walking With Our Sisters, a touring art installation to commemorate Missing and Murdered Indigenous Women of Canada, 2015.

above Kwanlin Dün and community members march in Take Back the Night, an international event and non-profit organization with the mission of ending sexual, relationship and domestic violence in all forms.

community to gain awareness of our country's residential school history. Three generations of Kwanlin Dün people were affected by the residential school system.

The Kwanlin Dün Cultural Centre hosted the first public hearings of the National Inquiry into Missing and Murdered Indigenous Women and Girls in 2017. Two years earlier, in April 2015, the Łu Zil Män room held the Walking with Our Sisters commemorative installation. The installation, which is made up of nearly two thousand moccasin vamps, or tops, was on a six-year national tour to draw attention to the loss of our women and girls, and the inadequate investigations into their disappearances. The moccasin vamps, laid out in concentric circles, provided a walking meditation on the tragedy and injustice of what we have all lost.

The thirty-foot dugout canoe housed at the Kwanlin Dün Cultural Centre is another symbol of healing. In summer 2009, nineteen youth spent two months on an island in the Yukon River carving the canoe under the guidance of Tlingit master carver Wayne Price. They held healing circles and sweat lodges together and learned from visits with Elders. They launched the canoe and paddled it to Whitehorse, from where it has since carried many more Kwanlin Dün on new journeys.

Doris Bill, Chief of KDFN, 2014–present: As a proud and vibrant Yukon First Nation, we treasure our collective values of wisdom, respect, humility, sharing, harmony, beauty, strength and spirituality. We must continue to root ourselves in the values, beliefs

above Paddlers in the dugout canoe *Spirit of Awakening*, created by the Sundog Carvers under the guidance of master carver Wayne Price (*far right*), arrive at the Whitehorse waterfront, 2009.

and traditions preserved and passed down through countless generations of our people. While some Kwanlin Dün citizens continue to suffer and struggle with the multi-generational impact of colonization, we must fight hard to help them restore a sense of hope and optimism for a better and stronger future for themselves and their loved ones. We must also continue to support our youth and young adults in achieving the dreams they set for themselves, and support our Elders in preserving and passing on our stories, languages, history and teachings.[19]

FAMILY FOCUS

Charles Chief

....

Charles Chief is a positive force in the Kwanlin Dün community. He's devoted, hard-working and caring—as a councillor in government, a construction and safety leader, and a loving father and grandfather. He stands out for having overcome obstacles and for making good decisions in life.

Born in 1962, Charles lived with his siblings and parents in a tiny one-room house by the water's edge, where the Yukon Legislature building is now. When he was around ten years old, they moved into a small log cabin purchased from the Indian agent at the Old Village. When he was sixteen, his family moved to the new McIntyre subdivision, into a house that awed them with multiple rooms and conveniences.

Charles grew up with parents who suffered the abuses of residential school and were alcoholics, but he has happy memories of a free and happy childhood exploring the riverside with his friends. Growing up, Charles made a few big decisions: he chose not to drink and instead pursued higher education and training—leading to rewarding employment and the ability to provide a stable, supportive upbringing for his children.

Charles' mother was Nina Chief, of Kaska descent, born at Hot Lake near Dease Lake, B.C. His father, Johnnie Tom Tom, was from Snag, Yukon, near Beaver Creek. They met in residential school, and although Johnnie was not Charles' biological father, he raised him as though he were. "Not many people know that," says Charles.

"They always assume Johnnie was my dad." He passed away when Charles was only sixteen because "he drank so much alcohol he just died." Despite his heavy drinking, Johnnie had a positive influence on Charles. "Johnnie treated me really good. He treated everyone really good. He had a really good heart," he recalls. "That's where I probably picked it up."

Both parents held down steady jobs, Johnnie as a track maintenance worker for the White Pass & Yukon Railway, his mom in various service jobs. The family always had food, clothes and wood for the stove. They were loving parents and never abusive—but they were always drinking. "How do you raise children like that?" Charles asks. "They were so heavy into alcohol, they just raised you. I found out later what it was all about and I was so disappointed. Everybody figured out it was because of residential school. Nobody talked about it back then." His mother has always been hard of hearing in one ear, and she told him she used to get hit a lot in that place and that's how she got deaf.

Living in Whitehorse away from their original homes, the family left behind many of their traditions and family ties. "I didn't know what First Nation I was. The older people knew but they never really talked about who's who." Although much was lost, Charles says some things are never taken away. "My mom lost her identity and I didn't know much about my culture. I hate to say it, but I lost it. It's there now. I still go back to the land and I can't get enough of it. I know how to go about it, but it wasn't taught at home.

"After my dad passed on, I wanted to get to know who my family was on my mother's side, so I ventured down to Kaska country, where I met my Grandpa Charlie Chief. Grandpa taught me so much about our land, the animals and nature at its best. At a young age, he taught me how to respect the land and that everything in and around it has a life and a purpose. Back then, I watched him hunt, trap and build his trapline. Grandpa Charlie knew every inch of his trapline. He lived a simple life. Grandpa said, 'This is my backyard,' as he showed me a valley with moose, 'take only what you need.' I am sure lucky to have known him, as he taught me the life on the land and now I have taken those teachings to my children and grandchildren."

The kids who lived along the river enjoyed a free childhood, playing, fishing and exploring. "The railroad track was there and we would play around that. Every time we saw a train, it would whistle. I remember the sound of the trains rumbling by all the time," recalls Charles. "We used to play where the ships were. We used to play tag. We used to sleep on the ships. Hang out there. We didn't do drugs, we didn't drink. We just played. I jumped from the top floor to the second floor. Nobody else could do that. We were all pretty athletic."

Charles has many positive memories of the Old Village. "Everybody was good. We enjoyed it down there. It was fun," he says. "I remember walking in big rubber boots around the whole village because there was so much water there in the spring." He enjoyed free rein as an older child. "We were so mature when we were kids, so independent. Just 'See you later Mom and Dad,' and we'd eat, change our clothes and take off again. Mom probably did worry about me a lot. Every mother does. She probably just knew I could handle it out there."

The kids fished on the riverbanks. "We'd catch grayling. We'd see salmon but we couldn't catch those. If you talked to the old-timers, they would tell you where they were catching the salmon. Everybody has a secret place," says Charles. "We'd go down there, catch grayling, hang out with the Dawsons, the Jacksons, the Smarches, the Smiths. Those were the main big families down there. We'd bring the fish back to my parents and they'd cut it up and fry it."

The Yukon River was a powerful force, and his parents always warned Charles to stay away from the swift current. "It was a dangerous river," he says. "One time, my mom went down to the river to get a pail of water and she was pregnant. She was big. I followed her. She slipped right off the edge and grabbed some branches. She was just hanging on. I was just looking at her. She screamed at me, 'Go get your dad!' Dad grabbed a hose and threw it down. She grabbed it and he pulled her in. She would have died."

There were a lot of negative experiences in the Old Village. "Booze and fights. The booze was the worst," says Charles. "It just wasn't a good scene. I thought it was normal. I started drinking when I was a teenager. I drank every now and then with my friends who were living down there. We had nothing else to do. We drank because our parents drank. They showed us how to drink. One day I just stopped. I knew it wasn't right." When he was sixteen, around the time his father Johnnie died, Charles started to think about drinking. "I didn't understand about death until my dad died.

work," says Charles. "I could provide right through. I helped build the Island Highway and did gas lines around the Island." When they moved back to Whitehorse, Charles' skills and experience were in high demand. He worked for Pelly Construction at various mine sites and for the Kwanlin-owned construction company. Then he spent ten years in Kaska country in northern B.C., working on the pipelines, and later worked in Saskatchewan and Manitoba. Charles missed home, so he came back to work for Kwanlin Dün's Canyon City Construction, repairing houses in the McIntyre subdivision. "Today I drive around this community and see all the work I did!"

Charles was the driving force behind Kwanlin Dün receiving the Certificate of Recognition (COR) workplace safety certification, the first Canadian First Nation to do so. In 2017, he was elected to Council, starting on a new path of learning: "When I first started in leadership, there was so much going on, one thing after another," he says. "I had a hard time learning. I'm still learning."

And that's his biggest piece of advice to young people in the community: "Just go to school. Stay out of the wrong crowd, don't drink, get educated, stay busy, stay active. It's hard to do when you think about it. For sure, alcohol and drugs are the worst enemies up here."

He says alcohol and drugs are a problem because of the intergenerational legacy of residential schools, but insists things are really starting to change. "A lot of people I talk to say, 'My parents went through residential. All they did was drink,' and they get stuck in it, too," he says. "But my generation is changing. I know that for a fact. My siblings, my children—we're not drinking. We're doing our best to survive."[20]

When he left, it was devastating on our family. Today I think about all my friends that have passed on, so many of them. Alcohol and drugs. Still going on today after how many years?"

At age twenty, Charles married Nancy Norby. They had two kids and lived in the McIntyre subdivision. "When my kids were born, that's when I really realized it," he says. "I don't want to raise my kids with alcohol. I want to be a part of their life, show them the way in life, never drink around them. Now, my daughter doesn't ever want to drink. I said, 'Yeah, don't do it, man.'"

Charles and Nancy moved to Vancouver Island so that she could go to nursing school. Charles earned a certificate as a heavy-equipment operator at Malaspina University-College in Nanaimo and immediately found steady employment while Nancy finished school. "There was so much

Our Rich First Nation Culture

DR. UKJESE VAN KAMPEN

When I walk downtown, and especially along the waterfront, I see many Aboriginal people hanging around doing what appears to be nothing. Some of these people were my schoolmates. I wonder—do they see themselves as having a rich culture? I say this because I often hear in media, government and other reports that Yukon First Nations have a "rich" culture. I have to ask: Where is the "rich" part for these people?

I note that we as a people have lost much of our culture. Our language is almost gone. Most of us no longer practise our spirituality to its full extent. Although there are exceptions, we no longer live off the land as we once did. So how have we responded to these drastic changes? Maybe the lifestyle of the people depicted in my photographs is to a certain extent a normal reaction to having their culture torn away from them. Their lifestyle in some respects is more traditional than the modern 9–5 wage economy. How so?

In the past we lived as hunter-gatherers with some traits that would now seem lazy and indeed were responsible for some people thinking of us as lazy. For example, when white people first started joining us in the winter wilderness for hunts or other purposes, they saw us erect a simple shelter, gather firewood and settle in for the night. The white person would state that the shelter was too simple and a better one had to be built. Their conclusion: the Indians must be lazy and simple.

What they did not understand is that our winter clothing was so superior that people could curl up in a snow bank, get a good night's

facing KDFN Councillor Charles Chief with his mother, Nina, near the site of their former home on the Whitehorse waterfront, 2020.

above *Left to right*: Greg Dawson, Cecelia Taylor, Keith Mintuk and Kim Johnnie. The portraits of KDFN citizens on this page and the following two pages are from the photo exhibition *Our Rich First Nation Culture*, by Dr. Ukjese van Kampen, which was displayed at the Yukon Arts Centre in 2015. Greg Dawson, Nora MacIntosh, and Adrian Ellis have since passed away.

left and right Nora MacIntosh (*left*) and Adrian Ellis (*right*), from *Our Rich First Nation Culture* by Dr. Ukjese van Kampen, 2015.

sleep and next morning brush off the snow and continue their journey. You cannot do that even with today's high-tech winter clothing. We "wore" our house, and the brush shelter was more of a convenience than a necessity. The white man in his factory-made clothing needed a more elaborate shelter to prevent him from freezing to death.

This brings us to the concept of work in our original lifeways. Work was done as the need arose—this often meant many days of walking and intense efforts during a hunt and afterwards preserving our food. We followed our food sources like caribou and fish on our seasonal rounds. We would never stay in one place for the full year. However—if there was no work to do, just relax! Relaxation was a big part of our culture. Next was the importance of gatherings, from potlatches to more informal get-togethers. They were a meaningful, fun part of our society and highlights of our year.

Although there are many negative reasons why people end up "on the streets," one aspect is that a true necessity to work is absent in present-day society where food is readily available. I feel that the people portrayed in these pictures reflect aspects of our traditional culture. With their free time they gather in public places, often along the waterfront, just like in the old days. They walk from place to place, or move from community to community. Before land claims we were all Yukon Indians. Today, we are more divided into separate First Nations. These people reflect a time when there were no white borders or First Nations boundaries. People were very mobile and intermarried throughout the region. We used to identify ourselves not as a First Nation member but as belonging to a particular clan coming from a particular area. Following that tradition, the people in these photographs are Wolf or Crow Clan, and I think of them as the Waterfront People.

Northern Tutchone Elder Emma Ina Shorty had a phrase for them: "Dän hʉ tthän do ádäw," meaning "People wander around, walking around anywhere." She always talked to them and kindly helped them according to our tradition of sharing.[21] Although problematic and sometimes tragic, their lives have many "rich" aspects in light of how they reflect some of our traditional ways.[22]

Connecting with Our Culture and Elders

Tut.Latseen—Victoria Fred, Citizen: I am thankful to be able to raise my daughter to not be afraid of who she is but to embrace her culture, to embrace her identity. That is her strength and that will give her the best ability to be a good person.[23]

Sean Smith: Focus on bringing back our culture, focusing on areas of that. Singing, dancing, making art, various other aspects to traditional lifestyles that were practised, not too long ago . . . Having that knowledge brings me to an understanding . . . to help develop things like the Cultural Centre here, because it's our house. It's our house to use as a means to teach culture, to express culture, to allow First Nation people here, in the Yukon, to be themselves, so they can take off whatever they're hiding and become themselves here, and practise traditions such as singing and dancing, with an open mind and an open heart. And having that, having that all together, is a means for people to heal, inside, because there's been lots done in our past, right? And it's important that we . . . take steps to really reaffirm who we really are as people, and to connect with that, and to connect with our history, and to practise our traditions . . . The whole meaning behind re-establishing our place along the waterfront, it carries a lot of significance, because, you know, it's our identity, it's who we are. Like, we're part of that river. We're part of the salmon, we're part of the fish, we're part of all the life that flows out to the ocean.[24]

above Karen Dawson, from *Our Rich First Nation Culture*, by Dr. Ukjese van Kampen, 2015.

above Elders Effie Campbell (*left*) and Annie Smith cut moose meat, with Phil Gatensby of Carcross/ Tagish First Nation in the background, at Jackson Lake camp, ca. 2000.

KDFN cultural revitalization is underway in many programs. Elders continue to carry and pass on our stories, languages, history and teachings. Elders share their knowledge when engaging in many aspects of our community. They form the Elders Council within KDFN government. They teach traditional skills at our Jackson Lake healing camps. They participate on many of the management committees established under the Final Agreement and in community consultations. Their knowledge is critical in projects like ice patch research, Chinook salmon studies, genealogy, health practices and much more.

The community works to support its Elders, who enjoy outings and events through the Elders' day program and a day camp at Jackson Lake. One of the earliest projects following signing of the Final Agreement was the construction of new Elders' homes in McIntyre. As Linda Huebschwerlen, an Elders' health worker, observes, "Our Elders thrive when involved in traditional cultural activities such as berry and medicine picking, setting rabbit and gopher snares, language lessons, singing and drumming, and telling stories. And they are crucial to sharing their skills with the community."[25]

Kwanlin Daghalhaan K'e (Amongst our relations) is a group of Kwanlin Dün dancers that was created for the opening of the Cultural Centre. Councillor Sean Smith, a key organizer of the group, said that the group "includes people from all over, because that's really what Kwanlin Dün is made of."[26] Kwanlin Daghalhaan K'e continues to grow in size and importance, as Smith explains:

We wanted a lot of people involved because it's really very touching to come back to this place, to reclaim this place, to be re-established along the waterfront, as one of the neighbours... within the City of Whitehorse. I know a lot has changed since the late 1800s, since this place was first colonized, but we've really come a long way, and... having a dance group is very, very empowering for our nation, and for our kids, too, because it's connecting the people with the history, and their culture and traditions. And it makes us very proud.[27]

In the McIntyre subdivision and throughout the city of Whitehorse, Dän K'é—the Southern Tutchone language—is appearing on signs and in other public works. Yukon First Nations artwork is seen on Whitehorse street banners and bus shelters. In 2017, we produced a series of children's books in Southern Tutchone. Teaching our languages ensures they will be increasingly used by our community, in the Dusk'a Head Start Family Learning Centre, on signage and in everyday conversations.

The efforts to make Kwanlin Dün culture more visible and accessible are working. Aurora Hardy, a KDFN youth, says, "I didn't have a lot of cultural connections and connections of Elders and coming back here, and in the past few years I've definitely been gaining that back and gaining more knowledge and skills."[28]

above Elder Lorraine Allen reads her book *Nán'j Yè Uka Nànnta— Hide and Peek* to children from the Dusk'a Head Start Family Learning Centre, along with Prince William (*centre*) and Kate, Duchess of Cambridge (*in red*), while Erin Pauls drums, MacBride Museum, September 28, 2016. The book was written in Southern Tutchone and funded by the Prince's Charities Canada, Dusk'a, the Yukon Native Languages Centre and other organizations.

FAMILY FOCUS

Skaaydu.oo—June Jules

It hasn't been an easy road for June Jules. Looking at her now—leading a fulfilling and successful life in Mexico, where she works as a teacher and is raising a son—you wouldn't guess she had a turbulent upbringing. "I faced many childhood traumas. So I have to say: Be the change you want to see in the world. Get support, learn a new way and build a new pattern." June found this through travel and schooling—and never giving up.

Born in Teslin but later moving to Whitehorse, June fantasized about travelling abroad to learn about other cultures and to experience other realities. Her birth father originated from the Czech Republic, adding to this allure. "I would listen to people speak of distant places and different languages," says June. "My interest in knowing more about what existed outside the limits of my community was piqued."

At fifteen, she raised her own funds and, with the support of her foster care mother, went to Ushiku, Japan, on a student exchange. "I was hooked. I set foot into another reality. I was immersed in a fascinating, rich culture, learning a foreign language and surrounded with new things that were once only imagined. From that trip I knew my life would never be the same and that I would venture further."

After graduating from high school in Whitehorse, she went to Simon Fraser University for a short while before realizing she had the urge to travel. "I was longing to escape the trials and tribulations that life was throwing my way. I left Canada as a lost young woman and came back as a young woman with her head held a bit higher with insight and a thirst for more." After a few years travelling and working in Europe, with a stint as a nanny in Rome, June returned to Canada and completed a certificate in school-age childcare. She found fulfilling work in her field but was soon yearning for more education. She completed a bachelor of arts degree in geography and environment at Simon Fraser University. Then she travelled in Mexico until she found a spot that just "finally felt like I returned home." She currently lives in Puerto Vallarta with her partner and young son.

"This is the role that travel and education have played in my life," says June. "I travelled when I felt like the ground beneath my feet was no longer steady, and I sought higher education during times I felt a need to understand the experiences I held or when I couldn't explain the human suffering I witnessed." Her university degree was only possible due to scholarships and awards she received from the university—as well as financial assistance from Kwanlin Dün First Nation. "Also, I rooted myself within the Indigenous groups on campus, which provided the cultural and moral support I needed to succeed."

Her sense of connection to her First Nations heritage and the Kwanlin Dün community has been a guiding force in her life.

June's First Nation name is Skaaydu.oo, the same as her grandmother's. "I was always told that I was special because I was her namesake." Her birth mother, Rose Marie Jules, and stepfather, Raymond Craft—both Kwanlin Dün citizens—as well as her foster mother, encouraged her to connect to her culture and traditions.

June has many positive memories of her upbringing that form the core of her identity. "I think back to hunting with my family. I remember freezing so that I thought my toes would fall off. I would feel so miserable dragging moose limbs out of the bush, but the reward of moose guts and cracklings makes my mouth water. I miss hearing the stories by my Elders, such as Grandma, or those of Kitty Smith, spoken in their own Native tongue. I miss the drumming. It's been a long time. I remember spending long days picking soapberries and making Indian ice cream. I loved bannock and still do. I remember learning to bead for moccasins. I admired the beads and ran them through my fingers. I pricked my fingers endlessly, but when I sold my first pair of moccasin tongues, I sure was proud. I miss being out fishing along the river and learning to gut fish. I would slide the fresh roe right out into my mouth. I love the smell of smoked salmon and I miss the festive mood of families and friends that were gifted with a good catch and the sharing."

June has fond memories of her time living in the McIntyre subdivision: Band office Easter egg hunts with her brother, house bingos with her mom, or gobbling peanut butter cookies made by her neighbour Charlene Tizya. She also remembers the strength of the people. "The community bonded together for people in times of loss and successes, and the fights, the tri-umphs," June recalls. "But I remember that even through the thick, unspoken, dark moments, people tried their best to create a positive vibe."

Along the way, June developed her own resilience. Although she had many setbacks and periods of self-doubt, she always persevered. "When I was young, I spent many moments imagining what life would be like if I could just leave and start new somewhere and leave my problems behind." Her advice to others comes from those experiences: "I would say that the choices I made along the way were difficult. They broke hearts, including my own. However, my choices have led me to being the woman I am today. The most profound experiences were the moments that were the most difficult and the most rewarding, but if I could offer any insight, it would be to follow your heart, make mistakes, fail, and when you fall, brush yourself off, get up and try again. If something isn't working, find a different way to succeed. There will always be people in your life that will try to bring you down. Equally, if you are open to what the world has to offer and search out opportunities, then you will be met with the right tools.

"There is no harm in trying, because the experience in itself will make you stronger and wiser. Go for it, and don't give up when it gets really hard. And yes, life will be so difficult sometimes that you might think it's not worth it, but it is. Think through those little decisions carefully as they are the ones that carve the way for the bigger ones. I fully stand firm that you need an education, whether it be through experience, travel, a trade, a degree, a master's or what have you. The reality of the world we live in today is that people are commodities, so get an education. Also, learn your traditions. Your roots are what will hold you up when you feel unsteady.

"Appreciate your friends, your family and the institutions that are by your side, because they are building you up and supporting you. Don't be over-confident, because there is always more to learn and more that you will become. Do not let your past define your future, and do not let it get the best of you when you fall, because regardless of what has happened to any one person, it is a part of who you are. Don't forget where you come from, because sometimes we all need a place to go back to in order to become grounded or to come back and make things right that were

wrong. Hold your family close, because the farther away you are, the more you wish they were closer, and sometimes that will rip your heart out. No matter how much I desire to seek the unknown, the biggest part missing is my family, and I long for them every day."

For the time being, June is happy living a simple, sunny, rewarding life in Mexico, but she says the time may come soon when she's ready to spread her wings and fly again, but this time "with a family under my wing."[29]

BUILDING ON THE STRENGTH
OF OUR PEOPLE

Chief Mike Smith: We are ... directing our own lives as our grand-mothers and grandfathers had always done until others interfered in our way of life.[30]

In 2005, Chief Mike Smith spoke of the power of the Final and Self-Government Agreements to help us recover from injustices and tragedies in our past, and to help us rebuild the proud identity that had been taken from us. He also recognized that while the agreements are important tools, it is the strong foundations of our ancestors, leaders and community members that allow us to flourish. With courage, healing and support for one another, the journey to create our new forms of governance and programs moves forward.

In the early years following the signing of the agreements, KDFN focused on re-establishing traditional governance responsibilities that had been taken away or eroded. These values are set out in the KDFN Constitution, which was adopted in 2005 along with the agreements. The Constitution promotes unity within the First Nation and supports our values of land, culture, well-being, diversity, Elders, spirituality and rights.

An early sign that we are doing government differently, and that citizens could be more fully engaged in their own government, was the 2010 referendum, required under the new Constitution, on three policies related to land use, investment of funds from the agreement, and consultations required for changing the agreement. A very high number of citizens turned out to pass these policies. The community celebrated this early success in exercising self-government powers with a big cake at a community barbecue on National Aboriginal Day.

In 2011, Chief Rick O'Brien reflected on the work done and on the work yet to come:

> Just six years into self-government, we quickly realized just how much work still needs to be done internally. So this year we also began building the structure and policies we need to be a stronger and more effective government. Council and senior staff took governance and leadership training to build our skills and knowledge. We also worked on developing Council's own policies and processes to help make our work more efficient, along with mandating our senior staff to develop or update a number of policies so that our government has clear guidelines to facilitate our work.[31]

above Naming ceremony at Dusk'a Head Start Family Learning Centre which is named for Dusk'a—Emma Burns. *From left to right*, the adults are Selena Pye, Temira Vance, U'yenets'echia—Sean Smith and Darlene Scurvey.

Our self-governing First Nation has five branches: General Assembly of citizens, Council of Chief and Councillors, Elders' Council, Youth Council and Judicial Council. All citizens are entitled to attend a General Assembly every year, at which time any citizen can bring forward issues of concern to them and resolutions for consideration. Our Council consists of an elected Chief and six elected Councillors, plus two non-voting members: one Elder appointed by the Elders' Council and one member of the Youth Council appointed by that Council.

Kwanlin Dün Council provides executive direction for our government and approves policies, budgets and program initiatives. The Elders' Council gives advice to Council on issues related to KDFN and arranges programs and services for Elders. All KDFN Elders who are sixty years and older may participate in the Elders' Council. All KDFN citizens between fourteen and twenty may sit on the Youth Council, which provides advice to Council on issues affecting KDFN youth, assistance to youth in learning about their culture and traditions, and leadership on other matters of concern identified by the Youth Council.

In the years since it began exercising these powers, our government has enacted seventeen pieces of legislation governing our affairs on taxation, financial administration, governance, elections, investments

top KDFN Council at the swearing-in ceremony, Kwanlin Dün Cultural Centre, April 27, 2017. *Front row, left to right*: Chief Doris Bill, Councillor Jessie Dawson. *Back row, left to right*: Councillors William Carlick, Dennis Calbery, Ray Sydney, Howard MacIntosh, Sean Smith. *Missing*: Councillor Charles Chief.

above All KDFN citizens over age sixty are members of the Elders Council, which advises KDFN Council. Some members of the 2012 Elders Council are pictured here. *Seated, left to right*: Elsie Cletheroe, Emma Sam, Judith Kuster, Louie Smith, Judy Gingell, Elizabeth Wilson. *Standing, left to right*: Billie Giroux, Betty Miller, Albert Webber, Malcolm Dawson, Bernice Empy, Harold Dawson, Serge Sawrenko, Hazel Campen, Patrick Boss, Ann Smith, Joey Lebarge.

and justice. We prepared a strategic plan to envision our overall government direction for 2012–2015. This was then renewed for 2014–2018, and again for 2018–2022. The strategic plan maps out a clear path for our future. Each department takes on responsibilities for implementing the agreements in keeping with its values, priorities and capacity. The branches of government are continually strengthened through policy and training work to formalize and integrate their mandates. Departments offer staff training and professional development, as well as a mentorship program for citizens.

The KDFN government takes a holistic and integrated approach, making connections between land, health, education, housing, employment, economic development and justice. While these may seem like separate services, they are linked by a common purpose: serving the people. Departments integrate their work and services to address the whole person. Our government programs also reflect the importance of circles of support in our community. KDFN programs draw on traditional values to encourage

people of all ages and life stages to follow their own pathways to healing, education, employment and empowerment.

The Health Centre has developed into a full-service agency that supports the mental and physical well-being of people and brings cultural practices, such as traditional or spiritual elements, into health services. The whole family is invited to be part of the Healthy Babies, Healthy Generations program.

The Education Department oversees the Dusk'a Head Start Family Learning Centre, the House of Learning and many programs in partnership with Whitehorse schools and Yukon College, which means one department encompasses citizens' education needs from pre-school to adult learner. In 2010 we renamed our daycare the Family Learning Centre, in recognition that the first circle surrounding a child is the family. Parents and Elders are welcome to come along with their kids. Cultural teachings start young at the Dusk'a Head Start Family Learning Centre. Southern Tutchone is taught and spoken. All new families make a drum for their child, which is gifted to the child on graduation. The House of Learning has grown to offer a wealth of programs, such as college courses and skill development on everything from chainsaw safety to traffic control. The college preparation courses are a significant stepping stone in the lives of students who have made the commitment to return to school to improve their lives and the lives of their families and community members. As Jason Charlie, who studied psychology at Thompson Rivers University in Kamloops, B.C., said, "After studying for a while, you notice the changes in yourself—the way you talk, the way you think, the way you question."[32]

above *Left to right*: David Taylor, Steve Kocsis, Darrell Charlie, Brian MacIntosh, Brad Bill and Brian Smith at a KDFN skills training course, 2011.

From the outset the Justice Department established programs rooted in traditional values. This includes the land-based healing program, which has since been transferred to the Health Department. Another significant program is restorative justice and its community-based circle approach to dealing with harm in the community. As a Justice Department report noted, "The circle is sacred and it is believed that all participants will experience healing and teaching from using a circle."[33] Following a lack of collaboration and consultation regarding child protection matters, KDFN took a stand in 2011 and negotiated a new agreement with the Yukon government for the delivery of child and family services in the community. This agreement has resulted in a major improvement in child and family service delivery, ensuring KDFN can advocate on behalf of its citizens on all child protection matters.

Since 2012, the department has been negotiating a new comprehensive administration of justice agreement with Canada and Yukon. The parties collaborated to create new processes, including a courts working group. This group identifies options to implement the KDFN justice model, with various elements to be phased in over a period of years. The intent is to transform all aspects of justice in the KDFN community and establish a KDFN court to adjudicate laws of general application (federal, territorial) and KDFN laws, including prosecutions, appeals and enforcement both on and off settlement land. The future agreement will include the joint appointment of judges to the KDFN court and the inclusion of KDFN staff working in Yukon correctional facilities (both adult and youth) to deliver programs and assist with community reintegration of offenders.

KDFN benefits from construction projects occurring in its territory through the Yukon Asset Construction Agreement (YACA) provisions negotiated in the Final Agreement. Through YACAs, the Yukon government is obliged to negotiate business, employment and training opportunities for Kwanlin Dün people when it plans to construct an asset worth over $3 million. By 2016, the Economic Development Department had been successful in negotiating twenty YACAs, which provided contracting, employment and training opportunities to KDFN businesses and people. KDFN citizens have filled many of the jobs on major construction projects around Whitehorse, including the new airport terminal building and the Whistle Bend subdivision. With YACA fuelling employment and business opportunities, the Economic Development Department has supported KDFN citizens on their pathways to employment. A labour survey in 2008 led the department to establish an employment centre, located beside the House of Learning, that helps map out training and work opportunities for citizens. KDFN has used funds earned from this activity to expand the House of Learning and upgrade the Jackson Lake Healing Camp.

The Heritage, Lands and Resources Department works to ensure that key elements of the Final and Self-Government Agreements are implemented. Since 2005 this has entailed working with the Yukon government on surveying settlement land, setting up Special Management Areas, managing fish and wildlife, planning land use and managing forests. The department provides input to the City of Whitehorse and Yukon Environment and Socio-economic Assessment Board (YESAB) on development proposals, and it reviews residential, business and agricultural projects and other issues that could have an impact on KDFN interests. Staff work with other First Nations on many collaborative heritage projects, researching and preserving critical authentic documentation with Elders and others regarding land use, languages and traditions. A milestone achievement was the passage of the Lands Act by the KDFN Council in March 2020.

Citizen Engagement

Chief Doris Bill: I wish to thank all citizens who are actively involved in keeping our community safe. It is our community and it is up to us to shape it into how we want to see it. Together we can make this a great place to live.[34]

Our government takes a consultative, collaborative approach to decision making, in keeping with the principles and structures in our Constitution. The importance of citizen involvement in government was recognized at a special General Assembly, Moving Forward Together, in 2013. It acknowledged the vital role that citizens play in shaping the First Nation's priorities and how the government programs and services benefit greatly from citizen involvement on the many boards and committees, and from community consultations. "Citizen input and involvement is a cornerstone of the way we are doing things in this government," said Chief Rick O'Brien, "and we are very fortunate to have such engaged and committed citizens."[35]

Our initiatives to improve community safety in McIntyre are a good example of citizens and government cooperating. In December 2012, Chief and Council focused government resources on developing an Action Plan for Community Safety and Well-Being. Directors from seven KDFN departments, along with five community members, including Elders and youth, came together to oversee the process. Several community open houses with a very high turnout resulted in a community-based plan for keeping community members safe and supporting healthier lives.

above An English and Southern Tutchone STOP sign in McIntyre subdivision.

Over the years, this community safety initiative has continued to grow. In 2013, KDFN worked out an agreement for an RCMP satellite office in the KDFN administration building. This office generated more police presence in the community, better understanding by the RCMP of the Kwanlin Dün community, and improved relationships with the RCMP. In 2015, KDFN carried out a major community cleanup and had a TIPS line set up as one way to, as Councillor Sean Smith put it, make "our community safe and secure for our Elders to live, our children to play and our citizens to work."[36]

Since 2015, KDFN staff and leadership have held Let's Keep Talking events, where community members have regular opportunities to voice concerns and contribute ideas on community safety and other topics. The ongoing participation of Elders and youth in committees and community consultations is contributing to strengthening our government foundations. Involvement in successful initiatives, such as community safety, is building the trust of KDFN citizens in their government.

As a true indicator of KDFN taking back responsibility in matters important to our people, in 2016–2017, KDFN hired and trained Community Safety Officers as the first point of contact for citizens in need of assistance. This steady progression from the initial vision of a safe, secure, closely connected and thriving community to actions that create change demonstrates how Kwanlin Dün citizens and their government are working together effectively.

Working Together in Collaboration and Partnership

Chief Doris Bill: As we continue this journey together and unlock the economic potential of our modern-day treaties, it is important that we strengthen relationships and establish partnerships with all levels of government and all who share our vision. It is equally important that we, collectively and individually, do our part for reconciliation. We are setting a new path with empathy, greater understanding of what we need to do, and a willingness for change.[37]

The Kwanlin Dün Traditional Territory overlaps the Traditional Territories of five other First Nations. About 75 percent of Yukon's population lives within KDFN's Traditional Territory. As a result, KDFN works government-to-government with the five other First Nations with overlapping territories, as well as with the municipal, territorial and federal governments with jurisdiction in its territory. Having large urban and rural landholdings and a large and diverse citizenry puts significant and unique demands on KDFN programs and services, but also brings opportunities. KDFN takes the approach of working collaboratively and building partnerships with governments, businesses and organizations that share common interests. And many other governments recognize the value of KDFN programs, such as the Jackson Lake Healing Camp, and see them as model examples of effective programs.

KDFN has reached formal agreements with these other governments. In 2013, after six years of work, KDFN reached an overlap agreement with Ta'an Kwäch'än Council (TKC), Carcross/Tagish First Nation (CTFN) and Champagne and Aishihik First Nations (CAFN), which enables the First Nations to move forward on implementing key provisions of the Final Agreement. In April 2016, KDFN participated in the first intergovernmental forum between Yukon First Nations and the territorial and federal governments to be held in many years.

The Kwanlin Dün Final Agreement assures KDFN's involvement in land and resource planning and management throughout its Traditional Territory. KDFN works jointly with other governments on several management committees set out in the agreement, including wildlife management, park and land use planning, and forest management. The traditional knowledge of Elders is brought together with scientific knowledge to inform this work. For example, KDFN has participated with other partners in twenty years of Chinook salmon research around Michie Creek, and in research on melting ice patches, which are revealing archaeological evidence of our ancestors.

KDFN's relationship with the City of Whitehorse has been growing over the years since the agreements came into effect. They include unique provisions to deal with KDFN's association with the Yukon River and Whitehorse waterfront and the urban aspects of KDFN's Traditional Territory. Initially, in working with the City of Whitehorse, KDFN participated in the City of Whitehorse Development Review Committee as the largest single landowner in the city. The relationship between the governments has evolved since then. In 2014, Chief Doris Bill and Mayor Dan Curtis held an

facing top KDFN Community Safety Officers pose with Constable Kerry Jury of the RCMP, 2017. *Left to right*: Tyler O'Brien, Jess Ryder, Constable Kerry Jury, Team Leader Elias Park.

facing centre Graduation ceremony of Community Safety Officers, ca. 2017. *Front row, left to right*: Hailey White, Rosie Smith, Sheila Caesar, Hank Henry, Susan Burns, Jess Ryder and Cynthia Taylor; *back row, left to right*: John Bunbury, Elias Park, Mike Carlisle, Cody Park, Tyler O'Brien and Dustin Greenland.

facing bottom First Nations leaders hold the newly signed overlap agreement, which addresses issues that overlap KDFN Traditional Territory, 2013. *Left to right*: Carcross/Tagish First Nation Chief Dan Cresswell, Champagne and Aishihik First Nations Chief James Allen, Ta'an Kwäch'än Council Chief Kristina Kane, KDFN Executive Elder Judy Gingell, KDFN Chief Rick O'Brien.

above Cutting meat at Jackson Lake Healing Camp, 2010.

top KDFN Chief Doris Bill (*right*), Ta'an Kwäch'än Council Chief Kristina Kane (*centre*) and Whitehorse Mayor Dan Curtis (*left*) pose in the city's council chambers with a photo of the Southern Tutchone addition to the Welcome to Whitehorse sign, January 2019.

above New signage at South Access Road leading into Whitehorse beside Chūlin (Whitehorse Rapids).

intergovernmental forum and identified many shared interests and a desire to work together. Chief Doris Bill said at the time, "There is a need and expressed desire by both governments to develop better relationships and work together more closely on improved services for the community and in dealing with issues of mutual interest."[38]

This collaboration led to KDFN and the City of Whitehorse holding a joint forum in April 2015 to talk about meeting the needs of vulnerable people. Hundreds of attendees came from Whitehorse and throughout the territory, representing a wide range of stakeholder groups, agencies and service providers. As a result, the four governments of KDFN, TKC, City of Whitehorse and Yukon partnered on the Vulnerable People at Risk Initiative in 2015, and Safe at Home: A Community-Based Action Plan to End and Prevent Homelessness in 2017. KDFN also co-hosted, with the Yukon government and the Council of Yukon First Nations, a mental wellness summit at the Cultural Centre in 2016, which featured a Blanket Exercise presented by KDFN youth to demonstrate the history and impacts of colonialism in Canada.[39]

KDFN is building other partnerships to augment the programs and services they offer to citizens. For example, the House of Learning frequently partners with Yukon College in training and education programs. Dusk'a Head Start Family Learning Centre has partnered with Yukon government on a Learning Together program. Other partnerships bring employment opportunities, such as the one between the Yukon government's Wildfire Management and KDFN. Building such partnerships contributes to the broader spirit of reconciliation. The community safety initiative improved not only KDFN community safety, but also the relationships with other partners in the process—City of Whitehorse By-Law Services, Correctional Services Canada, the Government of Yukon Public Safety Branch and the RCMP.

Protecting Our Land

> **Emily McDougall:** Look at the land and the trees and the mountains and stuff, and that's something that hasn't changed over time. When you look at a black-and-white picture, you think, "Oh, it must have been so different back then," but the landscape hasn't really changed that much.[40]

With the signing of our agreements we reclaimed our rights and responsibilities for stewardship, management and governance of our Traditional Territory. We retained title to over a thousand square kilometres on 264

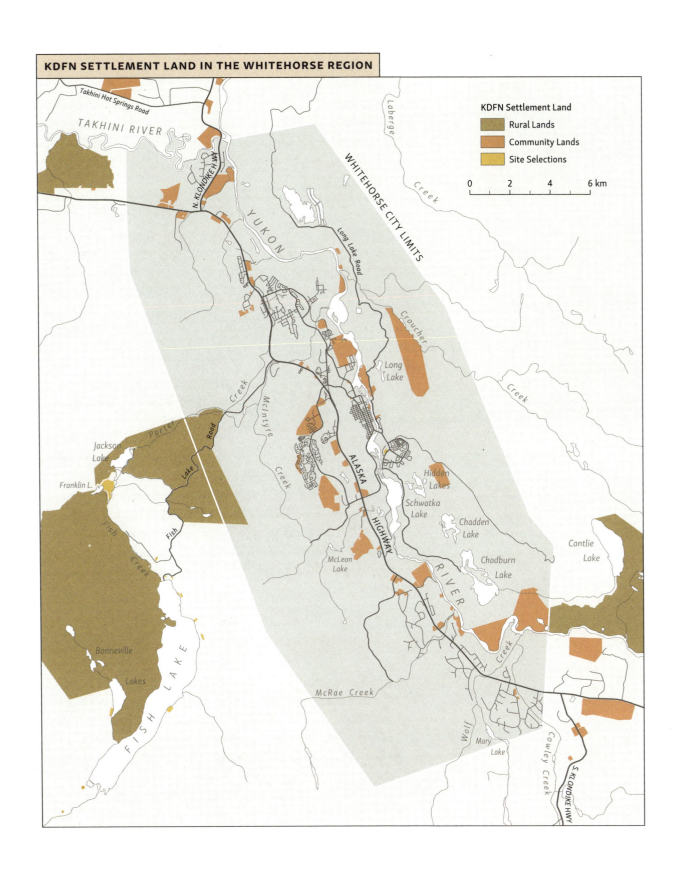

KDFN SETTLEMENT LAND IN THE WHITEHORSE REGION

KDFN Settlement Land
- Rural Lands
- Community Lands
- Site Selections

0 2 4 6 km

Takhini Hot Springs Road

TAKHINI RIVER

N. KLONDIKE HWY

Laberge

Creek

WHITEHORSE CITY LIMITS

YUKON

Long Lake Road

Croucher

Long
Lake

Creek

Creek

Jackson
Lake

Porter

Lake Road

McIntyre

Creek

Hidden
Lakes

Franklin L.

Fish

Creek

Schwatka
Lake

Chadden
Lake

Cantlie
Lake

ALASKA

HIGHWAY

Chadburn
Lake

McLean
Lake

RIVER

Bonneville

Lakes

FISH LAKE

McRae Creek

Creek

Wolf
Creek

Mary
Lake

Cowley Creek

S. KLONDIKE HWY

above New cemetery, Tágà Kwädän Tth'än K'è (River People Gravesite), on Long Lake Road, 2015.

parcels of settlement land, both urban parcels within the city of Whitehorse and larger, more rural and remote areas outside the city. KDFN's land and resource management responsibilities under the Final Agreement extend beyond the settlement land parcels, leading to collaborations with other governments on Local Area Plans and wildlife monitoring. Our intent is to protect the land base for future generations and to generate economic benefits from the land for our people. KDFN has worked since it signed its agreements to build the laws, policies and plans needed to fulfill that intention. "Slowly but surely, those structures have all gone into place," says Chief Doris Bill.[41]

One of the first steps in establishing a land protection, planning and management regime was to survey all the settlement land parcels, which we completed in 2010. We established the KDFN Lands and Resources Act in 2014, working closely with KDFN beneficiaries. Our Land Vision of 2016 guides planning and management of KDFN settlement land based on the well-being of the land and the well-being of the people, together with our principles of respect, caring for the land, considering future generations, and cooperation and community.

One of our first projects was the establishment of a new KDFN cemetery in 2013, high on a bluff overlooking the Yukon River and the Kwanlin Dün Cultural Centre. Elder George Dawson had identified this site decades earlier. With KDFN control over planning and development of our settlement land, we worked with Elders and other citizens to plan the cemetery.

Settlement land is key to securing prosperity for future generations. KDFN has a long-standing housing program, building and renting units for KDFN citizens. In 2015, we were one of the first urban First Nations in Canada to reach agreement with the First Nations Market Housing Fund, which creates further opportunities for KDFN to become a leader in housing development. In 2016, opportunities for KDFN citizens to benefit from our lands expanded with the ability to register settlement land in the Yukon land registry. This opened up more options for long-term residential and commercial leasehold interests for our citizens and others.

We work jointly with other First Nations and the Yukon government to manage wildlife, forest, fish and water within our Traditional Territory, according to provisions in the agreements. The Southern Lakes Wildlife Coordinating Committee includes KDFN, other First Nations and the governments of the Yukon, British Columbia and Canada working as a team to manage caribou, moose, sheep and other wildlife populations and their habitat. From 2008 to 2012, the committee developed a regional assessment of wildlife that included over eighty recommendations. To carry out its joint management responsibilities for the Traditional Territory, KDFN has worked with the Yukon government on protected area and land use planning, such as the Kusawa Park Management Plan and the Marsh Lake Local Area Plan. In 2017, we signed a charter to work with Ta'an Kwäch'än Council and Carcross/Tagish First Nation to work on a regional Indigenous land use plan.

KDFN Land Stewards have been out on KDFN settlement land since 2017, monitoring activities and educating citizens and visitors on appropriate and respectful use of the land. The Stewards work collaboratively with Yukon government conservation officers. The traditional values and knowledge of our Elders and other community members are brought into the work of managing lands and resources. Their knowledge enriches research on projects such as ice patch recording, archaeological surveys at McIntyre Creek and M'Clintock River, habitat mapping for planning, and thirty years of salmon research at Michie Creek.

In re-establishing our authority to make decisions about appropriate use of our lands, we are protecting the land as a vital foundation of our culture. Youth are getting back to the land through land-based camps and recreation programs at places their ancestors would have used, now protected on settlement land and through KDFN joint resource management. At a Celebration of the Land community dinner in 2015, Elder Irma Scarff said: "This is one of the first land celebrations in many years to honour the land. We once celebrated the land in every season."[42]

above KDFN Land Steward Manager Brandy Mayes inspects the settlement land parcel including her great-grandfather John Joe's trapline cabin near Cowley Lake, May 2019.

Securing Our Long-Term Prosperity

Rick O'Brien, Chair, Chu Níikwän Development Corporation: We are excited to introduce our development corporation to the development community. Kwanlin Dün will no longer be an observer. We are ready to go.

Having a large urban centre in the middle of our Traditional Territory brings challenges but also opportunities to generate wealth that is fully protected for our future generations. KDFN leaders and negotiators worked hard to secure land and business opportunities in the Final Agreement, and KDFN is now the largest landowner in the City of Whitehorse. Land development is key to our long-term economic sustainability. We have established the legal and regulatory structures to enable KDFN land to be planned, subdivided, leased and ultimately developed. Our strategy is to develop commercial and residential parcels that can be leased through our development corporation to generate revenue.

In 2014, we founded the Chu Níikwän Development Corporation with the vision of growing our Nation's equity and resources for the future benefit of all members. Chu Níikwän oversees a land leasehold and property management company; Kishwoot Enterprises, a gravel resources and small equipment company; and Canyon City Construction. The companies operate at arm's length from the KDFN government according to the terms of a business charter developed in 2014.

Chu Níikwän develops business partnerships with other companies with the purpose of providing long-term self-sufficiency for KDFN. Our development corporation is building a diverse and strategic portfolio of investments to generate wealth and prosperity for KDFN. Funds accrued from the Final Agreement are held in the KDFN Beneficiaries Trust, established in 2016.

FAMILY FOCUS

Geraldine Harris

....

Geraldine Harris reminds us that it's never too late to reconnect with your culture and heritage.

When she was only three years old, Geraldine and her family moved out of their home in the Old Village to a new life in Prince Rupert, where she grew up. "There was disconnection," she reflects. "We didn't learn any First Nations history in school. Everything I learned was from my visits back to the Yukon." Through the years, Geraldine loved her Yukon visits, especially to see her great-grandmother Sophie Smarch, who introduced her to many aspects of her Tlingit culture and Yanyèdí Clan heritage.

It wasn't until she was a young adult that she felt the calling to come back to the Yukon to live—with reconnection as her main goal. In 2016, she moved into a small four-season yurt on her Aunt Kim's property on the shores of Marsh Lake. Working as a tutor in the KDFN Education Department, she also attended many of the department's programs, immersing herself in traditional activities like the Elders Sewing Circle. "I was able to learn how to bead. We made gloves," she says. "And I spent my lunch breaks with Grandma, listening to her stories."

Sophie Smarch was a well-known and respected Elder and a fabulous storyteller. Geraldine was enraptured by the breadth of knowledge her great-grandmother shared with her and soaked it up like a sponge. "When I knew I was going to leave again, I spent even more time with Grandma," she says. "She helped me reconnect with my culture. She taught me songs that can only be sung by my clan, the Yanyèdí Clan. I think that is so special." One of her grandma's stories was about how her family ended up in Whitehorse. Sophie and her husband were forced to leave Teslin because their marriage wasn't accepted there.

Sophie also shared stories of growing up on the land with her mother and father on Teslin Lake. She loved to ski as a little girl, and it was her preferred way to get into town during the winter. That led to her first ever encounter with a white man. In Geraldine's words: "She was just a little girl and she went to the store to get some things for her grandma. She had to ski there. When she got there she saw a man who was pale and had blue eyes. She just left and went back home as fast as she could. 'Grandma, Grandma, grab the medicine! I met this man, he has blue eyes and he's pale and he's sick! We need to help him!' Her grandma got so mad at her and said, 'You can't talk like that. It's not appropriate!'"

Living in her yurt right through the winter helped Geraldine feel closer to the land, to her traditional territory and to her family history. With only a wood stove and no plumbing or indoor bathroom, it was an enjoyable challenge for her. "It was such an experience. When I think of Kwanlin Dün Traditional Territory, it's so beautiful. I'm thankful for being able to be a part of living so close to the land."[43]

facing KDFN grads stand with Community Education Liaison Coordinator Evelyn Troy and Councillor Jessie Dawson outside the Kwanlin Dün Cultural Centre, May 2019. *Left to right:* Evelyn Troy, Melia Hudgin, Alberta Sam, Tyreke Scurvey, Montana Dawson, Gracie Ekholm, Jessie Dawson, Isaac Bill.

OUR YOUTH ARE RISING

Tut.Latseen—Victoria Fred: Our children are the most important gift we can ever be given.[44]

Melia Hudgin, Youth: Young people need to play a lead role in reconciliation—especially in the area of strengthening intergenerational relations. We should be active in developing a generation of leaders and champions that will define and strengthen relationships between people, not only here in the Yukon but also across the country.[45]

Katelyn Dawson: We need to . . . make a change and . . . be strong leaders or role models, because I think . . . it'll be a better place up here . . . if we stand together and we make it . . . a better place for us and our children.[46]

Cheyenne Bradley, Youth: Our dream is for McIntyre to be part of Whitehorse. It seems like people in the rest of town don't know it. We want the stigma to be gone and not to feel judged for living here.[47]

Teagyn Vallevand, Youth: I see strong community that has strong roots, that knows itself and that knows its people. That has that full connection back with the river again. And . . . where everyone has that sense of love and belonging I guess. And identity.[48]

Building a legacy for future generations had always been the goal of land claims negotiations. As expressed in our 1973 statement of claims, "Together Today for our Children Tomorrow," "Our people have many deep feelings about our land and about the future of our children."[49] During the 2005 signing ceremony, Chief Mike Smith said, "We look forward at this time to pass on our legacy to future generations."[50] In later years he confirmed the significance of the agreements, saying: "We were finally accepted as real owners of this land. You reflect back on that, that was like turning a page for us, and really critical . . . We hope future generations would come back and think about that because it was really important, and especially for young people. They have to know, get some pride and realize that [the government or church] can't come and take you away anymore."[51]

That vision of our leaders is being fulfilled in many different ways. Despite multi-generational impacts of colonization, youth are finding their own ways to wellness and empowerment, supported by their families, Elders and leaders. Youth appreciate the support they receive from

their families and community as making all the difference in their growth. Reflecting on her graduation from the Red Seal carpentry program, Katelyn Dawson said, "I just wanted to make my mom proud and ... my parents, my dad, and ... my grandparents. I know they're probably watching over me, so I just ... want to do good, and you want a good life for not only me, but my family."[52] Cassis Lindsay, a champion swimmer, said, "I've just helped ... promote the image of all these people who have helped me and all these organizations that have helped me."[53]

Youth find unique ways to express their connection to their culture. In July 2018, a group of youth paddled the Yukon River from Whitehorse to Dawson as part of River Nation—Journey Through the Bloodlines—Our Land, Our Water, Our People. Teagyn Vallevand said of the experience: "I feel ... more connected ... to my ancestors and to my community. And it's more calming and serene ... One of my favourite things to do is probably go paddling. I really love being out on the river ... It's a really great place where you can kind of get your thoughts and emotions, and ... if you're going through a tough time or something, just being able to get that ... exercise ... It really helps calm you down, and then you can think out, and sort out your problem."[54] At Jackson Lake, many youth attend healing camps where they are guided by Elders in traditional teachings that connect them to themselves, the land and First Nations culture. KDFN youth

gathered with young people from across the Yukon at the 2015 Strength Within Circle: Youth Wellness Gathering, which empowered youth to have healthy minds, bodies, spirits and hearts.

Every spring, our community celebrates graduates of all ages, from pre-school to post-secondary—and the number of graduates listed in the KDFN newsletter keeps growing. "I did a speech for the valedictorian at the Native Grad," said Aurora Hardy, "and that was really good to just talk to all the graduates ... [to] represent them as well as speak to them ... about their accomplishments, and it felt so empowering for me and it's one of my biggest accomplishments to do that ... My main message was to love and respect yourself as much as you love your family. And just to hold yourself up and hold your community up."[55]

Young graduates are taking responsibility for their futures by finding employment and mentorship opportunities with our KDFN government and businesses. Katelyn Dawson worked her way through the Red Seal trades program in carpentry and applied her skills in the KDFN-owned Canyon City Construction, building homes for our citizens. "I wanted a better life for me and my son, and just having, you know, positive role models and good people behind you all the way to push you," said Katelyn. "Nothing's ever given to you ... you have to work hard for what you want and what you want in life, so that's what she [Mom] did and that's what I did and, you know, I'm not going to stop here, right? I'm going to keep going. I don't know what's next ... It opens up a lot of doors."[56]

Supporting the whole person is a strong value in KDFN, so the Health Department added recreation as a program in 2012. Youth are having fun at our on-the-land camps, on our ski and bike trails, and at the ball diamond and playground in McIntyre Village. Kids who participate in programs such as the Kwanlin Koyotes Ski Club learn much more than skiing. Going outside and being active connects them to the land and puts them on a pathway to culture and wellness. The program "is about giving kids a voice," says Gary Bailie, who has led the program for twenty years. "The Koyotes have a code of ethics: respect, dedication and attitude ... This program helps kids learn to be best buddies with themselves. It is a self-esteem builder."[57]

In February 2011, KDFN youth chose their first Youth Council spokesperson, Sarina Sydney, to fulfill the KDFN Constitution provision for youth representation in our government. Since 2017, the KDFN Youth Advisory Committee has held regular meetings with Chief and Council, participated in discussions with other organizations in Whitehorse and organized numerous youth-oriented projects and events. It has become a driving force for young people, organizing the 2018 Millennial Town Hall for over 125 youth from across the territory in partnership with *Shākāt Journal*. At the town hall, youth spoke openly and frankly on tough issues they face in their lives, such as homelessness, bullying and the use of opioids, and they presented a series of questions to political leadership.

Dawn Waugh, KDFN's Director of Education, says of our youth today: "So many of our young people are doing ... wonderful things. And it's not even about being in school ... They could be learning about their traditional ways or whatever it is ... that craving for knowledge. It's really, really exciting."[58]

With guidance from the Elders Council, youth were recruited for training in lateral violence prevention in 2016. These young leaders, calling themselves the V2K Warriors ("V2K" is short for "Violence to Kindness"), led community activities to counteract lateral violence—aggression acted out on others by people affected by multi-generation colonialism and other negative influences. They offered four workshops to youth to develop improved understanding and kinder communities. They have also contributed to broader reconciliation efforts in Whitehorse, as other community organizations outside KDFN have invited them to share their workshops.

We treasure our young people and we celebrate them with pride in their achievements. We stand beside them when they suffer. The youth of Kwalin Dün First Nation are rising up, using their power to shape their lives and the future of our nation.

> **Teagyn Vallevand:** Being in the Cultural Centre ... I think most KDFN citizens or just people in general ... when you walk into that building, you're just overwhelmed by ... awe, and you just feel so good about yourself, when you walk into that building. Because ... you think—look, we're still here![59]

facing top Red Seal carpenter Katelyn Dawson and father Howard MacIntosh at a worksite in McIntyre subdivision, 2011.

facing bottom Kwanlin Koyotes Ski Club with their coach Joseph Graham (*centre*), 2013.

above Elder Ashia—Ann Smith with Isabella Webb and Junkusiyi—Sarah Johnston Smith holding daughter Sadzeł–Azaria Rose at the Kwanlin Dün Cultural Centre, ca. 2017.

Acknowledgements

Many people and organizations contributed to developing the Kwanlin Dün First Nation (KDFN) Waterfront Heritage Project and this book. This project was a key provision of the 2005 KDFN Final Agreement. As of Fall 2020, the project has evolved through three of four planned phases:

PHASE 1: Archival Research and Bibliography
PHASE 2: Community Consultation and Research
PHASE 3: Publication
PHASE 4: Interpretation (for future development)

PHASE 1: Archival Research and Bibliography

Midnight Arts Consulting of Whitehorse (Helene Dobrowolsky and Rob Ingram) produced a report on existing waterfront interpretation and a comprehensive bibliography of archival resources related to KDFN history in the region.

PHASE 2: Community Consultation and Research

The KDFN Heritage, Lands and Resources (HLR) Department led this phase to develop themes and stories related to KDFN experiences on the waterfront, a series of video recordings with Elders, digitization of KDFN family photo albums, and consultations with the KDFN community. The following people contributed:

· Dave Sembsmoen, Director, HLR 2015–2017
· Geoff Cowie, HLR Project Manager
· Marie-Louise Boylan, KDFN Communications Officer
· Jason Shorty, Community Liaison
· Linda Johnson, Community Research Coordinator
· Tammy Joe, Lands Assistant

FOCUS GROUP: Jessie Dawson, Linda Harvey, Ukjese van Kampen, Ann Smith, Dianne Smith, Joan Viksten, Les Wilson, Executive Elder Judy Gingell

AUDIO AND VIDEO RESOURCES: Dennis Allen, Ronald Bill, Charlie Burns, Rose Charlie, Harold Dawson, Jessie Dawson, Katelyn Dawson, D'uska Head Start Family Learning Centre, Al von Finster, Barbara Fred, Judy Gingell, Leonard Gordon Sr., Aurora Hardy, Dinah Jim, Kanoe People, David Lebarge, Leonard Linklater, Richard Lawrence, Joanne Lindsay, Virginia Lindsay, Emily Lindsay McDougall, Roly Mitton, Erin Pauls, Trina Pauls, Mike Rudyk, Dorothy Sam, Irma Scarff, Emma Joanne Shorty, Ann Smith, Louie Smith, Mike Smith, Willie Smith, Betty Smith-Titus, Solid Sound, Robert Suits, Raymond Sydney, Unitech Sound and Lighting, Dawn Waugh, Albert Webber, Bill Webber, Frances Woolsey

WORKING GROUP: representatives from Canada, Government of Yukon, and City of Whitehorse

KWANLIN DÜN COMMUNITY MEMBERS: over two hundred KDFN citizens contributed ideas, images and information at community consultation meetings from 2014—2017

PHASE 3: Publication
The KDFN Heritage, Lands and Resources (HLR) Department led this phase to develop this book focused on KDFN history and experiences on the Whitehorse waterfront and surrounding region:

· Diane Reed, Director, HLR, 2017–2018
· Marlene Jennings, Director, HLR, 2018–2019
· Greg Thompson, Director, HLR, 2019–2020
· Rae Mombourquette, Project Coordinator, 2017–2018
· Diana Jimmy, HLR Heritage Projects Assistant
· Michele Taylor, HLR Administrator
· Linda Johnson, Content Editor

KDFN ADMINISTRATION: Gordon Campbell, Donna Holcomb, Chris Madden, Dorothy Sam, Roxanne Vallevand

KDFN COUNCIL

ELDERS COUNCIL

YOUTH COUNCIL

CHAPTER CONTENT AUTHORS: Jason Charlie, Lori Eastmure, Ruth Gotthardt, Gord Loverin, Gillian McKee, Sweeny Scurvey, Norma Shorty, Ukjese van Kampen

FAMILY FOCUS RESEARCH: Tyrell Brockman, Amanda Calberry and Family, Louie Carlick, Rose Charlie, Charles Chief, Richard Craft, Dawson Family, Barbara Fred, Geraldine Harris, Joe Family, June Jules, Joanne Luger, Jess Ryder, Katharine Sandiford, Darlene Scurvey, Norma Shorty, Louie Smith, Joan Viksten, Tina Williams

ARTWORK: Edith Baker, Evalena Beisser, Karen Bien, Kwanlin Dün Cultural Centre, Raymond Shorty, Ann Smith, Annie Smith and daughters, Irene Smith, Justin Smith, Gertie Tom, Wanda Webb, Yukon Permanent Art Collection

IMAGE RESEARCH AND DOCUMENTATION: Helene Dobrowolsky and Rob Ingram of Midnight Arts

INDIGENOUS LANGUAGE SPECIALISTS: Shirley Adamson, Lorraine Allen, Joe Binger, Nakhela Bunbury, Ida Calmegane, Bessie Cooley, Linda Harvey, Patrick Moore, Anne Ranigler, Sophie Smarch, Sean Smith, Daniel Tlen, Yukon Native Language Centre

HISTORY AND CULTURAL CONTENT: Ted Ackerman, Gail Anderson, Gary Bailie, Julie Cruikshank, Diana Dawson, Georgina Dawson, Hilda Dawson, Jessie Dawson, Loretta Dawson, Valerie Dawson, Starr Drynock, Patti Flather and Gwaandak Theatre, Victoria Fred, Sheila Greer, Greg Hare, Cathy Haydon, Ty Heffner, Donna Holcomb, Helen Holway, Linda Huebschwerlen, May Hume, Kwanlin Dün Cultural Centre, MacBride Museum, Sharon Mankowske,

Anne-Marie Miller, Dorothy Mitander-Graham, Linda Moen, Caroline Morrow, Wayne Price, Maverick Reindeer, Gary Rusnak, Edwin Scurvey, Melaina Sheldon, Jacquie Shorty, Norman Shorty Jr., Pearl Shorty, Sharon Shorty, Kuduat Shorty-Henyu, Ann Smith, Azaria Smith, Dianne Smith, Lisa Smith, Patrick Smith, Rosie Smith, Sarah Johnson Smith, Tyson Smith, Willie Smith, Ta'an Kwäch'än Council, Cynthia Taylor, Henry Taylor, Colin Teramura, Christian Thomas, Andrew Thompson, Louis Thompson, Natilee Thompson, Gertie Tom, Hiedi and Josh Cuppage of Transcripts North, Teagyn Vallevand, Les Walker, Cole Waugh, Colleen Williams, Bruce Wilson, Les Wilson, Yukon Archives

HLR MAP PRODUCTION: Richard Vladars

PHOTOGRAPHY: Gary and Brianne Bremner of GBP Creative, Geoff Cowie, CYFN Archives, John Meikle, *Whitehorse Star*

TECHNICAL REVIEW COMMITTEE: Pricilla Dawson, Barbara Fred, Judy Gingell, Sean Smith, Alicia Vance, Bill Webber

WORKING GROUP: City of Whitehorse, Government of Yukon, Canada representatives

PUBLISHER: Figure 1 Publishing, Vancouver

Many other people we may have missed by name—we are grateful to you all for your many valuable contributions!

Appendix: Chiefs and Councils

*MIDTERM REPLACEMENTS

1957–1965
CHIEF: Billy Smith
COUNCILLORS: Scurvey Shorty,
John McGundy

1965–1967
CHIEF: Elijah Smith
COUNCILLORS: Jimmy Charlie, Irene
MacIntosh, Clifford McLeod, Roy H. Sam

1968
ACTING CHIEF: Clifford McLeod
COUNCILLORS: Jimmy Charlie, Irene
MacIntosh, Clifford McLeod, Roy H. Sam

1969–1973
CHIEF: Johnnie E. Smith
COUNCILLORS: Ronald Bill, Freddy
Jackson, Irene MacIntosh, Roy H. Sam,
Sweeny Scurvey, Annie Burns,*
Richard Peters,* Andrew Joe*

1973–1977
CHIEF: Roy H. Sam
COUNCILLORS: Joe Shorty, Dennis Smith,
Jimmy Skookum, Johnny C. Smith,
Jackie Kodwat, Doris Charlie, Ronald Bill,
Sophie Smarch

1977–1981
CHIEF: Roy H. Sam
COUNCILLORS: Florence MacIntosh, Ann
Smith, Lesley Smith, Irene MacIntosh,
Edythe Kane, Mary Jane Jim, Louie Smith*

1981–1985
CHIEF: Johnnie E. Smith
COUNCILLORS: Howard MacIntosh,
Michael Smith, Wayne Jim, Mary Jane
Jim, Dianne Smith, Jackie Kodwat,
Annie Burns*

1985–1988
CHIEF: Johnnie E. Smith
COUNCILLORS: Larry Bill, Ronald Bill,
Howard MacIntosh, Roy H. Sam,
Sophie Smarch, Shirley Smith

1988–1990
CHIEF: Ann Smith
COUNCILLORS: Lena Johns, Joanne Bill,
Billie Smith, Russell Burns, Watson
George, John Edzerza

1990–1993
CHIEF: Lena Johns
COUNCILLORS: Norman Shorty Sr.,
Malcom Dawson, Roy H. Sam, Charlene
Burns, Edwin Scurvey

1993–1996
CHIEF: Lena Johns
DEPUTY CHIEFS: Albert Webber,
Malcolm Dawson
COUNCILLORS: Dianne Smith, Allan
Taylor, Patrick Boss, Malcolm Dawson,
Richard Peters, John Edzerza

1996–1999
CHIEF: Joe Jack
DEPUTY CHIEF: Pat Joe
COUNCILLORS: Jason Shorty, William Carlick, Helen Charlie, Ann Smith, Colleen Williams, John Edzerza

2000–2003
CHIEF: Rick O'Brien
COUNCILLORS: Edith Baker, Jessie Dawson, Leonard Gordon Sr., Darwin O'Brien, Lesley Smith, Allan Taylor

2003–2005
CHIEF: Mike Smith
COUNCILLORS: Edith Baker, Jessie Dawson, Leonard Gordon Sr., Jason Shorty, Lesley Smith, Allan Taylor

2005–2008
CHIEF: Mike Smith
COUNCILLORS: Edith Baker, Jessie Dawson, Shirley Dawson, Ann Smith, Allan Taylor, Bill Webber

2008–2011
CHIEF: Mike Smith
COUNCILLORS: Edith Baker, Helen Charlie, Jessie Dawson, Shirley Dawson, Jennifer Edzerza, Ray Webb
ELDER: Bill Webber
YOUTH: Aaron Holway, Doronn Fox*

2011–2014
CHIEF: Rick O'Brien
COUNCILLORS: Charlene Charlie, Jessie Dawson, Jennifer Edzerza, Ron MacIntosh, Ray Sydney, Alicia Vance
ELDER: Judy Gingell
YOUTH: Sarina Sydney

2014–2017
CHIEF: Doris Bill
COUNCILLORS: Dennis Calbery, Charlene Charlie, Jessie Dawson, Howard MacIntosh, Sean Smith, Alicia Vance
ELDER: Judy Gingell
YOUTH: Tayler Vallevand-Vance

2017–2020
CHIEF: Doris Bill
COUNCILLORS: Dennis Calbery, Charles Chief, Jessie Dawson, Howard MacIntosh, Sean Smith, Ray Sydney
ELDER: William Carlick

2020–2023
CHIEF: Doris Bill
COUNCILLORS: Charlene Charlie, Charles Chief, Jessie Dawson, Jess Ryder, Ray Sydney, Rosemary Waugh-Wilson
ELDER: Judy Gingell

Notes

1: Adaalàl Kwàch'e Kwadą̂y (It is spring time long ago)

1 This phrase is borrowed from the title of Kàdùhikh—K'aɫgwach—K'odetéena—Kitty Smith's book *Nindal Kwädindür: "I'm Going to Tell You a Story,"* recorded by Julie Cruikshank (Whitehorse: Council for Yukon Indians and Government of Yukon, 1982).

2 Angela Sidney's biographical details were compiled from *Tagish Tlaagú: Tagish Stories* (Whitehorse: Council for Yukon Indians and Government of Yukon 1982); and from "Introduction" in Julie Cruikshank in collaboration with Angela Sidney, Kitty Smith and Annie Ned, *Life Lived Like a Story*, pp. 27-28.

3 Angela Sidney published an English version of this story in Angela Sidney, Kitty Smith and Rachel Dawson, *My Stories Are My Wealth*, as told to Julie Cruikshank (Whitehorse: Council for Yukon Indians, 1977), pp. 90-92. At the end of her story she said, "Somebody was watching all this from way back there, his name is *Tudecha'de*, means 'duck head feathers' in Tagish language." Another English version of this story was published in Julie Cruikshank in collaboration with Angela Sidney, Kitty Smith and Annie Ned, *Life Lived Like a Story* (Vancouver: UBC Press, 1990), pp. 44-48. In endnote 15 on page 361, Cruikshank cites Mrs. Sidney's further explanation that "*Tudech'ade* was a man of the *Dakl'aweidí* clan who watched the process and learned the songs, so that today Tagish *Dakl'aweidí* have the right to sing them."

James Teit published a Tahltan version of the story in "Tahltan Tales," *Journal of American Folklore* (1919): pp. 230-32. Catharine McClellan described Tlingit and Tagish traditions relating to Game Mother in *My Old People Say* (Ottawa: National Museums of Canada, 1975), pp. 117-18. The Tagish orthography used in this story is the same as that used by the Yukon Native Language Centre http://ynlc.ca/index.html.

4 Victor Golla recorded *Aadakoon.áa(gen)* as a Tlingit name for Montana Mountain with Angela Sidney in 1976. However, it has not been attested in other sources to date. Angela Sidney's 1980 book *Place Names of the Tagish Region, Southern Yukon* provided *Tsálgi Shaayí* as the Tlingit name she recorded with Julie Cruikshank for Montana Mountain.

5 Recorded by Angela Sidney at the 1990 Tagish Language Workshop, Tagish Water Centre, as heard originally by Tù de Ch'ah. Mrs. Sidney explained that a long ago Tagish ancestor called Tù de Ch'ah or Tù de Ch'ahdè' ("Duck Hat," so named because he wore a hat made from the green neck feathers of mallard ducks), who was hunting by Bennett Lake, watched as the animals danced on the swing while Game Mother sang for each of them.

6 Louie Smith recorded his biographical details in *Ajänath'a, Kwanlin Dün Elders Portrait Project, Kwanlin Dün Cultural Centre* (Whitehorse: Kwanlin Dün Cultural Centre, 2015), p. 11. Southern and Northern Tutchone names were verified by Louie Smith in collaboration with Nakhela—Hazel Bunbury in December 2019.

7 Nakhela—Hazel Bunbury developed her biographical details for this publication in November 2019.

8 Anne Ranigler developed biographical details for her mother, Emma Ina Shorty, for this publication in January 2020.

9 The recording is available on YouTube at https://www.youtube.com/watch?v=y5aXtkEO8KM.

10 Sophie Smarch recorded her biographical details in *Ajänath'a, Kwanlin Dün Elders Portrait Project, Kwanlin Dün Cultural Centre*, p. 9, and family members contributed additional details in December 2019.

2: Ịmè Kwàch'e (It is summer time)

1 From "Big Raft Story," Kwanlin Dün First Nation: Heritage, Lands & Resources, 1993 Fish Lake Project, transcripts, pp. 16–20.

2 Virginia Smarch quoted in Catharine McClellan, *Part of the Land, Part of the Water: A History of the Yukon Indians*, with Lucie Birckel, Robert Bringhurst, James A. Fall, Carol McCarthy and Janice R. Sheppard (Vancouver: Douglas & McIntyre, 1987), p. 1.

3 May Hume, Kwanlin Dün First Nation: Heritage, Lands & Resources, 1993 Fish Lake Project, transcripts.

4 May Hume recorded her biographical details in *Ajänath'a, Kwanlin Dün Elders Portrait Project, Kwanlin Dün Cultural Centre* (Whitehorse: Kwanlin Dün Cultural Centre, 2015).

5 Gladys Huebschwerlen, Kwanlin Dün First Nation: Heritage, Lands & Resources, 1993 Fish Lake Project, transcripts.

6 Biography of Gladys Huebschwerlen provided by daughter Linda Huebschwerlen, 2020.

7 Ronald Bill, Kwanlin Dün First Nation: Heritage, Lands & Resources, 1996/97 Land Use Planning Project, transcript of interview with Mark Lindsay and Hank Henry, August 5, 1996.

8 Ronald Bill recorded his biographical details in *Ajänath'a, Kwanlin Dün Elders Portrait Project, Kwanlin Dün Cultural Centre*, p. 1.

9 Johnnie Smith, Kwanlin Dün First Nation: Heritage, Lands & Resources, 1993 KDFN Cultural History Project, transcript.

10 Biography of Johnnie Smith provided by daughter Judy Gingell, 2020.

11 Rachael Dawson recorded this story in English with Julie Cruikshank for publication in Angela Sidney, Kitty Smith and Rachel Dawson, as told to Julie Cruikshank, *My Stories Are My Wealth* (Whitehorse: Council for Yukon Indians, 1977), pp. 93–95.

12 Rachael Dawson's daughters Hilda Dawson and Edna Rose, and grandchildren Jessie Dawson, Kathleen Dawson and Diana Dawson developed her biographical details in December 2019. Note that her English name is spelled Rachel in several publications; however, her given name is Rachael (with a second a) as recorded by family members.

13 Catharine McClellan, *My Old People Say* (Ottawa: National Museums of Canada, 1975), p. 75.

14 Angela Sidney in Julie Cruikshank in collaboration with Angela Sidney, Kitty Smith and Annie Ned, *Life Lived Like a Story* (UBC Press: Vancouver, 1990), pp. 48–49. Cruikshank also discusses the White Winter World in *Reading Voices Dan Dha Ts'edenintth'e: Oral and Written Interpretations of the Yukon's Past* (Vancouver: Douglas & McIntyre, 1991).

15 McClellan, *My Old People Say*, pp. 74-75; McClellan, *Part of the Land, Part of the Water*, p. 253.

16 Jeffrey Bond, "Late Wisconsinan McConnell Glaciation of the Whitehorse Map Area (105D), Yukon," in D.S. Emond and L.L. Lewis, eds., *Yukon Exploration and Geology 2003* (Yukon Geological Survey annual report, 2004), pp. 73–88.

17 Louie Smith, Kwanlin Dün First Nation: Heritage, Lands & Resources, Waterfront Heritage Project 2017 Story-Weaving Workshop, transcript.

18 Giant animals have been described in many stories, including Annie Ned's stories of giant wolverines in *Life Lived Like a Story*, pp. 282–85; Jessie Jonathan's "Äsùya and the Giant Wolverine Man" in Margaret Workman, *Kwadây Kwändür: Traditional Southern Tutchone Stories* (Whitehorse: Yukon Native Language Centre, 2010), p. 108, as well as "Äsùya and the Giant Bear" (p. 93); "Äsùya and the Eagle" (p. 95); "Äsùya and the Big Worm" (p. 98); "Äsùya and the Big Water Snake" (p. 103); and "Äsùya and the Giant Animal" (p. 112); and Marge Jackson's "Smart Man" story about making wolverines small in McClellan, *Part of the Land, Part of the Water*, p. 305.

19 Ukjese van Kampen developed these "Life Imagined" segments for this book in 2019.

20 Jessie Scarff, Kwanlin Dün First Nation: Heritage, Lands & Resources, 1993 Fish Lake Project, transcript.

21 Ibid, revised transcript 2019, p. 20.

22 Ruth Gotthardt and Greg Hare, *Łu Zil Män Fish Lake: Uncovering the Past* (Whitehorse: Kwanlin Dün First Nation, 1994).

23 Norman Easton, "Regional Archaeological Sequences," in *Archaeological Excavations at the Little John Site (KdVo-6), Southwest Yukon Territory—2011* (Whitehorse: Yukon College, 2011), pp. 20-41. Norman Easton, personal communication to Ukjese van Kampen, 2016. Note that Little John site obsidian is from Wiki Peak.

24 Ben A. Potter, Joel D. Irish, Joshua D. Reuther and Holly J. McKinney, "New Insights into Eastern Beringian Mortuary Behaviour: A Terminal Pleistocene Double Infant Burial at Upward Sun River," *Anthropology*, PNAS Early Edition (2014). https://doi.org/10.1073/pnas.1413131111.

25 Todd J. Kristensen, P. Gregory Hare, Ruth Gotthardt, Ty Heffner, Norman A. Easton, John W. Ives, Robert J. Speakman and Jeffrey T. Rasic, "The Movement of Obsidian in Subarctic Canada: Holocene Social Relationships and Human Responses to a Large-Scale Volcanic Eruption," *Journal of Anthropological Archaeology*, vol. 56 (December 2019): 1-18, 101114. https://doi.org/10.1016/j.jaa.2019.101114.

26 Greg Hare, *The Frozen Past: The Yukon Ice Patches* (Whitehorse: Government of Yukon, 2011).

27 McClellan, *My Old People Say*, p. 77.

28 Irene Smith, personal communication to Ukjese van Kampen, 2004, 2005, 2009. Johnnie Smith, personal communication to Ukjese van Kampen, 2004, 2005.

29 Ukjese van Kampen, *History of Yukon and Regional Warfare*, unpublished manuscript (Whitehorse: Yukon College, 2015).

30 Annie Ned, *Old People in Those Days: They Told Their Story All the Time* (Whitehorse: Yukon Native Language Centre, 1984).

31 Violet Storer, Ta'an Kwäch'än Council, *Ta'an Kwäch'än Cultural History Project*, transcript of interview by Linda Johnson with Violet Storer at Naalin, October 10, 1989, p. 151.

32 Yukon Native Language Centre, *Kwadą̄y Kwadań: Traditional Southern Tutchone Stories* (Whitehorse: Yukon Native Language Centre, 2000), p. 12.

33 Ida Calmegane, Kwanlin Dün First Nation: Heritage, Lands & Resources, Project Louie, transcript of Session 4, September 11, 2019. Interview with Ida Calmegane, Louie Smith, Frances Woolsey, Linda Johnson and John Meikle at Ida's residence in Tagish. Ḵaax' anshée—La.oos Tláa—Ida Calmegane was born in Tagish to Angela and George Sidney in 1928. She grew up listening to traditional stories told by her mother and other relatives in the Tagish and Tlingit languages. Ida continues her family's tradition of storytelling to preserve and pass on her culture and language.

34 Ukjese van Kampen, *History of Yukon First Nations Art* (PhD dissertation, Leiden University, 2012), openaccess.leidenuniv.nl; Joseph Andrew Park Wilson, *Material Cultural Correlates of the Athapaskan Expansion: A Cross-Disciplinary Approach* (PhD dissertation, University of Florida, 2011).

35 Frederick Schwatka, *Along Alaska's Great River* (New York: Cassell & Company, 1885).

36 Quoted in Edward Curtis, *The North America Indian*, vol. 18 (Massachusetts: The Plimpton Press, 1928), p. 25, http://curtis.library.northwestern.edu/curtis/viewPage.cgi?showp=1&size=2&id=nai.18.book.00000049&volume=18#nav.

37 Clifford Wilson, *Campbell of the Yukon* (Toronto: Macmillan of Canada, 1970), p. 77. Annie Ned reported the purchase price of a musket was equal to its height in furs in *Life Lived Like a Story*, p. 281.

38 Dominique Legros, *Oral History as History: Tutchone Athapaskan in the Period 1840-1920* (Whitehorse: Government of Yukon, 2007), pp. 114-23.

3: Nùchū Kwàch'e (It is fall time)

1 Ronald Bill, Kwanlin Dün First Nation: Heritage, Lands & Resources, 1995 KDFN Canyon City Project, transcript.

2 Lucy Wren, Kwanlin Dün First Nation: Heritage, Lands & Resources, 1993 KDFN Cultural History Project, transcript.

3 Lucy Wren's biographical details were compiled from "Lucy Wren—*Ḵu̱' Eyû. At Home. Tagish Story Book*" on the Yukon Native Language Centre website. Retrieved from http://ynlc.ca/languages/tagish/book_tagish_1.html on May 10, 2010.

4 Angela Sidney, compiled by Julie Cruikshank, *Haa Shagoón (Our Family History)* (Whitehorse: Yukon Native Languages Project, 1983), xii.

5 Angela Sidney in Julie Cruikshank in collaboration with Angela Sidney, Kitty Smith and Annie Ned, *Life Lived Like a Story* (Vancouver: UBC Press, 1990), p. 52.

6 Sweeny Scurvey, Whitehorse Area Chiefs, 1898-1998, Kwanlin Dün First Nation: Heritage, Lands & Resources. Whitehorse: KDFN, 1998.

7 Ida Calmegane, Kwanlin Dün First Nation: Heritage, Lands & Resources, KDFN Project Louie, transcript of Session 4, September 11, 2019.

8 Kwanlin Dün First Nation: Heritage, Lands & Resources, Waterfront Heritage Project, Elders Input Meeting Notes, January 9, 2017.

9 Ronald Bill, Kwanlin Dün First Nation: Heritage, Lands & Resources, 1995 KDFN Canyon City Project, transcript.

10 Violet Storer, ibid.

11 Louie Smith, ibid.

12 Ronald Bill, ibid.

13 Violet Storer, Kwanlin Dün First Nation: Heritage, Lands & Resources, 1996/97 Land Use Planning Project, transcript.

14 Hoodlua—Kitty Smith, Kwanlin Dün First Nation: Heritage, Lands & Resources, 1995 KDFN Canyon City Project, transcript.

15 Violet Storer, ibid.

16 May Hume, ibid.

17 Ibid.

18 Ronald Bill in *Ajänath'a, Kwanlin Dün Elders Portrait Project, Kwanlin Dün Cultural Centre* (Whitehorse: Kwanlin Dün Cultural Centre, 2015), transcript.

19 Hoodlua—Kitty Smith, Kwanlin Dün First Nation: Heritage, Lands & Resources, 1995 KDFN Canyon City Project, transcript.

20 Johnny McGundy, Kwanlin Dün First Nation: Heritage, Lands & Resources, 1996/97 Land Use Planning Project, transcript.

21 Effie Campbell, ibid.

22 Lily Kane, Kwanlin Dün First Nation: Heritage, Lands & Resources, 1993 KDFN Cultural History Project, transcript, June 24, 1993.

23 Violet Storer refers here to Dan Snow. This was undoubtedly Whitehorse resident Dan Snure, as reported in the *Whitehorse Star*, January 23, 1923: "Dan Snure will shortly be taking charge of the Whitney Fox Ranch." Some people pronounced his name "Snow."

24 Violet Storer, Kwanlin Dün First Nation: Heritage, Lands & Resources, 1993 KDFN Cultural History Project, transcript, June 24, 1993.

25 Hoodlua—Kitty Smith, Kwanlin Dün First Nation: Heritage, Lands & Resources, 1995 KDFN Canyon City Project, transcript.

26 Lily Kane, Kwanlin Dün First Nation: Heritage, Lands & Resources, 1993 KDFN Cultural History Project, transcript.

27 Ronald Bill, Kwanlin Dün First Nation: Heritage, Lands & Resources, 1995 KDFN Canyon City Project, transcript.

28 Don McKay, Kwanlin Dün First Nation: Heritage, Lands & Resources, 1993 Fish Lake Project, transcript.

29 John McGundy, ibid.

30 Polly Irvine, ibid.

31 Sophie Smarch, Kwanlin Dün First Nation: Heritage, Lands & Resources, Before and After Whitehorse Dam, 1995 interview transcript.

32 Shorty or Henry Roils' name appears in government records with this spelling, but it is sometimes pronounced "Royle."

33 Compiled from notes contributed by Joe family members, February 2020.

34 Ronald Bill in *Ajänath'a, Kwanlin Dün Elders Portrait Project, Kwanlin Dün Cultural Centre*, transcripts.

35 Renee Peter, Kwanlin Dün First Nation: Heritage, Lands & Resources, 1995 KDFN Canyon City Project, transcripts.

36 Hoodlua—Kitty Smith and Fred Smith, ibid.

37 Ronald Bill in *Ajänath'a, Kwanlin Dün Elders Portrait Project, Kwanlin Dün Cultural Centre*, transcript.

38 Violet Storer, Kwanlin Dün First Nation: Heritage, Lands & Resources, 1996 KDFN Traditional Economics Project, transcript.

39 Compiled from notes contributed by Dawson family members, February 2020.

40 Compiled from notes recorded with Louie Smith, February 2020.

4: Yúk'e Kwàch'e (It is winter time)

1 Jessie Scarff, Kwanlin Dün First Nation: Heritage, Lands & Resources, 1993 Fish Lake Project, transcript.

2 Irene Smith told this story to her daughter Linda Rose Harvey in 2007 at the Yukon Native Language Centre in Whitehorse where they both worked for many years recording, preserving and teaching their Southern Tutchone language.

3 Irene Smith's biography was compiled from information provided by her daughter Linda Rose Harvey in February 2020.

4 "A Cordial Welcome," *Whitehorse Star*, April 10, 1942.

5 "The Old Town Has Gone," *Whitehorse Star*, May 8, 1942.

6 Sweeny Scurvey, "Disturbing the Peace," in *A Glimpse of Peace* (Whitehorse: Sweeny Scurvey, 1996), p. 18.

7 Biographical details of Sweeny and Edwin Scurvey compiled from *Ajänath'a, Kwanlin Dün Elders Portrait Project, Kwanlin Dün Cultural Centre* (Whitehorse: Kwanlin Dün Cultural Centre, 2015), p. 17.

8 Emma Joanne Shorty, Kwanlin Dün First Nation: Heritage, Lands & Resources, 1996 Land Use Planning Project; Waterfront Heritage Project, 2015 video interview transcript.

9 Jessie Scarff, Kwanlin Dün First Nation: Heritage, Lands & Resources, 1993 Fish Lake Project, transcript.

10 Frances Woolsey, Kwanlin Dün First Nation: Heritage, Lands & Resources, Waterfront Heritage Project, March 6, 2016 video interview transcript.

11 Ronald Bill, *Ajänath'a, Kwanlin Dün Elders Portrait Project, Kwanlin Dün Cultural Centre*, transcript.

12 Sweeny Scurvey, "The Seasonal Rounds," in *A Glimpse of Peace*, p. 14.

13 Charlie Burns, *Ajänath'a, Kwanlin Dün Elders Portrait Project, Kwanlin Dün Cultural Centre*, transcript.

14 Ronald Bill, *Ajänath'a, Kwanlin Dün Elders Portrait Project, Kwanlin Dün Cultural Centre*, transcript.

15 Emma Joanne Shorty, Kwanlin Dün First Nation: Heritage, Lands & Resources, 1996 Land Use Planning; Waterfront Heritage Project, 2015 video interview transcript.

16 Jessie Scarff, Kwanlin Dün First Nation: Heritage, Lands & Resources, 1996 Land Use Planning Project, Land Use Planning Project, transcript.

17 Johnnie Smith, Kwanlin Dün First Nation: Heritage, Lands & Resources, 1996 Land Use Planning Project, transcript.

18 Darlene Scurvey, Kwanlin Dün First Nation: Heritage, Lands & Resources, Waterfront Heritage Project, 2018 Community Writing Project. Mile 932 on the Alaska Highway is about twenty miles west of Whitehorse.

19 Biographical details of Elsie Suits were compiled by her daughter Joan Viksten with Suits and Webber family members, February 2020.

20 Charlie Burns, Kwanlin Dün First Nation: Heritage, Lands & Resources, Waterfront Heritage Project, March 5, 2016 video interview transcript.

21 Harold Dawson, Kwanlin Dün First Nation: Heritage, Lands & Resources, Waterfront Heritage Project, March 5, 2016 video interview transcript.

22 Ann Smith, Kwanlin Dün First Nation: Heritage, Lands & Resources, Waterfront Heritage Project, 2017 video interview transcript.

23 Emma Joanne Shorty, Kwanlin Dün First Nation: Heritage, Lands & Resources, 1996 Land Use Planning Project, transcript.

24 Ronald Bill, *Ajänath'a, Kwanlin Dün Elders Portrait Project, Kwanlin Dün Cultural Centre*, transcript.

25 Charlie Burns, *Ajänath'a, Kwanlin Dün Elders Portrait Project, Kwanlin Dün Cultural Centre*, transcript.

26 "Tears Shed as Bulldozer Pushes Condemned Shacks Into Slough," *Whitehorse Star*, June 6, 1953.

27 Helene Dobrowolsky and Linda Johnson, *Whitehorse: An Illustrated History* (Vancouver: Figure 1, 2013), pp. 194–97, 212–15.

28 Dorothy Webber biographical details were compiled by her son Bill Webber in February

2020 and from the transcript of his interview for *Ajänath'a, Kwanlin Dün Elders Portrait Project, Kwanlin Dün Cultural Centre*.

29 Julie Cruikshank in collaboration with Angela Sidney, Kitty Smith and Annie Ned, *Life Lived Like a Story* (Vancouver, UBC Press, 1990), pp. 263-77.

30 Bridget Lee Baumgarte, "Alaska Natives and the Power of Perseverance: The Fight For Sovereignty and Land Claims in Southeast Alaska, 1912–1947" (master's thesis, University of Nevada, Las Vegas, 2015), 82, https://digitalscholarship.unlv.edu/thesesdissertations/2466.

31 Quoted in Department of Indian Affairs and Northern Development, "Report of the Indian Act Consultation Meeting, Whitehorse, October 21, 22 and 23, 1968," p. 4. Retrieved from http://publications.gc.ca/collections/collection_2017/aanc-inac/R5-288-10-1968-eng.pdf on May 8, 2020.

32 Ibid., p. 9.

33 Ibid., p. 22.

34 From article in *Whitehorse Star*, October 21, 1968.

35 Bill Webber, *Ajänath'a, Kwanlin Dün Elders Portrait Project, Kwanlin Dün Cultural Centre*, transcript.

36 Emma Joanne Shorty, Kwanlin Dün First Nation: Heritage, Lands & Resources, Waterfront Heritage Project, 2017 video interview transcript.

37 Biography compiled by Elder Gertie Tom, sister of Norman Shorty Sr.; Norma Shorty, daughter of Emma Joanne and Norman Shorty Sr.; and other family members in October 2019.

38 Yukon Native Brotherhood, "Together Today for Our Children Tomorrow" (Whitehorse: Council for Yukon Indians, 1973), p. 17.

5: Adàką (Light dawning over the mountains)

1 "Video: Together Today for Our Children Tomorrow" on the Mapping the Way: Yukon First Nation Self-Government website. Retrieved from http://mappingtheway.ca/stories/video-together-today-our-children-tomorrow on May 5, 2020. The website includes a video clip from the CBC Archives dated February 14, 1973, that shows the historic meeting.

2 Kitty Smith recorded this version of her story with Julie Cruikshank for publication in Angela Sidney, Kitty Smith and Rachel Dawson, as told to Julie Cruikshank, *My Stories Are My Wealth* (Whitehorse: Council for Yukon Indians, 1977), p. 15.

3 Kitty Smith's biographical details were compiled from Julie Cruikshank in collaboration with Angela Sidney, Kitty Smith and Annie Ned, *Life Lived Like a Story* (Vancouver: UBC Press, 1990), pp. 159-63.

4 From article in *Yukon News*, June 14, 1973.

5 Chief Sitting Bull quote from https://www.allgreatquotes.com/authors/sitting-bull-quotes/, retrieved May 4, 2020.

6 Judy Gingell in Linda Johnson, *At the Heart of Gold: The Yukon Commissioner's Office 1898–2010* (Whitehorse: Legislative Assembly of Yukon, 2013), p. 268.

7 "The White Paper 1969," on the Indigenous Foundations website. Retrieved from https://indigenousfoundations.arts.ubc.ca/home/ on April 24, 2020. Naithan Lagace and Niigaanwewidam James Sinclair, "The White Paper, 1969," in *The Canadian Encyclopedia* online, Historica Canada. Article published September 11, 2015; last edited November 12, 2015, www.thecanadianencyclopedia.ca/en/article/the-white-paper-1969.

8 John Hoyt, "Kishwoot, Elijah and the Class of '73," p. 371, unpublished manuscript in Yukon Archives, John Hoyt Collection 2019/6.

9 Quoted in J.R. Miller, *Skyscrapers Hide the Heavens: A History of Indian-White Relations in Canada*, 3rd ed. (Toronto: University of Toronto Press, 2000) p. 343. See also "Honouring Our Past—Dr. Frank Calder" on the Nisga'a Lisims Government website. Retrieved from https://www.nisgaanation.ca/news/honouring-our-past-dr-frank-calder on May 7, 2020.

10 From article in *Yukon News*, April 19, 1973, in Yukon Archives Search Files, Yukon Land Claims.

11 Bill Webber, personal communication to Lori Eastmure, March 5, 2018.

12 "Yukoner Appointed to Land Claims Treaty," *Whitehorse Star*, March 4, 1974.

13 Judy Gingell in Johnson, *At the Heart of Gold*, p. 268.

14 Bill Webber, personal communication to Lori Eastmure, March 5, 2018.

15 Libby Barlow, "Sharp Meets Hostility," *Whitehorse Star*, July 21, 1978.

16 Thomas Berger, *Northern Frontier, Northern Homeland* (Ottawa: Supply and Services Canada, 1977).

17 Kenneth M. Lysyk, Edith E. Bohmer and Willard L. Phelps, *Alaska Highway Pipeline Inquiry*. (Ottawa: Supply and Services Canada, 1977).

18 Bill Webber, personal communication to Linda Johnson, May 6, 2020.

19 Ken McKinnon in Johnson, *At the Heart of Gold*, pp. 251–54.

20 Bill Webber, personal communication to Lori Eastmure, March 5, 2018.

21 Judy Gingell, Kwanlin Dün First Nation: Heritage, Lands & Resources, Waterfront Heritage Project, 2015 video interview transcript.

22 Inventory to the records of the Yukon Indian Arts and Crafts Co-operative Ltd. fonds held at the Yukon Archives, March 2009, http://www.tc.gov.yk.ca/findingaids/yiacc.pdf. The Yukon Indian Craft Society restructured as the Yukon Indian Arts and Crafts Co-operative Ltd. in 1980 to better serve its members as an economic development initiative. As a cooperative, members could earn a profit from the sale of their arts and crafts.

23 Articles from *Yukon News*, April 19, 1973, March 7, 1979, in Yukon Archives Search Files, Yukon Land Claims.

24 Adeline Webber, personal communication to Lori Eastmure, March 9, 2018.

25 Ibid.

26 Bill Webber, personal communication to Linda Johnson, November 2019.

27 Jess Ryder, Kwanlin Dün First Nation: Heritage, Lands & Resources, Waterfront Heritage Project, 2018 Community Writing Project.

28 Sweeny Scurvey, "Gopher Gopher," in *A Glimpse of Peace* (Whitehorse: Sweeny Scurvey, 1996), p. 41.

29 Biography of Renee Peters and Field Johnny compiled by granddaughter Tina Williams, November 23, 2017.

30 Judy Gingell, Kwanlin Dün First Nation: Heritage, Lands & Resources, Waterfront Heritage Project, 2017 video interview transcript.

31 Quoted in "Framework Finally Signed," *Dan Sha News*, June 1989.

32 Provision 12 of Yukon First Nations Land Claims Settlement Act S.C. 1994, c. 34.

33 "Kwanlin Dün Takes On New Constitutional Discussions," Kwanlin Dün newsletter, Land Claims Special, July 2001, p. 7.

34 Chuck Tobin, "First Nation Now Eyes High-End Hotel," *Whitehorse Star*, November 15, 2004. Retrieved from newspapers.com, May 6, 2020.

35 Chief Mike Smith, Kwanlin Dün First Nation: Heritage, Lands & Resources, Waterfront Heritage Project, 2015 video interview transcript.

36 Kwanlin Dün First Nation, Constitution of the Kwanlin Dün First Nation (Whitehorse: KDFN, 2005), p. 7.

37 Sophie Smarch, Kwanlin Dün First Nation: Heritage, Lands & Resources, Before and After Whitehorse Dam, 1995 interview transcript.

38 Chief Mike Smith, Kwanlin Dün First Nation: Heritage, Lands & Resources, Waterfront Heritage Project, 2015 video interview transcript.

39 "Lot 226 Receives Reserve Status," Kwanlin Dün newsletter, Land Claims Special, July 2001, p. 7.

40 Chief Rick O'Brien, "It Is the Beginning of a New Future," *Whitehorse Star*, February 21, 2005.

41 Minister Andy Scott, ibid.

42 Chief Mike Smith quoted in "About Us" on the Kwanlin Dün website, retrieved from kwanlindun.com on May 5, 2020.

43 Barbara Fred and her family prepared this biography based on personal recollections and information in *Ajänath'a, Kwanlin Dün Elders Portrait Project, Kwanlin Dün Cultural Centre* (Whitehorse: Kwanlin Dün Cultural Centre, 2015), transcript.

6: Shakaat (A hunting and gathering trip in late summer)

1 Chief Doris Bill in *Kwanlin Dän Ch'a* newsletter, January 2017, p. 2.

2 "Letter from the Chief," *Kwanlin Dän Ch'a* newsletter, December 2006.

3 Johnnie Smith, Kwanlin Dün First Nation: Heritage, Lands & Resources, Kwanlin Dün Cultural History Project, July 30, 1993, interview transcript.

4 In this story the fish are the same as people in that they have their own society and way of being, much like humans. In long ago times, people and animals were able to talk to one another and live together, even sharing similar ways of travel, as seen here where the fish have boats because they are like people. It was much easier to communicate with each other and travel between societies and worlds. This story illustrates how disrespecting the salmon resulted in the boy being taken by them to learn respect. This concept is also presented in "The Girl Who Married the Bear."

5 Dawn Waugh, Kwanlin Dün First Nation: Heritage, Lands & Resources, Waterfront Heritage Project, 2016 video interview transcript.

6 Teagyn Vallevand, Kwanlin Dün First Nation: Heritage, Lands & Resources, Waterfront Heritage Project, 2016 video transcript.

7 "Chief and Council Message," *Kwanlin Dän Ch'a* newsletter, October 2012.

8 Elder Emma Joanne Shorty in Kwanlin Dün First Nation, *Back to the River: Celebrating our Culture* (Whitehorse: Kwanlin Dün First Nation, 2003), p. 26.

9 Cassis Lindsay, Kwanlin Dün First Nation: Heritage, Lands & Resources, Waterfront Heritage Project, 2016 interview transcript.

10 Emily McDougall, Kwanlin Dün First Nation: Heritage, Lands & Resources, Waterfront Heritage Project, 2015 video interview transcript.

11 Katelyn Dawson, Kwanlin Dün First Nation: Heritage, Lands & Resources, Waterfront Heritage Project, 2016 video interview transcript.

12 Sweeny Scurvey, "The Waterfront," in *A Glimpse of Peace* (Whitehorse: Sweeny Scurvey, 1996), p. 40.

13 Joanne Luger, Kwanlin Dün First Nation: Heritage, Lands & Resources, Waterfront Heritage Project, community interviews by Katharine Sandiford, 2017.

14 Chief Mike Smith in *Uyid Ynji Tl'aku ~ I let it go now* (Whitehorse: Kwanlin Dün First Nation, 2010), p. 2.

15 Elder Judy Gingell in *Kwanlin Dün First Nation Strategic Plan 2018-2022* (Whitehorse: Kwanlin Dün First Nation), p. 10.

16 Councillor Sean Smith, Kwanlin Dün First Nation: Heritage, Lands & Resources, Waterfront Heritage Project, 2016 video interview transcript.

17 Quoted in *Kwanlin Dän Ch'a* newsletter, October 2010, p. 2.

18 Councillor Ann Smith in *Kwanlin Dän Ch'a* newsletter, October 2010, p. 11.

19 Chief Doris Bill in *Kwanlin Dün First Nation Strategic Plan 2018-2022* (Whitehorse: Kwanlin Dün First Nation), p. 1.

20 Charles Chief, Kwanlin Dün First Nation: Heritage, Lands & Resources, Waterfront Heritage Project, community interviews by Katharine Sandiford, 2017.

21 Elder Anne Ranigler, personal communication to Linda Johnson, December 2019.

22 "Our Rich First Nation Culture" is adapted from an essay Dr. Ukjese van Kampen wrote to accompany the 2015 photo exhibit at Yukon Arts Centre. It was adapted for this book and for the Kwanlin Dün First Nation: Heritage, Lands & Resources, Waterfront Heritage Project, January 2020.

23 Victoria Fred in *Uyid Ynji Tl'aku ~ I let it go now* (Whitehorse: Kwanlin Dün First Nation, 2010), p. 29.

24 Councillor Sean Smith, Kwanlin Dün First Nation: Heritage, Lands & Resources, Waterfront Heritage Project, 2016 video interview transcript.

25 Linda Huebschwerlen in *Kwanlin Dän Ch'a* newsletter, January 2017, p. 10.

26 Councillor Sean Smith, Kwanlin Dün First Nation: Heritage, Lands & Resources, Waterfront Heritage Project, 2016 video interview transcript.

27 Ibid.

28 Aurora Hardy, Kwanlin Dün First Nation: Heritage, Lands & Resources, Waterfront Heritage Project, October 2016.

29 June Jules, Kwanlin Dün First Nation: Heritage, Lands & Resources, Waterfront Heritage Project, community interviews by Katharine Sandiford, 2017.

30 Chief Mike Smith in *Kwanlin Dän Ch'a* news-letter, March 2008, p. 1.

31 Chief Rick O'Brien in Kwanlin Dün First Nation, *Annual Report 2011–2012*, p. 2.

32 Jason Charlie in *Kwanlin Dän Ch'a* newsletter, January 2016, p. 11.

33 Kwanlin Dün First Nation, *Dädze Nasat. Our Strong Heart* newsletter, October 2009, p. 6.

34 Chief Doris Bill in *Kwanlin Dän Ch'a* news-letter, January 2016, p. 2.

35 Chief Rick O'Brien in Kwanlin Dün First Nation, *Annual Report 2011–2012*, p. 3.

36 Councillor Sean Smith in *Kwanlin Dän Ch'a* newsletter, January 2016, p. 14.

37 Chief Doris Bill in Kwanlin Dün First Nation, *Annual Report 2016–2017. Lat'adinch'é. Connections*, p. 5.

38 Chief Doris Bill in *Kwanlin Dän Ch'a* news-letter, Fall/Winter 2014, p. 2.

39 The Blanket Exercise was developed by KAIROS in response to recommendations in the 1996 *Report of the Royal Commission on Aboriginal People*. The Blanket Exercise offers an experiential workshop covering more than 500 years of history shared by Canada's Indigenous and non-Indigenous peoples. For more information, see the KAIROS website: https://www.kairosblanketexercise.org/about/#history.

40 Emily McDougall—granddaughter of Frank Slim—Kwanlin Dün First Nation: Heritage, Lands & Resources, Waterfront Heritage Project, 2015 video interview transcript.

41 Chief Doris Bill in *Kwanlin Dän Ch'a* news-letter, Winter 2018, p. 6.

42 Elder Irma Scarff in *Kwanlin Dän Ch'a* news-letter, January 2016, p. 4.

43 Geraldine Harris, Kwanlin Dün First Nation: Heritage, Lands & Resources, Waterfront Heritage Project, community interviews by Katharine Sandiford, 2017.

44 Victoria Fred in *Uyid Ynji Tl'aku ~ I let it go now* (Whitehorse: Kwanlin Dün First Nation, 2010), p. 29.

45 Melia Hudgin in Kwanlin Dün First Nation, *Annual Report 2017–2018. Shro kwathan nii. It's good to see you*, p. 20.

46 Katelyn Dawson, Kwanlin Dün First Nation: Heritage, Lands & Resources, Waterfront Heritage Project, 2016 video interview transcript.

47 Cheyenne Bradley, Kwanlin Dün First Nation: Heritage, Lands & Resources, Waterfront Heritage Project, Diana Jimmy, transcript of youth comments at Advisory Council Meeting, February 12, 2020.

48 Teagyn Vallevand, Kwanlin Dün First Nation: Heritage, Lands & Resources, Waterfront Heritage Project, October 2016.

49 Yukon Native Brotherhood, "Together Today for Our Children Tomorrow" (Whitehorse: Council for Yukon Indians, 1977), p. 7.

50 Chief Mike Smith quoted in "About Us" on the Kwanlin Dün website, retrieved from kwanlindun.com on May 5, 2020.

51 Chief Mike Smith, Kwanlin Dün First Nation: Heritage, Lands & Resources, Waterfront Heritage Project, 2015 video interview transcript.

52 Katelyn Dawson, Kwanlin Dün First Nation: Heritage, Lands & Resources, Waterfront Heritage Project, 2016 video interview transcript.

53 Cassis Lindsay, Territorial Swimmer of the Year, Kwanlin Dün First Nation: Heritage, Lands & Resources, Waterfront Heritage Project, 2016 interview transcript.

54 Teagyn Vallevand, Kwanlin Dün First Nation: Heritage, Lands & Resources, Waterfront Heritage Project, October 2016.

55 Aurora Hardy, Kwanlin Dün First Nation: Heritage, Lands & Resources, Waterfront Heritage Project, October 2016.

56 Katelyn Dawson, Kwanlin Dün First Nation: Heritage, Lands & Resources, Waterfront Heritage Project, 2016 video interview transcript.

57 Gary Bailie in *Kwanlin Dän Ch'a* newsletter, December 2006, p. 6.

58 Dawn Waugh, Kwanlin Dün First Nation: Heritage, Lands & Resources, Waterfront Heritage Project, 2016 video interview transcript.

59 Teagyn Vallevand, Kwanlin Dün First Nation: Heritage, Lands & Resources, Waterfront Heritage Project, October 2016.

Selected Bibliography

Almstrom, Marjorie E. *A Century of Schooling: Education in the Yukon 1861–1961.* Whitehorse: Marjorie E. Almstrom, 1990, revised 1991.

Bartlett, Richard H. "Citizens Minus: Indians and the Right to Vote." *Saskatchewan Law Review*, vol. 44, no. 2 (1979–1980): 163–94.

Baumgarte, Bridget Lee. "Alaska Natives and the Power of Perseverance: The Fight For Sovereignty and Land Claims in Southeast Alaska, 1912–1947." Master's thesis, University of Nevada, Las Vegas, 2015. https://digitalscholarship.unlv.edu/thesesdissertations/2466.

Berger, Thomas R. *Northern Frontier, Northern Homeland: The Report of the Mackenzie Valley Pipeline Inquiry.* Vol. 1. Ottawa: Supply and Services Canada, 1977.

Bond, Jeffrey. "Late Wisconsinan McConnell Glaciation of the Whitehorse Map Area (105D), Yukon." In D.S. Emond and L.L. Lewis, eds., *Yukon Exploration and Geology 2003*, 73–88. Yukon Geological Survey annual report, 2004.

Canada. Department of Indian Affairs and Northern Development. "Report of the Indian Act Consultation Meeting, Whitehorse, October 21, 22 and 23, 1968." http://publications.gc.ca/collections/collection_2017/aanc-inac/R5-288-10-1968-eng.pdf.

Canada. Treaties and Historical Research Centre, P.R.E. Group. *The Historical Development of the Indian Act.* Ottawa: Indian and Northern Affairs, 1978.

Coates, Kenneth. *The Alaska Highway: Papers of the 40th Anniversary Symposium.* Vancouver: UBC Press, 1985.

Coates, Kenneth. *Best Left as Indians: Native-White Relations in the Yukon Territory, 1840–1950.* Montreal: McGill-Queen's University Press, 1991.

Coates, Kenneth. *Furs along the Yukon: Hudson's Bay—Native Trade in the Yukon River Basin, 1830–1893.* Master's thesis, University of Manitoba, 1980.

Cruikshank, Julie. *Reading Voices Dan Dha Ts'edenintth'e: Oral and Written Interpretations of the Yukon's Past.* Vancouver: Douglas & McIntyre, 1991.

Cruikshank, Julie, and Jim Robb. *Their Own Yukon.* Whitehorse: Yukon Indian Cultural Education Society and Yukon Native Brotherhood, 1975.

Cruikshank, Julie, in collaboration with Angela Sidney, Kitty Smith and Annie Ned. *Life Lived Like a Story: Life Stories of Three Yukon Native Elders.* Vancouver: UBC Press, 1990.

Dawson, George. *Report of an Exploration in the Yukon District, N.W.T. and Adjacent Northern Portion of British Columbia 1887.* Montreal: William Foster Brown & Co., 1889. Reprint, Whitehorse: Yukon Historical and Museums Association, 1987.

Dobrowolsky, Helene, and Linda Johnson. *Whitehorse: An Illustrated History.* Vancouver: Figure 1 Publishing, 2013.

Gotthardt, Ruth, and Greg Hare. Łu Zil Män Fish Lake: *Uncovering the Past.* Whitehorse: Kwanlin Dün First Nation, 1994.

Hare, Greg. *The Frozen Past: The Yukon Ice Patches.* Whitehorse: Government of Yukon, 2011.

Johnson, Linda. *At the Heart of Gold: The Yukon Commissioner's Office, 1898–2010.*

Whitehorse: Legislative Assembly of
Yukon, 2013.

Johnson, Linda. *The Kandik Map: Cultural
Exchange along the Yukon River*. Fairbanks,
AK: University of Alaska Press, 2009.

Johnson, Linda. *With the People Who Live Here.
The History of the Yukon Legislature, 1909–
1961*. Whitehorse: Legislative Assembly of
Yukon, 2009.

Kristensen, Todd J., P. Gregory Hare, Ruth
Gotthardt, Ty Heffner, Norman A. Easton,
John W. Ives, Robert J. Speakman and Jeffrey T. Rasic. "The Movement of Obsidian
in Subarctic Canada: Holocene Social
Relationships and Human Responses to
a Large-Scale Volcanic Eruption." *Journal of Anthropological Archaeology*, vol. 56
(December 2019): 1–18, 101114. https://doi
.org/10.1016/j.jaa.2019.101114.

Kwanlin Dün Cultural Centre. *Ajänath'a,
Kwanlin Dün Elders Portrait Project, Kwanlin
Dün Cultural Centre*. Whitehorse: Kwanlin
Dün Cultural Centre, 2015.

Kwanlin Dün First Nation. *Kwanlin Dün First
Nation Strategic Plan 2018–2022*. Whitehorse: Kwanlin Dün First Nation, 2018.

Kwanlin Dün First Nation. *Uyid Ynji
Tl'aku ~ I let it go now*. Whitehorse: Kwanlin
Dün First Nation, 2010.

Legros, Dominique. *Oral History as History:
Tutchone Athapaskan in the Period 1840–
1920*. Whitehorse: Government of Yukon,
2007.

Lysyk, Kenneth M., Edith E. Bohmer and
Willard L. Phelps. *Alaska Highway Pipeline
Inquiry*. Ottawa: Supply and Services
Canada, 1977.

McCandless, Robert G. *Yukon Wildlife: A Social
History*. Edmonton: University of Alberta
Press, 1985.

McClellan, Catharine. *My Old People Say:
An Ethnographic Survey of Southern Yukon
Territory, Part 1 and 2*. Ottawa: National
Museums of Canada, 1975.

McClellan, Catharine, with Lucie Birckel,
Robert Bringhurst, James A. Fall, Carol
McCarthy and Janice R. Sheppard. *Part
of the Land, Part of the Water: A History
of the Yukon Indians*. Vancouver: Douglas
& McIntyre, 1987.

Miller, J.R. *Skyscrapers Hide the Heavens: A
History of Indian-White Relations in Canada*.
3rd ed. Toronto: University of Toronto
Press, 2000.

Ogilvie, William. *Early Days on the Yukon and
the Story of the Gold Finds*. Ottawa: Thor-
burn & Abbott, 1913.

Potter, Ben A., Joel D. Irish, Joshua D. Reuther
and Holly J. McKinney. "New Insights into
Eastern Beringian Mortuary Behaviour:
A Terminal Pleistocene Double Infant
Burial at Upward Sun River." *Anthropology*,
PNAS Early Edition (2014). https://doi
.org/10.1073/pnas.1413131111.

Schwatka, Frederick. *Along Alaska's Great
River*. New York: Cassell & Company, 1885.
Reprint, Anchorage: Alaska Northwest
Publishing Co., 1983.

Scurvey, Sweeny. *A Glimpse of Peace*. Whitehorse: Sweeny Scurvey, 1996.

Sidney, Angela. *Place Names of the Tagish
Region, Southern Yukon*. Whitehorse:
Yukon Native Languages Project, 1980.

Sidney, Angela. *Tagish Tlaagú: Tagish Stories*.
Whitehorse: Council for Yukon Indians
and Yukon Government, 1982.

Sidney, Angela, compiled by Julie Cruik-
shank. *Haa Shagoón (Our Family History)*.
Whitehorse: Yukon Native Languages
Project, 1983.

Sidney, Angela, Kitty Smith and Rachel
Dawson. *My Stories Are My Wealth*, as told
to Julie Cruikshank. Whitehorse: Council
for Yukon Indians, 1977.

Smarch, Sophie. "The Woman Who Married
the Bear." September 27, 2015. YouTube
video, 17:19. https://www.youtube.com/
watch?v=y5aXtkEO8KM.

Smith, Kitty. *Nindal Kwädindür: "I'm Going to
Tell You a Story,"* recorded by Julie Cruik-
shank. Whitehorse: Council for Yukon
Indians and Government of Yukon, 1982.

van Kampen, Ukjese. *History of Yukon
First Nations Art*. PhD dissertation,
Leiden University, 2012. openaccess
.leidenuniv.nl.

Wilson, Clifford. *Campbell of the Yukon*.
Toronto: Macmillan of Canada, 1970.

Workman, Margaret. *Kwadĝy Kwändür:
Traditional Southern Tutchone Stories*.

Whitehorse: Yukon Native Language Centre, 2010.

Wren, Lucy. "Lucy Wren—*Ḵu' Eyû. At Home. Tagish Story Book.*" Yukon Native Language Centre website. http://ynlc.ca/languages/tagish/book_tagish_1.html.

Wright, Allen. *Prelude to Bonanza: The Discovery and Exploration of the Yukon.* Sidney, BC: Gray's Publishing, 1976.

Ye Sa To Communications Society. *In Their Honour.* Whitehorse: Ye Sa To Communications Society, 1989.

Yukon Native Brotherhood. *Together Today for Our Children Tomorrow.* Whitehorse: Council for Yukon Indians, 1973.

Newspapers

Dan Sha News, KDFN website
Kwanlin Dän Ch'a, KDFN website
Whitehorse Star, 1906–1961, microfilm, Yukon Archives.
Yukon News, 1960–2020, Yukon Archives.

Government Documents

Kwanlin Dün First Nation: Heritage, Lands & Resources

1993 Fish Lake Project, transcripts.

1993 KDFN Cultural History Project, transcripts.

1995 KDFN Canyon City Project, transcripts.

1996 KDFN Traditional Economics Project, transcripts.

1996/97 Land Use Planning Project, transcript of interview with Mark Lindsay and Hank Henry, August 5, 1996.

2015–2017 Waterfront Heritage Project, video interview transcripts.

2017 Waterfront Heritage Project Story-Weaving Workshop, transcripts.

2018 Waterfront Heritage Project, Community Writing Project.

2019/2020 Project Louie, transcripts.

Yukon Archives

Yukon Council. Journals; Votes and Proceedings; Revenues and Expenditures.

Yukon Record Group 1. Yukon Government Records, 1898–1948.

Manuscripts

Hoyt, John. "Kishwoot, Elijah and the Class of '73." Unpublished manuscript in Yukon Archives, John Hoyt Collection 2019/6.

van Kampen, Ukjese. *History of Yukon and Regional Warfare.* Unpublished manuscript. Whitehorse: Yukon College, 2015.

Map

The Kohklux Map, 1969. The Bancroft Library, University of California, Berkeley: G4370 1852 K6.

Image Credits

LISTED BY PAGE NUMBER

87 Richard Vladars, KDFN; Todd Kritensen

89 John Meikle, KDFN

90 (top, bottom left and right) GBP Creative, KDFN

91 (top left) John Meikle, KDFN

91 (top right) Geoff Cowie, KDFN

91 (bottom) John Meikle, KDFN

92 (left and right) John Meikle

93 Richard Vladars, KDFN as adapted from Rob Ingram, Midnight Arts. Adapted from J.F. Lerbekmo, "The White River Ash: Largest Holocene Plinian Tephla," *Canadian Journal of Earth Sciences* (2008) 45: 693–700

94 ROM, D.A. Cameron coll.

95 John Meikle

96 John Meikle

97 Linda Johnson

99 Courtesy of the Bancroft Library, University of California Berkeley. G4370 1852.K6, Map Collection

101 (left, centre and right) KDCC collection

102 GBP Creative, KDFN

104–5 Geoff Cowie, KDFN

106 John Meikle

108 KDFN

109 GBP Creative, KDFN

110 University of Washington Libraries, NA 2345, PH coll. 274, Eric A. Hegg coll.

111 YA, Pam 1897-067, Veazie Wilson, p. 33

113 (top) YA, Emil Forrest fonds, 80/60 #6

113 (bottom) University of Washington Libraries, PH coll. 373-5, #3347, neg. # UW37630

114 (top) US Geological Survey, Charles W. Hayes coll. #334

114 (bottom) Evan A. Sather photo. YA, Robert Coutts fonds, 82/358 #3

116 University of Washington Libraries, #28675

117 In Fred H. Lysons, *Map-Guide: Seattle to Dawson over Chilkoot* (Seattle: Humes, Lysons, and Sallee, 1897)

118 Raymond Shorty, KDFN

119 Museum of Canadian History, C. McClellan coll., #J6186

120 (left) YA, Raymond Craft fonds, 94/92 #1, PHO 477

120 (right) YA, E.J. Hamacher fonds (Margaret & Rolf Hougen coll.), 2002/118 #174

121 Yukon Archives, Indian Affairs 82/130 Re: Chief Jim Boss 1902 GOV 1313 f3; copied from LAC, RG 10 Records of Indian Affairs Program, vol. 4037, file 317050, General Correspondence regarding Yukon Treaty, 1902–1907. Colourized from a b&w photocopy of the original letter.

122 (top) YA, Louis Irvine fonds, #1900

122 (bottom) YA, Frank Slim fonds, 2003/121 #37

123 (top) M. McCarthy photo. YA, VPL coll. #2273

123 (bottom) MacBride Museum of Yukon History 1989.29.27

124 YA, Chris Everest Webb fonds, 80/87 #40

126 YA, E.J. Hamacher fonds (Margaret & Rolf Hougen coll.), 2002/118 #530

127 Richard Vladars, KDFN

129 Tammy Joe, KDFN Family Photo Collections

130 (top, centre and bottom) Tammy Joe, KDFN Family Photo Collections

131 YA, E.J. Hamacher fonds (Margaret & Rolf Hougen coll.), 2002/188 #289

132 Joan Viksten, KDFN Family Photo Collections

133 YA, Evelyn Brunlees fonds, 2001/139R, #14

134 (left) YA, Amy Lebarge Clethero fonds, 2001/44 #3

134 (right) YA, Amy Lebarge Clethero fonds, 2001/44 #2

135 YA, Dawson family fonds 99/84 #2

136 (top and bottom) Dawson Family Collection

137 Norma McBean

139 Jim Robb

140–41 KDFN

142 John Meikle, KDFN

144 KDFN

Index

berries, preservation of, 118
Bien, Karen, 240
Big Salmon Charlie, 36, 138
Big Salmon George, 132
Bill, Brad, 264
Bill, David, 68, 152
Bill, Doris (Chief): on citizen engagement, 265; on healing, 248-49; on KDFN community, 229; with KDFN Council, 262; on land protection, 270; on partnerships, 266, 267-68, 268; with Youth Council, 263
Bill, Isaac, 263, 275
Bill, Jasmine, 263
Bill, Ronald: biography, 68; "Cannibal Lake Story," 68; on Cloud People, 114; on housing, 167-69; on living in Whitehorse, 133-34; on Miles Canyon and Whitehorse Rapids, 107, 112; on residential school, 154-55; on Taylor & Drury, 131; on trapping, 125; on wartime years, 152; on wood camps, 122
Bill C-31, 187, 201
Billy, Frank, 153
Billy, Mary, 110, 161
Binger, Joe, 51n
bison, 78, 78, 79
Bison Hunting Man, 76-77
Black, Lynn, 223
black berry (moss berry, crow berry), 29
Blackjack, Clyde, 111
Blackjack, Roddy, 111
Blackwell, W.G., 120
Blake, Margaret, 243
Blanket Exercise, 268, 292n39
blueberries (kanat'a), 51, 164, 175
Bluefish Caves, 77
Borgford, Shari, 214
Boss, Annie, 110
Boss, Fred, 176, 177
Boss, Jenny (Tusáxal), 110, 135
Boss, Jim (Kashxóot; Chief): ceremonial outfit of, 137; family of, 110, 135, 138; Kishwoot Hall and, 180; land claims attempt, 121, 181; photographs, 120, 177
Boss, Kathleen, 110
Boss, Maude, 110
Boss, Patrick, 262
boughs (haw), 57
Bourassa, Ernie, 216

bow and arrow, 93
Bowe, Hailey, 210
Bradley, Cheyenne, 263, 274
Branigan, Don, 204
Breen, Mrs., 151
Britannia Creek archaeological site, 77, 78
Broeren, Henry, 110, 214
Broeren, Maggie (Shuwateen), 144
Bunbury, Hazel (Nakhela): biography, 42; "Chùnäy Yè Ts'urk'i Kwǎndur" ("Eagle and Crow Story"), 42-44, 46n; "Chùnäy Yè Ts'urk'i Kwǎndur" ("Eagle and Crow Story") English interpretation, 45; Louie Smith's story and, 37n
Bunbury, John, 266
burials, 85, 86, 117. See also cemeteries
Burns, Annie (née Broeren), 153, 155, 169-70, 170, 214, 223
Burns, Bessie, 110, 170
Burns, Charlie, 154, 155, 164, 169-70, 170, 223
Burns, Donnie, 214
Burns, Emma (Dusk'a), 236
Burns, Joe, 170
Burns, Susan, 266

C

Cadieux, Pierre, 211, 212
Caesar, Sheila, 266
Calbery, Dennis, 262
Calder v British Columbia (1973), 194
Calmegane, Ida (Kaax' anshée—La.oos Tláa), 27n, 100, 110, 111-12, 286n33
Campbell, Big Jonathon (Chief), 135
Campbell, Bruce, 214
Campbell, Effie, 122, 124, 198, 256
Campbell, Ellen, 135, 135
Campbell, Mary (née Alfred), 70, 135, 135
Campbell, Robert, 103, 135
Campen, Hazel, 214, 262
cannibals, 74; "Cannibal Lake Story" (Bill), 68
Canol Pipeline and refinery, 147, 148, 167
Canyon City, 114, 173
Canyon City Construction, 252, 272, 272, 276
Canyon City Historic Site, 219
Canyon Johnnie, 117
Carcross/Tagish First Nation (CTFN), 215, 219, 267, 271
caribou (wajìh), 28, 88-89, 90, 93, 129; in "Xī`h Mā" ("Game Mother"), 26-35